MW00532124

Foundations of Education

Foundations of Education

A Christian Vision

Edited by
Matthew Etherington

With a Foreword by Edwin Boyce

WIPF & STOCK · Eugene, Oregon

FOUNDATIONS OF EDUCATION
A Christian Vision

Wipf & Stock
An Imprint of Wipf and Stock Publishers
199 W. 8th Ave., Suite 3
Eugene, OR 97401

www.wipfandstock.com

ISBN 13: 978-1-60608-579-0

Manufactured in the U.S.A.

Last Update: June 18, 2014

Dedicated to Harro Van Brummelen:
Teacher, Scholar, Mentor and Friend

Contents

Foreword

Dr. Edwin Boyce

To understand the foundations of education from a Christian perspective we need to have an understanding of the spiritual dimension of existence and of the concept of biblical revelation. More directly, in establishing a Christian vision for education we need to understand the teachings of Christ. From Matthew 22:34–40, in Christ's response to the Pharisee's question of what God requires of humanity, we are provided with an understanding that is both classical and radical. Here, within the educational context of Old Testament history, Jesus emphasizes the first and greatest commandment, which is to "Love the Lord your God with all your heart and your mind and your soul." This was the classical response, consistent with the orthodoxy of the day. This commandment goes before all others and in this statement Jesus effectively connects the classical to the Christian imperative of bringing glory to God in all of our lives, including through our educational processes. The radical element in Jesus' response to the question was to teach that we should "love our neighbors as ourselves." Here Jesus asserts that the concept of loving others as ourselves, of acceptance and care of others and acceptance and care of ourselves, is an expression of the first commandment in a new and different way. In Galatians 5:14 the Apostle Paul teaches us that "All of the commandments are summed up in one: Love your neighbor as yourself." In James 2:8 we learn that if you follow the royal law of Scripture "to love your neighbor as yourself" you are doing right. In these two statements we see a continuation of the expression of the Christian vision first presented by Jesus in his response to the question of the Pharisee, which gives us a foundation from which education should be practiced and a reason for which education should be pursued.

Throughout history many Christian educators have made an impact on the educational thinking of their time because of their Christian perspective. Of particular historical importance are the writings in the fourth century of St. Augustine, the bishop of Hippo. His writings feature a foundational concept that supposes that faith leads to understanding. Augustine's constructive argument teaches us that any vision for understanding anything from a Christian perspective must have its basic assumptions in the teachings of the Bible and particularly in the teachings of Jesus.

A number of writers, theologians, and philosophers (among them a number of contributors to this book) have left an imprint on the sphere of education as a result of applying their Christian perspective to their thinking about education. These writers have come from many different contexts, and therefore provide different emphases. The common thread among them, however, is that the teachings of the Bible are foundational to how Christian educators view education in our world at any point in history and in respect to any culture. There are many focal points for people's thoughts and writings but, in the end, a Christian vision of our foundations must relate to the truth of God revealed to us through Scripture.

In framing a philosophy that is from a Christian perspective, the presuppositions we employ should always be based on a theological understanding that is reflective of the truth expressed in God's revelation. As we adopt this way of thinking, we will understand the place of truth, grace, mercy, justice, and peace. In doing so our vision of education from a Christian perspective will be a process that brings glory to God and that is manifested through the ways in which the educators and the educated impact society, particularly through Christian service. In 1 Peter 4:10 we read, "Each one should use whatever gift received to serve others, faithfully administering God's grace in its various forms." This statement implies that a Christian vision for education is not properly understood until there is the practice of service in the process of being educating.

The sociological foundations of a Christian vision of education will include the view of the school as community. The German concept of *Gemeinschaft*, developed in the writings of Tönnies, highlights aspects of relationships that contribute to learning within community. An understanding of this concept is vitally important as we develop a contemporary application of the enduring foundational principles of Christian education in the digital age that will remain applicable as innovations occur in the future.

A Christian vision of the foundations of education leads us to a model of education that is based on the revelation of God's truth in the Bible and that is built on a framework in which service and relationships within community are the hallmarks of our understanding and practice.

Introduction

Matthew Etherington

The Purpose of Christian Education

Does a Christian vision for education have anything substantial to offer schooling in the twenty-first century? Given a comprehensive investigation into the historical roots and positive influence that Christianity has had on Western society, the increasing religious pluralism and multiculturalism of Western societies, the number of bestselling Christian books, documentaries, and websites for and against Christianity, conflicts and events motivated by religious beliefs, the ongoing discussion over the compatibility of science and religion, and the substantial claims that Christianity makes about the meaning and purpose of life, it would be reasonable to propose that a Christian vision for education should have a significant presence in the educational marketplace. In fact, to keep religion out of the public arena is becoming less and less sustainable. Brewer[1] argues that religion itself is not a private experience anymore as some would have us believe, but is better described as a "public religion" with an increasing resurgence of importance within society. Brewer goes on to suggest that religion is

> . . . affecting ethical debates about access to medical care and the desirability of certain forms of treatment. Geopolitics has given the 'war on terrorism' a religious dimension. The elision of culture and religion in many places ensures that ethnic minorities couch their demands for equality in religious terms and that the

1. John Brewer, "Sociology and Theology Reconsidered: Religious Sociology and the Sociology of Religion in Britain," *History of the Human Sciences* 2 (2007) 7–28.

> multicultural mosaic also represents a religious plurality that mono-religious cultures are having difficulty in adjusting to as some believers expect their beliefs to count in public affairs.[2]

A close inspection of the public school curriculum, however, does not necessarily reflect this reality. School students attending public institutions graduate with only a secular view of the world and a minimal cognitive understanding of how the Christian religion impacts and shapes people's thinking and behavior.[3] To offer students a comprehensive education, schools must include all live options for analysis and consideration. A Christian worldview is a live option; therefore it follows that educators have an obligation to acknowledge and include Christian views of interpreting both subject matter and the world.

In fact, this conclusion is not as radical as some might suggest. In Canada, a Justason Marketing poll commissioned by the B.C. Humanist Association found that more than 77 percent of British Columbians would actually approve of religious worldview education reinstated and included in public schools.[4] The majority of Canadians in British Columbia want schools to teach religious education and perspectives. Regarding religious diversity in British Columbia, Paul Bramadat, director of the University of Victoria's Centre for Studies in Religion and Society, states that the idea that public education or any public arena should or can be free of religion is an assumption that is being questioned more and more. Bramadat maintains that we need a broader society where the religious and non-religious can engage in discussion. He notes that public institutions need to recognize how religious people want things to be in the public arena.[5]

How Christianity Changed Education

The authors of *Foundation of Education: A Christian Vision* agree that for over two thousand years the Christian world- and life-view has been

2. Ibid., 9.

3. Read Warren Nord, *Does God Make a Difference?: Taking Religion Seriously in Our Schools and Universities* (Oxford: Oxford University Press, 2010); and Stephen Prothero, *Religious Literacy* (New York: HarperCollins, 2007).

4. See the *Vancouver Sun*, "Education, and World Religions: 4 out 5 want them taught in B.C. Public Schools," http://blogs.vancouversun.com/2013/04/30/world-religions-8-of-10-want-them-taught-in-b-c-public-schools/.

5. See Paul Bramadat video interview, "Experts on Statistics Canada Census Release on Immigration, Religion and Ethnic Diversity," http://communications.uvic.ca/releases/tip.php?date=08052013.

a motivating force to make education more equitable and available for all groups of people. From the first century AD, the Christian religion has had a positive influence on education. For example, Alvin Schmidt[6] highlights the catechetical schools of the early church in AD 150 with its strong literary emphasis; early Christians innovated coeducation; they offered universal education rather than confining it to the privileged as the Greeks and Romans practiced; cathedral and episcopal schools of the fourth to tenth centuries taught a liberal education consisting of logic, arithmetic, music, geometry, and astronomy; Martin Luther was motivated in the sixteenth century to cultivate the mind and advocated for compulsory tax-supported public education to give all children the right of an education; the French theologian John Calvin advanced universal coeducation; the bishop of the Moravian Brethren, John Comenius, pushed for education of the poor and all social classes; the Lutheran layman John Sturm (1507–1589) introduced graded levels of education to assist with academic motivation; the devout Christian Friedrich Froebel (1782–1852) invented the kindergarten school; the strong Christian convictions of Abbe Charles Michel de l'Eppe, Thomas Gallaudet, and Laurent Clerc inspired them to educate the deaf. In particular Eppe, an ordained priest, developed sign language for school use in Paris in 1775. In the first half of the nineteenth century, Louis Braille, a dedicated Christian, enabled the blind to read with their fingers. In 1780, Robert Raikes, a committed Christian who aimed to help deprived children by teaching them on Sunday, invented Sunday schools. Finally, universities and colleges were founded by Christians. It is clear that the Christian vision has had the most positive impact on education.

The Purpose of Education

Christian educators are well aware of the different views concerning the purpose of an education. Some of the more popular views are to build physical fitness, to develop good character, to express effective understanding, to equip young people to think, to make good citizens, to learn practical skills, and to relate life to its source and goals.[7] John Dewey's definition of the purpose of education was to reconstruct or reorganize experience, and traditions were only relevant if they served this purpose; otherwise they

6. Alvin Schmidt, *How Christianity Changed the World*, (Gran Rapids: Zondervan, 2004) 170–91.

7. Herman Horne, *Jesus the Teacher: Examining His Expertise in Education* (Grand Rapids: Kregel, 1998) 18–19.

were oppressive.[8] One might ask which of these goals the Christian educator should accept and/or reject. If we read about the life and work of Jesus of Nazareth the response could involve the following. Horne[9] notes that for Christ physical fitness was obviously important to his ministry—he healed the bodies of men and women and made them whole. He developed good character by living and teaching the highest standards of moral character. He pointed to the beauties of nature. He taught ethical and spiritual truths and trained the minds of his disciples. He was a good citizen and taught obedience to civil authority. He was a carpenter and taught the economic virtues. And finally, Jesus was the Son, and he taught the spiritual content of life. Horne goes on to suggest that Jesus of Nazareth practiced a complete education and pedagogy; the great objective was that, through the physical, moral, esthetic, intellectual, social, vocational, and spiritual aspects, people would attain their own state of mind.[10] Dewey's notion of tradition as oppressive, however, does not square well with the Christian tradition—nor is it compatible with indigenous cultures around the world where tradition and the passing of knowledge from one generation to the next is central to identity and community.

In 1912 mathematician, philosopher, and ordained Anglican priest Alfred North Whitehead presented a lecture on the purpose of education. He opened his talk by observing that to gain more knowledge is surely not the purpose of education. "A well-informed man," Whitehead argued, "is the most useless bore on God's earth."[11] He then went on to suggest that the purpose of education should be to inculcate "duty and reverence."[12]

I submit that Whitehead was heading in the right direction. Knowledge in itself does not bring ultimate purpose or meaning to one's life. As the philosopher and historian Isaiah Berlin said, "Although knowledge is indeed worth striving for, it is not necessary to believe that all knowledge makes people happier or freer or morally better."[13] Berlin went on to argue that some knowledge, i.e., scientific, has actually increased oppression, danger, and misery as well as diminished people in other spheres.[14]

8. C. A. Bowers, *The False Promises of Constructivist Theories of Learning* (New York: P. Lang, 2005) 18.

9. Ibid.,19.

10. Ibid.

11. Alfred North Whitehead, *The Aims of Education and other Essays* (New York: The Free Press, 1929) 1.

12. Ibid.,14.

13. Isaiah Berlin, *The Power of Ideas*, ed. Henry Hardy (New Jersey: Princeton University Press, 2001) 215.

14. Ibid., 290.

In 1943 English professor William DeVane maintained that the purpose of education is to correct mass tendency and to make learners real three-dimensional persons of wisdom, individuality, and conscience.[15] I suggest that DeVane was fundamentally on the right path. To make a three-dimensional person, education would have the task of reshaping the structure of modern society by educating its students for a better world, a world where people can flourish due to an education that is grounded in community, tradition, truth, justice, and peace.

The Anglican churchman, scholar, and later Roman Catholic cardinal John Henry Newman said that what students need from their education are not the newest tricks of the trade, but rather the implications of research and reflection for the best practice of their chosen vocation.[16] The educator thus seeks to interpret the world, but also to provide a dialectic platform for students so they can change the world for the better. The educator also has a responsibility to provide intellectual and philosophical nurture for the moral outrage and social idealism of its students, by exposing them to a wide range of serious reflections (religious and non-religious) about the nature of the good life and the good society. Neither governments nor intergovernmental bodies can undertake the task by themselves,[17] and when they do carry on such research it needs to be reviewed and verified by educational wisdom and scholarship.

The sociology professor emeritus at Eastern University, pastor and activist Tony Campolo, asks the question, why educate?[18] He suggests that students are often led to believe that education is about getting a good job and acquiring lots of assets. As a Christian person he rejects this view, arguing that education should equip people to serve others in the name of Jesus Christ. So is the purpose of an education to provide students with the necessary skills for economic competition, social success, and purchasing assets that make living easier or indeed more interesting? This view is not at all reflective of the Christian vision for education. The primary vision of a Christian education is to be incarnational, to be like Christ in serving oth-

15. This quote by William DeVane is located in Jaroslav Pelikan, *The Idea of the University: A Reexamination* (New Haven, CT: Yale University Press, 1992).

16. John Henry Newman, *The Idea of a University* (Washington, DC: Regnery, 1999).

17. See, Jonathan Chaplin, "A Case for Pluralism in Public Policy," in *Agenda for Educational Change*, edited by John Shortt and Trevor Cooling (Suffolk: Apollos, 1997) 62–71.

18. Tony Campolo delivered this sermon on January 1, 2000. Campolo calls us to not conform to the materialistic values of our secular society, but to live out the vision of meaningful service to others prescribed by Christ. The audio recording is available at http://tonycampolo.org/sermons/2000/01/the-last-great-idea/.

ers, liberating and bringing hope to the lives of people who have little hope or minimal opportunity in life. The secondary vision is to ordain justice, bring peace, defend truth, reject evil, love wisdom, and uphold conscience and moral integrity. These things reflect a Christian vision for education. Schools and universities are in the business of teaching what is true—so a pursuit of these truths is necessary. If learners and teachers pursue wisdom and conscience, then a pursuit of what is true must be considered a good in itself.

Shalom and Education

Shalom means to be at peace with God. Jesus of Nazareth asked his followers to love others and to be stewards or trustees of the earth until his return. The God of the Bible provides a foundation and source for the motivation to be excellent in everything one does, to love other people and care for the earth. One could ask if non-believers might approve of this goal; after all, non-believers are not committed to a worldview with God as the foundation. Consequently, there is no need to be at peace with God. Nevertheless, the understanding of shalom, that is, to be at peace with God, may I suggest, can still be achieved by non-believers without a categorical belief in God. Shalom can signify being at peace with God's representatives, that is, people of faith. To be in harmony with those with whom you most disagree is restorative to the soul and body. Modern psychology describes such harmony as forgiveness—whereby one is released from the anxiety, frustration, and anger that bedevils one when worldviews collide. Governments sometimes describe it as reconciliation. In society, others describe it as tolerance—to stand up for, but not necessarily agree with, those who hold to different worldviews.

Individualized and personalized education is important and many ministries of education are happily heading in this direction[19]; however, shalom incorporates community and not just a collection of individuals each set out to make their way in the world.[20]

19. See British Columbia Ministry of Education, *BC's Education Plan* (Personalized Learning), http://www.bcedplan.ca/actions/pl.php.

20. Nicholas Wolterstorff, *Educating for Life: Reflections on Christian Teaching and Learning* (Grand Rapids: Baker Academic, 2002) 102–3.

The Christian Vision

This book is called *Foundations of Education: A Christian Vision*. What are the foundations of education when understood from the Christian tradition? The book comprises the work of a number of scholars and educators in the field who have thought carefully about the philosophical ideas that have shaped Christian education, the historical events leading to public and Christian schooling, and the sociological influences that have formed society and schools. If we consider what it is to have a Christian vision for education, we undertake this to mean that all students are created in the image of God, and that they can think reflectively and make meaningful decisions in regards to their own course of action and destiny. Students are educated and encouraged to think for themselves rather than merely be trained to respond to environmental cues.

The Christian vision upholds the view that students should think and act reflectively for themselves, rather than just to respond to what the world deems important. This is necessary in terms of both mental and moral development. Self-control, rather than externally imposed control, is central. Students are brought to a place where they can think critically about their faith, make their own decisions and be responsible for those decisions without continually being coaxed, directed or forced by the short term pleasures of this world. This means that the context in which we teach will be as important as the content. The Christian vision includes preparing both educators and students to express themselves with humility and love by maintaining an emphasis on servanthood and Christ's lordship within a Christian setting.

This is just as it should be because authentic and viable curricula must be developed out of, and consistent with, their metaphysical and epistemological basis. Christian education develops an integrated balance that is focused on the whole person—the physical, social, spiritual, and intellectual. The educational experience is therefore wider than the subject matter developed in the formal curriculum and taught by teachers in the classroom. The school also has an informal curriculum with a significant impact.

From a Christian perspective, neutrality is impossible within education. Teachers must therefore ask what the effect of any activity is on a student's character. The educational philosopher John Dewey once said that schools should be designed to demonstrate what the best and wisest parent wants for his child. While we would hope that the best and wisest parent would focus on truth and wisdom, there is skepticism that, in an age of entertainment, individualism, and consumerism, there would be much importance placed on truth or wisdom. The theologian R. C. Sproul has called this period of history the most anti-intellectual age. The importance of education for defending truth and wisdom was discussed by Aristotle. On one occasion, when asked how much educated people were superior to the uneducated, he replied, "As much as the living are to the dead."

If an aim of education is to correct mass tendency and make graduates real three-dimensional persons of wisdom, individuality, and conscience,[21] then we have much to do. The economist Ernst Schumacher,[22] reflecting on these problems and the inadequacy of education, warned that

> the problems of education are merely reflections of the deepest problems of our age. They cannot be solved by organization, administration, or the expenditure of money, even though the importance of all these is not denied. We are suffering from a metaphysical disease, he said, and the cure must therefore be metaphysical. Education which fails to clarify our central convictions is mere training and indulgence. For it is our central convictions that are in disorder, and, as long as the present anti-metaphysical temper persists, the disorder will grow worse. Education, far from ranking as man's greatest resource, will then be an agent of destruction, in accordance with *corruptio optimi pessima.*[23]

If Schumacher is right, the Christian vision of schooling has the task of metaphysical reconstruction—that is, to focus on what is real in the world and to help students arrive at their place of purpose. In fact, all educational communities, then, face the tension and challenge that accompany the question: What should our schools teach and why? In Victorian education, a philosophy known as utilitarianism approved schoolchildren to be systematically denied any expression of emotion and creativity, reduced to reciting monotonous facts, such as defining horses.[24] Consequently, the why question was not encouraged. Today the why question is still claimed by some to be a silly question and not worth pursuing. Biologist Richard Dawkins and Peter Atkins are of this view.[25] And yet asking why is what makes us human. It is one of the most fundamental existential questions that human beings can

21. Read in Jaroslav Pelikan, *The Idea of the University: A Reexamination* (Michagan: Yale University Press, 1992).

22. Ernst Schumacher, *Small Is Beautiful: A Study of Economics as If People Mattered* (New York: Harper and Row, 1973).

23. Ibid.,107.

24. Patrick Bradley, "Victorian Lessons: Education and Utilitarianism in Bentham, Mill, and Dickins," *Concord Review* 10/99 (1999) 74.

25. Howard Taylor, "Why the Universe Must Have a Purpose," http://www.hgtaylor.net/purpose.htm.

ask and, in a real sense, separates us from non-humans. Socrates was right when he said that "the unexamined life is not worth living." The words of the great teacher remind us that there is hardly a more influential force than education; education provides the mind with life and shapes the whole person.[26] Without tension and dialogue, education will not progress but regress, because when such tensions cease to exist the educational community is either dying or in a chaotic state.[27] Dialogue, exploration, tradition, tension, and asking why are thus critical for a good and healthy community.

Christian educators are reminded that truth by its very nature diversifies human thought and discovery, and is rarely found on only one side of complex issues. If Christian educators are silent on complex matters, or do not or cannot respond to complex questions in the classroom, they are not truly qualified to be instructors, for they are depriving students of areas of inquiry that are important for their nurture and understanding.

The Elimination of the Philosophy of Education from Teacher Education

In the noble pursuit of developing the best teacher, open any book on teacher education and you will probably find the debate over whether teaching is more of a science or an art. Although by the end of a university education degree teacher candidates are well versed in scientific pedagogical and psychological principles, they soon realize that, while scientific judgments are valuable, most often our decisions are based on metaphysical judgments.

As teacher educators, we are deeply rooted in our metaphysical judgments. To test this, include a "value line" activity at the beginning of a class for a new cohort of pre-service teachers using the question, "Is teaching a science or an art?" Ask them to form an imaginary line with one end of the line being art and the other end science. Students get out of their seats and, depending on their sense of the answer to the question, they stand at their chosen positions on the imaginary line. After everyone has selected a place on the line, lively discussion follows as students defend their choice. Refrain from offering an opinion, taking, instead, a facilitator role. At the end of the cohort program, ask the same question and have the group repeat the activity. It's remarkable to hear the more thoughtful opinions and see fewer teachers standing at either end of the line. They soon discover that

26. Michael, L. Peterson, *Philosophy of Education: Issues and Options* (Downers Grove, IL: InterVarsity) 13.

27. Anthony J. Diekema, *Academic Freedom and Christian Scholarship* (Grand Rapids: Eerdmans, 2000) 40.

many decisions about teaching strategies, responses to student misbehavior, or selection of materials and assessment techniques, while benefiting from scientific research, often must take into consideration more subjective judgments. Having the skills of thought is important. We must never become complacent in our beliefs. Christianity is a reasonable faith. Through our commitment to research, evidence, reflection, and service to others, Christian education will continue to produce tomorrow's Christian leaders in the respective fields.

Yet the dominance that scientific enquiry and cognitive science enjoys today has displaced tradition and metaphysical accounts of inquiry. This no doubt explains the decline in recent years of philosophy of education courses and learning theory.[28] Theory helps us to see practice as part of a bigger project. Theory has purpose and, as Stuart Hall and Lawrence Grossberg have argued, we take "detours" through theory in pursuit of understanding some phenomenon or process in a new way.[29] School curriculum is an interdisciplinary enterprise, and so the Christian world- and life-view of education has a natural and much-needed metaphysical role to play in all areas of the school curriculum and in education in general. In fact, some of the most important decisions made in education are metaphysical. When educators talk about the nature and structure of policy, course selection, what is important to learn and experience, or what to leave out of the curriculum, they are engaging in metaphysical discussion.

The Foundations of Education: A Christian Vision

This book is organized into three sections: the historical underpinnings of education, the philosophical issues of education, and the sociological questions pertaining to education.

Part 1: Historical and Religious Foundations

The Christian foundation of schooling and education is discussed by Dr. Harro Van Brummelen. A detailed historical overview (breadth and depth) of Christian thought and action together with the central leading figures in

28. Donald Kerr, David Mandzuk, and Helen Raptis, "The Role of the Social Foundations of Education in Programs of Teacher Preparation in Canada," *Canadian Journal of Education* 34/4 (2011) 120–34.

29. Greg Dimitriadis and George Kamberelis, *Theory for Education* (New York: Routledge, 2006).

Christian education is given. Anyone interested in the progressive influence that Christianity had on education should read this chapter.

Dr. Jan Hábl presents the life and teachings of the great Christian educator and pioneering figure Johan Amos Comenius (1592–1670). He argues that Comenius understood a proper education to be a key means for the creation of a more tolerant and humane world and ultimately the restoration of humanity.

In attention to gender and the Christian women who influenced education, Dr. Allyson Jule highlights four women who were motivated by Christian principles of justice, equality, and care. She considers their main contributions to education and relates their achievements and convictions to the gospel message.

The historical influence of Christianity on special education and, in particular, the deaf and the blind, is discussed by Dr. Matthew Etherington. For the blind and the deaf Christianity offered protection from society, fought against injustice, and liberated the oppressed from a world that assumed and still assumes perfection. He notes that while secular incentives for launching institutions for the disabled were to protect society *from* the handicapped, Christian monasteries and hospices arose to save handicapped people from society.

Science and religion continues to be a topic of fascinating discussion and debate and scientist Dr. Arnold Sikkema contributes to the discussion. He deliberates upon the relationship that religion and science share and carefully highlights the inadequate epistemological claims often made by both scientists and evangelicals. He refers to the types of knowledge that each activity brings to the discussion and encourages school students in Christian education to be informed both scientifically and theologically.

Dr. June Hetzel and Dr. Tim Stranske explore the notion of educating for faithful presence. The aim of the educator, they argue, is to first "respond to God's faithful presence in his or her own life, to model it, to practice it, and to encourage its development in his or her students' lives—through relationship and through the curriculum—and then watch the Spirit of God produce the fruit and encourage youth to himself." When Christian educators educate for faithful presence, they prepare students to live the Christian life by being genuinely present to God and others.

Part 2: Philosophical Foundations of Education

Dr. Perry Glanzer considers an education for moral and ethical life. He maintains that educating for the good life must involve helping students understand the moral elements of their various identities. He argues for the pursuit of a moral education with a grand narrative. The Christian tradition sufficiently grounds a divine nature and human purpose in life.

Evangelism in the classroom is introduced by Dr. Elmer John Thiessen. The essay explores what is and what is not acceptable by way of evangelism or proselytizing in the classroom. Although the opposition to evangelism in the classroom is acknowledged and understood, Thiessen highlights that "It not easy to separate teaching about religion from the teaching of religion." He suggests that, in light of postmodern epistemology, the ideal of neutrality is increasingly problematic, and thus it is more difficult to use neutrality as an argument against evangelism in the classroom.

Dr. Nicholas Wolterstorff reflects upon "The Peculiar Hope of the Educator." Without hope we have nothing. Although hope is central to our work as teachers, it is rarely mentioned or discussed in any depth. Wolterstorff was invited to reflect on this very topic as it relates to teaching and learning and to share his thoughts to a live audience of education faculty, teachers, and student teachers at Trinity Western University. This essay is the outcome of his live presentation.

A balanced understanding of truth, traditionalism, and constructivism is discussed by Rev. Keith Mitchell. In light of all truth being God's truth, Mitchell argues for an alliance to a biblical framework that can be adopted when integrating constructivist thought against traditional methodologies. He suggests that, from a biblical worldview, traditional teaching methods and constructivism have their place alongside each other in the schema of pedagogical practice and can thus be combined appropriately and successfully.

The aims and definitions of education are discussed by Dr. Ted Newell. He argues for the importance of traditions in education so as to resist a modernity that "subordinates local Stories to the technological promises of progress." He promotes a cultivational model approach to education, which includes cultural participation in all its dimensions and ultimately aimed toward godly wisdom.

The importance of the humanities in education is explored by Dr. Karen Swallow Prior. Humanities education is experiencing a crisis. One challenger is a modern progressive education that is overwhelmingly pragmatic in purpose, utilitarian, and career oriented. Prior argues for a proper balance of church and culture and encourages a thinking Christian faith of both intellect and spirit. So, can a humanities education in a Christian setting strengthen faith? If students are challenged to defend their Christian identities, then yes. Faith-based institutions can be the cause of a fragile faith, however, because students are surrounded almost uniformly by like-minded peers and graduate without having their faith and thinking challenged.

Part Three: Sociological Foundations of Education

From a British context, Dr. Elizabeth Green draws on experience and recent debates concerning the Dual System and the evolution of school choice policies in the UK. She examines the history of the Dual System and the evolution of school choice policies and considers what is distinctive about church school provision in the marketplace. She reflects upon the claim that church schools perpetuate structural inequalities in the system by actively selecting their pupils and fostering segregation along sectarian lines. She then gives thought to the claim that tolerance and community cohesion can only be achieved by mixed schooling.

How does a scholar-teacher impart awareness of the timeless (the eternal) in an age of constant change? Dr. Grant Havers explores this question. Working from a Christian perspective, Havers contrasts two views of the timeless—those of the German-Jewish philosopher Leo Strauss and media theorist Marshall McLuhan. He seeks to understand how the timeless transcends a world that is in a constant state of flux. He then considers the observations made by the so-called moderns (reason plus science) and premoderns (tradition plus reason) involving what counts as legitimate and worthwhile knowledge.

The relationship of religion, secularity, and education is presented by Dr. Douglas Blomberg. Schooling that focuses on the transmission of knowledge and skills, Blomberg notes, while avoiding the formation of character, creates a particular worldview of what it means to be a mature person. Blomberg argues that the financial support for faith-based public schooling is essential "if we are justly to accommodate all citizens and their children in religiously plural societies." He maintains that there is a straightforward way to disestablish the two-school system in Ontario, Canada: regulate and authorize, yes, but most importantly, empower all schools financially.

Dr. David Long and Dr. William Van Arragon discuss some of the issues significant to Aboriginal education. The issues they raise are grounded in their own personal experience and, as such, are pertinent to any course on Aboriginal education—the insufficiency of apology, the suspicion we have of the "other," the filters that have been set by European analysis, and the weariness of students saying sorry. The way forward for non-Aboriginal people is to walk humbly with Aboriginal people in a way that Martin Buber called the I-Thou experience. Non-Aboriginal people should see and treat their Aboriginal sisters and brothers in the same way that Jesus saw and treated all "others"—with dignity, respect, and love. In other words, treating one another with dignity, respect, and love is not only the way forward in all our relations—it is at the heart of the gospel.

What should be the goal of education? Dr. Angus Brooks considers this philosophical question from the perspectives of ancient and medieval thinkers. He argues that "educating for public life, within the Sophistical tradition, signified an education in the basic arts such as grammar, law, and rhetoric with an orientation towards self-interested engagement in public life." He considers an alternative model of education that is helpful for those who react against the self-interested model of educating for public life. Brook discusses the alternative account of education given by Plato, which was reoriented towards a notion of freeing up a human being through the investigation of reality and a pursuit of virtue. A sufficient model of educating for public life, he says, could be a love of truth, a commitment to a good human life, and a notion of community participation for the common good.

The school as community (including the role of service learning) is explored by Dr. Stephen J. Fyson. He questions a teaching and learning environment that encourages educational egotism. We must ask what the purpose of school is. Is it information transfer according to an agenda that is presented in an environment of competition? Should student self-advancement be given the priority in education that it currently enjoys? Fyson suggests that ambition is contrary to the teaching of Christ, which has as its goal "service of God and his creatures, so that his justice and *shalom* might be at least pastorally restored."

All of the articles are written by experts with experience in their fields. This book offers readers an understanding that Christian education has and continues to take an interest in the personal life, character development, academic growth, and moral habits of students, with a mission that is historically grounded, philosophically significant, and sociologically applicable.

If Christianity is a public religion with a public truth, then students need comprehensive diverse schools where the Christian worldview is included and valued—culture demands it. We need inclusive schools where children with special needs and their parents are involved and valued. We need schools that teach students how to serve and love others. We need schools that promote justice, wisdom, and human flourishing. We need schools that promote peace and community. And, finally, we need schools that uphold truth. This is the Christian vision of education.

Contributors

Dr. Harro Van Brummelen is professor emeritus and former dean of the School of Education at Trinity Western University. His best-known books are *Walking with God in the Classroom: Christian Approaches to Teaching and Learning* (2nd ed., 1998), and *Steppingstones to Curriculum: A Biblical Path* (1994), both available in a number of languages. Van Brummelen has written widely about curriculum issues as well as about religion and education. He was involved in the Cardus Foundation study on the effectiveness of religiously based schools in North America. He is co-editor of *Metaphors We Teach By: How Metaphors Shape What We Do in Classrooms* (2012).

Rev. Dr. Jan Hábl is a professor of pedagogy at J. E. Purkyne University in Ústí nad Labem (Czech Republic) and a pastor in the Církev bratrská (Free Evangelical Brethren Church). He studied education at J. E. Purkyne University (M.Ed.), theology at EMF School of Biblical Studies in England, and philosophy at University of Wales (PhD). He has taught systematic theology and apologetics at Evangelical Theological Seminary in Prague and is known as a gifted biblical preacher and a Christian apologist in the tradition of C. S. Lewis. He also taught philosophy of education, ethics education, and the history of pedagogy at University Hradec Králové. Since 2004 he has been associated with the Comenius Institute. He is completely in love with the phenomenon of education as he has found it to be both one of the most fundamental needs and one of the most fascinating merits of human nature.

Dr. Allyson Jule, PhD, is professor of education and co-director of the Gender Studies Institute at Trinity Western University in Langley, Canada. She is the author of *A Beginner's Guide to Language and Gender* (2008) and *Gender, Participation and Silence in the Language Classroom: Sh-Shushing the Girls* (2004), and the editor of two collections of sociolinguistic scholarship: *Gender and the Language of Religion* (2005) and *Language and Religious Identity: Women in Discourse* (2007), and co-editor with Bettina Tate-Pedersen of *Being Feminist, Being Christian: Essays from Academia*

(2006). Allyson Jule is also the media reviews editor for *Women and Language* journal and serves on the advisory council for the International Gender and Language Association (IGALA).

Dr. Matthew Etherington achieved his PhD in the philosophy of education from Macquarie University in Sydney Australia and at the Ontario Institute for Studies in Education (OISE) at the University of Toronto, Canada. He is presently an associate professor in the School of Education at Trinity Western University in Langley, Canada. His primary interests are in metaphysics, epistemology, apologetics, Aboriginal pedagogy, and the philosophy of education. Matthew has published one book, *Changing Careers to Become a Teacher: A Study of Mature Age Preservice Teachers in Career Transition.* He has published over twenty scholarly articles on a variety of topics such as e-learning pedagogy, Christian education, play and childhood, the Pygmalion effect and learning, the philosophy of mathematics, and many other topics within the philosophy of education.

Dr. Arnold E. Sikkema earned his PhD in theoretical physics at the University of British Columbia, and has been involved in Christian higher education since 1997, first at Dordt College in Iowa, and since 2005 at Trinity Western University, where he is professor of physics and chair of the Mathematical Sciences Department. His research interests focus on emergence and reductionism, considering both collective motion in biophysical systems and Christian philosophical perspectives on the connections between physics and biology. He is president of the Canadian Scientific & Christian Affiliation, and regularly presents workshops at teachers' conventions, driven by his experience in and enthusiasm for both science education and faith-and-science dialogue.

Dr. Karen Swallow Prior, professor of English, earned her PhD and MA at the State University of New York at Buffalo and her BA at Daemen College. She was the 2003 recipient of the President's Award for Teaching Excellence. In 2006 she received the Sigma Tau Delta (LU chapter) Teacher of the Year Award. She was named Faculty of the Year by the Multicultural Enrichment Center in 2010 and won a Chancellor's Award for Teaching Excellence in 2013. She is a member of the graduate faculty and teaches British literature primarily, with a specialty in eighteenth-century British literature, which she loves for its emphasis on philosophy, ethics, aesthetics, community, and the "middle way." Her scholarly work has appeared in *1650–1850: Ideas, Aesthetics, and Inquiries in the Early Modern Era*; *The Shandean*; and *The Scriblerian*. She is a contributing writer for *Christianity*

Today, *The Atlantic*, and *Think Christian* and the author of *Booked: Literature in the Soul of Me* (T. S. Poetry Press, 2012). Her writing has also appeared in *Comment*, *Relevant*, *Books and Culture*, and *Salvo.* A biography of the nineteenth-century social reformer and abolitionist Hannah More is forthcoming from Thomas Nelson in 2014. Prior is a member of the Redbud Writers Guild and the Faith Advisory Council of the Humane Society of the United States.

Dr. Grant Havers is professor of philosophy and chair of the Department of Philosophy (with a cross-appointment in the Department of Political Studies) at Trinity Western University, Langley, Canada. He has published and lectured widely on political philosophy, especially the conservative tradition. Havers' first book, *Lincoln and the Politics of Christian Love*, was published by the University of Missouri Press in late 2009. His second book, *Leo Strauss and Anglo-American Democracy: A Conservative Critique*, was published by Northern Illinois University Press in 2013.

Dr. Perry L. Glanzer is professor of educational foundations at Baylor University and a resident scholar with Baylor Institute for Studies of Religion. He is the co-author with Todd Ream of *The Idea of a Christian College: A Reexamination for Today's University* (Cascade, 2013), *Christianity and Moral Identity in Higher Education* (Palgrave-Macmillan, 2009), *Christianity and Scholarship in Higher Education* (Jossey-Bass, 2007), and *The Quest for Russia's Soul* (Baylor University Press, 2002). In addition, he has published over forty journal articles and book chapters on topics related to religion and education, and moral education.

Dr. Elmer J. Thiessen obtained his PhD from the University of Waterloo, and is now a semi-retired philosopher, having taught at Medicine Hat College in Alberta for thirty-six years. He has published three books, *Teaching for Commitment*, *In Defence of Religious Schools and Colleges* (McGill-Queen's University Press, 1993, 2001), and *The Ethics of Evangelism: A Philosophical Defense of Proselytizing and Persuasion* (Paternoster and IVP Academic, 2011). He is presently an adjunct professor at Emmanuel Bible College, and also teaches regularly in the LALL program at Wilfrid Laurier University. His latest overseas teaching stints were at Meserete Kristos College in Ethiopia in the summer of 2011, and at the Caribbean Graduate School of Theology in Jamaica in 2013.

Dr. Nicholas Wolterstorff is Noah Porter Professor Emeritus of Philosophical Theology at Yale University, fellow of Berkeley College at Yale University, and senior research fellow of the Institute for Advanced Studies in Culture, University of Virginia. He graduated from Calvin College in 1953 and received his PhD in philosophy from Harvard University in 1956. After teaching philosophy for two years at Yale, he returned to the philosophy department at his alma mater in 1959. He returned to Yale in 1989, where he was on the faculty of the Divinity School and associate faculty of the Philosophy Department and the Religious Studies Department. He retired from Yale at the end of 2001. He also taught, during leaves of absence, at Haverford College, the University of Michigan, the University of Texas, the University of Notre Dame, Princeton University, and the Free University of Amsterdam.

Recent publications are *Justice: Rights and Wrongs* (Princeton, 2008), *Hearing the Call* (Eerdmans, 2011), *Justice in Love* (Eerdmans, 2011), *The Mighty and the Almighty* (Cambridge, 2012), and *Understanding Liberal Democracy* (Oxford, 2012). Among his earlier publications are *Until Justice and Peace Embrace* (Eerdmans, 1983), *Art in Action* (Eerdmans, 1980), *Works and Worlds of Art* (Oxford, 1980), *Divine Discourse* (Cambridge 1995), *John Locke and the Ethics of Belief* (Cambridge1996), *Thomas Reid and the Story of Epistemology* (Cambridge 2001), *Educating for Life* (Baker 2002), and *Educating for Shalom: Essays on Christian Higher Education* (Eerdmans 2004).

He has been president of the American Philosophical Association (Central Division) and president of the Society of Christian Philosophers. He is a fellow of the American Academy of Arts and Sciences. Among the named lectures he has given are the Wilde Lectures at Oxford University, the Gifford Lectures at St. Andrews University, the Taylor Lectures at Yale Divinity School, and the Stone Lectures at Princeton Seminary.

Dr. Doug Blomberg has spent most of his life in Australia, where he earned a PhD in Education (Sydney) and, after nearly thirty years experience as a teacher and administrator in high school and teacher education, an EdD (Monash). He is currently Professor of Philosophy of Education and Academic Dean at the Institute for Christian Studies, Toronto, Canada. He edited and co-authored *A Vision with a Task: Christian Schooling for Responsive Discipleship* (1993) and wrote *Wisdom and Curriculum: Christian Schooling after Postmodernity* (2007). Doug has published many articles for professional and academic journals on a wide range of educational and other topics.

Dr. June Hetzel completed doctoral studies in education at Claremont Graduate University. She currently serves as Dean of Education at Biola University, La Mirada, California. She teaches philosophy of Christian education as well as curriculum and instruction coursework. Her primary interests are spiritual formation, literacy, curriculum, and philosophy. She has served in the roles of teacher, administrator, curriculum specialist, writer, editor, professor, chair, and dean. She currently serves as a series editor for Passport to Adventure, an English as a Foreign Language series (Purposeful Design); is the co-author of *The Literacy Gaps: Bridge-Building Strategies for English Language Learners and Standard English Learners* (Corwin, 2009); and has just completed a study of "The Spiritual Lives of Teachers," a survey of over 1,500 teachers in 38 countries. She has a heart for global outreach and has served in Thailand, North Africa, and England.

Dr. Tim Stranske completed his doctoral studies in education at Claremont Graduate University. He is presently the assistant dean of the School of Education at Biola University and graduate chair in the School of Education. His primary interests are philosophy of education and educational psychology. He currently teaches philosophy of Christian education. Dr. Stranske has served as a K-12 Christian school teacher and administrator for thirty years and has most recently worked with the Minister of Primary and Secondary Education in Burundi to enhance their educational system. This partnership has involved participation in several Burundian educational conferences and the development of nine teacher-preparation DVDs in French and English, using all African teachers and narrators. He has also published articles on biblical integration.

Keith Mitchell undertook initial theological studies at Morling Theological College, Australia, and then after over seventeen years pastoral experience commenced as Lecturer in Pastoral and Practical Studies at Morling College. He has completed a Masters of Adult Education at the University of Technology, Australia, and is currently a PhD candidate researching pastoral burnout and sustainability. His main areas of Christian education are in pastoral care, ministry formation, pastoral leadership, supervised field education, Christian worship, and family studies.

Dr. Angus Brook obtained his PhD in philosophy from the University of Sydney and is presently an associate professor in the School of Philosophy and Theology at the University of Notre Dame Australia, Sydney. His primary teaching and research areas are in metaphysics, particularly that of Aristotle and St. Thomas, ontology, phenomenology, and the philosophy of education.

Dr. Stephen J Fyson obtained his PhD in community psychology from Edith Cowan University, Western Australia. His academic interests are in understanding the nature of God, personhood and community, and the consequent implications for the social sciences—notably psychology and education. He has co-authored two books on Christian Life Studies, and published in international journals and professional support publications. He has also been a conference speaker in Australia and internationally, and is involved in Christian school development work in a number of countries. Stephen has worked in welfare, health, and education, and is currently the principal of a Christian special needs school in Newcastle, Australia.

Dr. Elizabeth Green is director of the National Centre for Christian Education Research at Liverpool Hope University. Elizabeth gained her doctorate in education from the University of Oxford, Green Templeton College, and her research interests include Christian education, social theory in education, and institutional ethos and culture. Previously Elizabeth has worked as a history teacher and pastoral head in UK secondary schools. Her publications include articles in journals such as the *British Journal of Sociology of Education* and the *Cambridge Journal of Education*.

Dr. David Long has been in the sociology department at The King's University College since he and his wife, Karen, moved with their children from Southern Ontario to Edmonton, Alberta, in 1989. He recently guest-edited a special edition of the *Native Studies Review* in tribute to the life and work of his long-time mentor and colleague Dr. Olive Patricia Dickason, and is currently putting together the fourth edition of *Visions of the Heart: Issues Involving Aboriginal People in Canada*. Along with his academic writing, David has long been committed to engaging various levels of government and the public at large on issues having to do with Aboriginal/non-Aboriginal relations, male health and well-being, and fathering. Much of the focus of his "community service" work with First Nation communities, men's groups, non-profit human service organizations, and government is largely on raising awareness and promoting positive change in the development of support services for males in all their diversity.

Dr. William Van Arragon is Associate Professor of History at The King's University College in Edmonton, Alberta, where he has taught since 2007. He received his BA from Calvin College and his PhD from Indiana University, where he studied early American religious history, and he is currently completing a book on Cotton Mather, the eighteenth-century Boston cleric and theologian. In addition, he is involved in ongoing projects in Canadian environmental history, especially focusing on Edmonton's beautiful urban river valley, and on Christian philosophies/theologies of history.

Dr. Ted Newell obtained his EdD from Teachers College, Columbia University, in 2004 and is an associate professor who teaches education and worldview at Crandall University, Moncton, Canada. He published the definitive study of Catholic religious educator James Michael Lee's theory, *"Education Has Nothing to Do with Theology"* (Princeton Theological Monograph Series, 2006), and has written on Jesus as a teacher, Christian liberal arts education, narrative approaches to education, and philosophy of education in the *Journal of Education & Christian Belief*, *Journal of General Education*, and elsewhere. He researches the influence of worldview on ways of educating, often taking a comparative and historical approach. He can be found online at linkd.in/lnbfti.

Dr. Edwin (Ted) Boyce received his PhD in education from the University of Alberta and then spent one year as a visiting scholar at Regent College, Vancouver. As well as being principal of Pacific Hills Christian School in Sydney, Australia, for almost thirty years, Dr. Boyce is also executive principal of Pacific Coast Christian School and Pacific Valley Christian School in Australia. For twenty-eight years he has been principal and then president of an institute of higher education, Southland College, based in Sydney, Australia. His primary interests in scholarship are in theology, philosophy, and comparative and international education. Dr. Boyce travels widely speaking at conferences throughout the world and had presented courses in Christian education in more than fifty countries. He is the founder of the Global Christian Schools Network, which seeks to promote service and mission through Christian school communities around the world.

PART ONE

Historical and Religious Foundations

1

The Christian Roots of Public Schooling in North America

Harro Van Brummelen

A remarkable educational event took place around 450 BC. In a large square in Jerusalem, the priest Ezra taught a large proportion of the fifty thousand Jews who had returned from captivity in Babylon. For eight days, Ezra and his helpers taught them the Law, the *Torah*, "making it clear and giving the meaning so that the people could understand what was being read." It became a joyful celebration, with the governor Nehemiah supplying "choice food and sweet drinks."[1]

This account is just one example of how the Judeo-Christian tradition has championed the importance of education. As this chapter describes, in the Western world it was Christian leaders who founded schools. They believed that serving God and neighbor demanded widely available schooling for all children. They were intent to foster an educated citizenry that could contribute responsibly and significantly to all aspects of society.

1. Neh 8:8, 10.

Education in Biblical Times

Long before Ezra, education was already important to the Jews. Teachers—originally priests and parents—instructed children with knowledge and authority. Teaching the Law and Israel's cultural narrative gave children an anchor in life. They learned about their responsibilities to God, their community, and their fellow human beings. Psalm 78 points out the importance the Jewish nation put on education. Children were to be taught "things we have heard and known" and "the praiseworthy deeds of the Lord" (vv. 3–4). Those praiseworthy deeds, as God made clear when he spoke to Job, were not restricted to religious knowledge but also included the marvels and intricacies of the physical world.[2]

In the century before the birth of Jesus the Jews established schools in every synagogue in Israel. These schools offered instruction to both boys and girls until age ten. This was the first school system in the world that was universal, compulsory, and supported by a tax (levied by the high priest). At the time of Jesus, 480 synagogue schools existed in Jerusalem alone. Students attended every day, even on the Sabbath, with sessions in the early morning and late afternoon. Apparently boys used the time in between to learn a craft, often the trade of their fathers, and girls performed duties in the home. Teachers were highly respected. As a popular saying put it, "Respect your teacher as you would God."[3]

Thus it was a mark of esteem that the Jews called Jesus a rabbi or teacher who taught with unusual authority.[4] Jesus testified to the truth. He taught people, as the Old Testament had enjoined teachers, God's marvelous deeds as well as the way they should live. He took persons where they were at and encouraged them to change and enrich their lives. He encouraged meaningful response and personal responsibility. He lived what he taught, showing genuine respect and concern for others. He demonstrated empathy and compassion while modeling humility, self-sacrifice, and integrity. Jesus has been a compelling and influential model for teachers ever since he lived on earth.

The last instruction that Jesus gave his followers was to teach all nations "everything I have commanded you."[5] The disciples and the Apostle Paul therefore stressed the importance of teaching. A large part of Paul's letter to Titus, for instance, discusses what it means to teach with integrity,

2. Job 38–41.

3. Kienel, *History of Christian School Education*, 30.

4. Matt 7:29.

5. Matt 28:20.

seriousness, and soundness of speech.[6] For Jesus' followers, education was important. It initiated children into their faith tradition, and it helped them "assess and synthesize their Christian life with the best of secular culture."[7]

Education in the Early Church

During the first few centuries after Jesus' death, Christians set up few schools. Their small communities often suffered persecution. They considered religious and moral education to be primarily the responsibility of parents. Therefore early Christians stressed education in homes and churches rather than in schools. They taught mainly religious history and doctrines that prepared for baptism.

Gradually larger centers established catechetical schools. Like the synagogue schools, but unlike the Roman ones, they taught both boys and girls. Their programs included both theological and literary emphases. In the second century, Justin Martyr in his catechetical school advanced the concept that all knowledge stems from God. Therefore Christians should study not only theology but also philosophy and literature. Two centuries later Augustine built on this. He said that Christians should be well grounded in classical and general studies since all truth belongs to God. At the same time, the intent of such study should be to understand how to serve God. Reason, while important, is to be used within the biblical framework of faith, hope, and love. The catechetical schools were the first Christian ones that influenced culture beyond the church.[8]

During the medieval period in Europe, education was the virtual monopoly of the Catholic Church. Most parishes had a school. However, usually only boys who were academically inclined and belonged to higher social classes had access. Monastic and convent schools prepared their students primarily for religious vocations. Despite the fact that Emperor Charlemagne at the end of the eighth century issued several directives that boys should learn to read in schools, the universality of education in Jesus' time no longer existed. Also, those who wrote about education addressed mainly the study of theology. Neither Jesus' example of master teaching nor some rudimentary pedagogical thought by Christian thinkers such as Augustine seems to have had much effect on medieval schools.

6. Titus 2.

7. Gangel and Benson, *Christian Education*, 81.

8. Schmidt, *Under the Influence*, 2001.

Christians Lead the Way to Universal Education in Europe

The sixteenth-century Reformers revitalized universal elementary education, and for the first time did so across a cluster of countries. Martin Luther (1483–1546) argued that a lack of education was a "great and murderous harm." It was shortsighted for parents not to send their children to school. Society needed not only clerics but also lawyers, secretaries, teachers, and doctors. Moreover, merchants and miners and other "common folk" were also God's servants and would therefore also benefit from schooling.[9]

In 1524 Luther wrote a lengthy letter to the mayors and councilors of all cities in Germany that it was their duty to maintain schools for all boys and girls.[10] Schools would provide spiritual, material, and political benefit for the German nation. They would promote the fear of God, faith, and good works in the service of others. God's Word was to be a central focus of the curriculum. Nonetheless, since all truth is from God, children would also study languages, history, music, and mathematics. Luther's letter about schooling led to the establishment of schools throughout Germany, ones where the poor were assisted to attend. Luther is recognized as one of the outstanding figures in promoting popular education in the Western world.

Later in the sixteenth century John Calvin (1509–1564) together with his former Latin teacher, Mathurin Cordier, set out to set up schools in Switzerland and France. They began one of the first free and compulsory public education systems in the Western world. The curriculum included reading, writing, arithmetic, history, catechism, the singing of Psalms and, later, Latin. Even more notable for the time was that education deliberately began with the simple and moved to the more advanced, and was administered with gentleness and moderate discipline. Cordier's book for teaching Latin was so innovative pedagogically that it became one of the main ones used for several centuries throughout the Western world, including North America. It also encouraged virtues such as diligence, courtesy, honesty, respect, and love and fear of God. Calvin and Cordier's influence resulted in a network of two thousand French Protestant public schools prior to their demise because of the severe persecutions that began in the 1560s.

Calvin-inspired Swiss, French, Dutch, and Walloon municipalities supported universal education for all boys and girls. The desire that all children should read the Bible as well as a progressive spirit of inquiry led to what was the earliest acceptance of general tax levies for schooling in the Western world. Schools were to be for rich and poor alike. Ministers were

9. Luther, "Sermon on Keeping Children in School."

10. Ibid.

required to visit schools frequently to encourage teachers and to assess both their spiritual atmosphere and their quality of education. Public schools abounded throughout the Netherlands, and there was a zealous interest in sustaining them.[11] Calvin and Cordier determined the framework that guided Dutch and Swiss schooling for several centuries.

One of the greatest pedagogical thinkers that the world has seen was John Amos Comenius (1592–1670). Like Melanchton and Cordier, he wanted education to lead children to faith and piety, to moral virtue, and to knowledge of languages and the arts. Through a broad-based knowledge people would come to know God, the source of all truth, and this would lead to world peace. On this score he was overly optimistic, of course. Still, this conviction led him to be the first educator to write about stages of readiness and how to make learning attractive and interesting for children, "God's most precious gifts." He insisted that the classroom atmosphere should be encouraging and pleasant. Kindergarten-age children were to learn through play. Playing "house" or "father and mother" through the use of toys would enable them to understand the function of different members of the family. Comenius developed the first textbook with pictures, which for a century was the most popular text in Europe.

Comenius was persecuted for his faith but his resulting travels meant that he impacted schooling throughout central and western Europe. Governments in countries like Poland, Sweden, and England used him as a consultant to structure school systems and determine how learning would take place. He was even asked, but declined, to become the president of Harvard. He is still justly called "The Father of Modern Education."[12]

The Impact of Protestant Christians on Schooling in America

Calvin's influence on schooling was not limited to Western Europe. The Calvinist Puritans and Scottish Calvinist Presbyterians "profoundly colored all early American education."[13] The Massachusetts Law of 1642, passed by the Puritans, was the first one in the English-speaking world where a government required all children to be taught to read. In 1647 an additional law required each town of at least fifty households to appoint a teacher of reading and writing, and each town with one hundred or more households

11. Cubberley, *History of Education*, 335.
12. Lockerbie, *Passion for Learning*, 184, 204.
13. Cubberley, *History of Education*, 299.

to provide a secondary grammar school. These laws resulted from the Calvinistic conviction that the state should provide schooling for all children. "It can be safely asserted, in the light of later developments, that the two laws of 1642 and 1647 represent the foundations upon which our American state public-school systems have been built."[14]

The early schools in New England used the Bible and a catechism as texts. For more than a century after 1690, American schools used many editions of *The New England Primer*, a collection of readings based on Christian doctrine and morality ("In Adam's Fall / We sinned all"). Later, Presbyterian pastor and university professor William McGuffey wrote his famous McGuffey Readers in an effort to improve pedagogical materials for public schools, as well as to promote Christian faith and morality. McGuffey's stories, illustrations, and questions held the interest of children. From 1837 to 1922 more than one hundred million copies were printed. Until 1870, Calvinist theology dominated the readers, including sermon excerpts from McGuffey's friend, Lyman Beecher.

Lyman Beecher's daughter Catherine was able to motivate many women to travel to the western United States in the mid-nineteenth century to be teachers in the expanding settlements. Catherine Beecher believed that this would result in domestic, moral, and religious blessings for both the teachers and their communities. Most of these women were Protestant Christians and did so to serve God. One of Beecher's intents was to help women avoid exploitation by industrial capitalists, and instead to use their God-given gifts as followers of Christ instead for the "noble profession" of educating children.[15]

Beecher worked closely with her brother-in-law Calvin Stowe, a professor of biblical literature who was a leading common school advocate. Stowe's 1836 report for the Ohio legislature on the Prussian school system was used by at least six states to establish their public school curriculum. Like Egerton Ryerson in Canada ten years later, Stowe promoted non-sectarian Christian faith and morality. The public school curriculum was to show the glory of God in creation and undertake activities to help pupils develop their intellectual abilities and think about their duties. His belief that teachers should be well trained to implement this type of education stimulated the growth of state-supported teacher training in the U.S.[16]

Horace Mann (1796–1859) is often referred to as the father of the American public school for his role in establishing common schools

14. Ibid., 366.

15. Lockerbie, *Passion for Learning*.

16. Watras, *Foundations of Educational Curriculum and Diversity*.

in Massachusetts. A contemporary of Calvin Stowe, he left Calvinism to become a Unitarian. However, "the influence of his early [Calvinist] training manifested itself in the moralism of his intellectual and personal temperament."[17] Like Stowe, he promoted a nondenominational "common Christianity" based on the truths of the Bible as an essential ingredient of public schooling. He was proud that he restored Bible reading in the schools so that Christian precepts and doctrines would be upheld.[18]

What is clear from these few examples is that Christians and persons with a strong Christian heritage not only founded but also put a lasting stamp on early schooling in the United States. Without them, the development of universal, free schooling would have taken much longer, and the schools would likely not have emphasized as strongly the importance of morals and values.

The Christian Ethos of English Canada's Early Schools and Sunday Schools

Christian churches and organizations opened the early English-speaking Canadian schools. In many ways developments were similar to those in the northeastern United States and also reveal how schooling today owes much to Christian churches and Christian educational leaders. So I discuss the development of schooling in Canada as a case study that has its parallels in other English-speaking nations, parallels that worked themselves out somewhat differently in different locations as a result of the particular leadership given by prominent educational leaders.

The first common schools in the Atlantic provinces in eastern Canada were founded and supported in the eighteenth century by the Anglican Society for the Propagation of the Gospel in Foreign Parts (SPG). Young clergymen from England sent out by the SPG started schools with themselves as teachers. The SPG and other Christian charitable organizations enabled many children, especially the poor and dispossessed, to attend school. However, as in England, a common public school system with government grants was established only very gradually.

In the English-speaking parts of the central provinces of Quebec and Ontario, it was most often Protestant clergy who brought about the decision to build a schoolhouse. Many clergy also became informal or appointed

17. Cremin, in Mann, *Passion for Learning*, 4.

18. Gutek, *History of the Western Educational Experience*; Mann, *Republic and the School*, 202.

superintendents of one or more schools. The schools had a strong Christian basis. A common reader was Murray's 1823 *English Reader*, which contained passages on biblical persons such as Joseph, whose "integrity and prudence" enabled him to be "justly raised to a high station, wherein his abilities were eminently displayed in the public service."[19] Teachers were expected to promote the principles of Christian faith and morality.

Early in the nineteenth century free Sunday schools, often operated by the non-denominational Sunday School Union Society of Canada, complemented regular fee-based schools. They were set up not only to promote literacy, but also to combat poor physical health and immorality. Volunteers provided weekly education from three to six hours, mainly but not exclusively for poor children. In 1832 between 350 to 400 Sunday schools taught some 10,000 students in English-speaking Canada. They stressed memorizing and understanding Bible texts and "placed much emphasis on literacy as a means of gaining religious knowledge and achieving moral behaviour."[20] The Sunday Schools provided not only rudimentary literacy for children who had no other schooling opportunities, but also what was often the only source of public reading material in the community.

The Christian Educational Legacy of Egerton Ryerson

A Christian ethos was also a main impetus in the establishment of nineteenth-century Ontario public schools. Ontario's 1836 Duncombe report on education stated that

> Those great [Christian] principles of religious truths and moral duty in which all agree, are the only ones which are needed in the moral education of children at school. . . . One thing is certain, if religious influences are banished from our provincial system of education, every denomination will be injured in its most vital interest.[21]

The Dunscombe Report was also one of the first to propose that schools were to be universally accessible so that all inhabitants would gain "virtuous intelligence."

Dunscombe's thinking was actualized by Egerton Ryerson, who is justifiably called the father of public schooling in Ontario. Ryerson also had

19. Brown, *Schooling in the Clearings*, 32.

20. Ibid., 39.

21. Guldemond, *Ontario's Educative Prejudice*, 51–52.

momentous influence on the expansion of all English-speaking schools in Canada. Ryerson, a Methodist minister, gained widespread support as he opposed Anglican control of Ontario's schools. Instead, he promoted a common Protestant public school. He held that denominational schools would fragment enrollments and therefore Canadian society. Ryerson was appointed superintendent of Ontario's schools in 1846. He set about to create a public school system that promoted the common principles of evangelical Christianity as the foundation of a healthy society. He reluctantly allowed only Roman Catholics to operate "separate" but government-controlled schools. Their strong opposition to common schools might, Ryerson felt, undermine the latter's viability.

For Ryerson, schooling was to be based on generic Christian moral principles buttressed by reason. That basis would lead to a prosperous and happy country in which ignorance, vice, and crime could be overcome. Instilling a common Christian morality as children were educated would be the best security of proper governance of self and hence to peace, order, liberty, good government, and prosperity. Ryerson's 1846 *Report on a System of Public Elementary Instruction Education for Upper Canada*[22] set out his blueprint for Ontario's public school system. In it, he devoted more than thirty pages to the teaching of religion and morality, including biblical instruction. Ryerson emphasized the "*absolute necessity of making Christianity the basis and cement of the structure of public education*."[23] He regularly reiterated that Christian faith should be the all-pervading principle of education. For instance, natural history "prepares the mind and heart to contemplate, admire and adore the wisdom and beneficence of the Creator."[24] Education was beneficial only if first of all it nurtured Christian faith and morality.

To accomplish this, Ryerson set up a centralized school system. By 1871, the schools were free, universal, and compulsory. All had opening and closing exercises consisting of the Lord's Prayer and readings from the Bible. They promoted virtue and obedience by teaching the Ten Commandments and through a system of merits and demerits.[25] Ryerson's efforts, driven by his faith commitment, firmly established a school system that was based on Christian moral principles, that taught a relevant program of studies, and that was accessible to the whole population.

22. Ryerson, *Report on a System of Public Elementary Instruction for Upper Canada.*
23. Ibid, 32 (italics original).
24. Ibid, 136.
25. Curtis, *Building the Educational State*, 103–5.

The legacy of Ryerson's universal, Christian system of schooling was felt long after his death in all of Canada, except for Quebec and Newfoundland.[26] In western Canada, for instance, the structure of the school systems, their curricula, their prescription of uniform textbooks, and their religious instruction were all strikingly similar to those that Ryerson had implemented in Ontario. That meant that a broad Protestantism framed nineteenth-century public schools in English-speaking Canada. For instance, British Columbia's public school system was established in 1872 to be "non-sectarian." Nevertheless, the prescribed readers were Ryerson-inspired ones that taught that God was the creator the universe and that children should read the Scriptures daily in order to absorb his goodness. Similarly, the 1888 curriculum guide for the North-West Territories (encompassing Alberta, Saskatchewan and northern Canada) stated that teachers should discuss "the duty of believing in, fearing, and loving God, cleanliness, and neatness, honesty, truthfulness and obedience."[27]

Without Ryerson's leadership, the establishment of public schools would have lagged and been much more fragmented. Ryerson was also able to draw together the views of most Protestant Christians to support providing education for all that reflected Christian principles and morality. While the latter has faded, the structure of Canadian public schools is still a direct result of Ryerson's leadership.

The Waning of the Christian Legacy in Canadian Schooling

Ryerson and other Christian leaders gave the impetus for accessible, free public schools in English Canada. However, that the Christian foundation of public education gradually eroded is clear from the textbooks that schools used to transmit cultural values. The textbooks prescribed for public schools late in the nineteenth century all promoted orthodox Christian doctrines based on the Bible. They emphasized morals rooted in Christian faith.

26. Tomkins, *Common Countenance*, 47–49, 56, 69.

27. Sheehan, "Indoctrination." I do not want to imply that all the work of religious leaders yielded positive educational results. Two glaring shortcomings were (1) the Catholic's Church's lack of support of compulsory schooling in French-speaking Canada, and (2) the heart-rending involvement of churches in setting up and operating federally-funded residential schools, schools aimed at the elimination of indigenous culture, which was often tragically accompanied by physical, cultural, and sexual abuse. Describing the complexity of the roots and praxis in these educational situations would require separate chapters.

Early in the twentieth century, social gospel thinking gradually replaced an emphasis on personal salvation, but Christian morals were still highlighted. Churches no longer existed to convert people to Christian faith, but to improve the moral and social conditions of society and thus be a civilizing force. Obedience to God was replaced by virtues for citizenship such as courage, loyalty, and justice. Until the mid-century they upheld Christian morality as something of central concern in the lives of Canadians. By the 1960s, however, very little of Canada's Christian heritage remained in its school textbooks—and, therefore, in the teaching and learning taking place in the schools.[28]

While the Bible became less directly relevant to public education, until the mid-twentieth century the Christian faith of most educational leaders and teachers resulted in a deep commitment to provide free, quality education for all within a Christian ethical framework. Hilda Neatby, author of the well-known *So Little for the Mind*, together with philosopher George Grant were the last persons to gain national attention with their belief that "a divine purpose within history" and "God-given laws of morality" should be the basis for schooling.[29] While Neatby's critique of progressive education played some part in restoring the formal teaching of the disciplines, it was no longer possible to capture the public mood with her Christian ideals.

Early in the twenty-first century most Canadian educational leaders have forgotten the role and contributions of Christianity to education. Most promote the ideals that educated persons are to be autonomous and self-sufficient, productive and thoughtful, and respectful and tolerant. Respectful and tolerant, however, is often interpreted as uncritical acceptance or celebration of all points of view. Notably missing are Christian values such as compassion, forgiveness, moral uprightness, humility, and self-sacrifice—traits considered essential in the Christian tradition. In this way, Canadian schooling now often contributes to rather than redresses the societal malaise of self-centered self-fulfillment.

Past, Current, and Future Christian Influences on Education

Both in Europe and in North America, Christians were the first to recognize the importance of schooling for all children. The sixteenth-century Reformers reawakened the support for universal schooling that was prevalent

28. Van Brummelen, "Faith on the Wane."

29. Tomkins, *Common Countenance*, 289.

among the Jews in Jesus' time. They wanted children to be well versed in the Bible, but also in more general studies so that they could understand and contribute to society. This influence was carried over to the "New World." There Christians were usually the founders of the first schools and systems of schools. It was their faith that instilled in them the dedication to set up and operate schools—and to persevere under what were often trying circumstances. It was their faith that set the stage for free and universal schooling. And it was their faith that caused them to do so according to Christian guidelines and values.

In English-speaking Canada, the Protestant Christian consensus that dominated public education for many decades gradually crumbled. However, that does not mean that Christians no longer have an impact on Canadian schooling. First, individual Christian leaders today still impact education on the basis of their Christian faith. For instance, Michael Tymchak's Christian faith led him to be a pioneer in Aboriginal teacher education in Saskatchewan. After serving as Dean of Education at the University of Regina, he authored a report for the provincial government that makes the case that effective schools are ones where the culture of the children and the culture of the supporting community are strongly reflected in the school. Such schools, he holds, must ensure that parents are valued as partners and have meaningful involvement in the school's goals and program design.[30] Tymchak's report provided a basis for educational improvement in his province. It is recognized to have the potential of making a unique contribution to Canadian schooling.

Second, more educators are once again realizing that the consideration and study of religion can help restore education's transformative edge. Books and journal articles that discuss the importance of spirituality and religion in the curriculum are once again being published. Some Christian teachers in public schools are using a renewed societal interest in spirituality to discuss questions of ultimate meaning. They teach about religion and spirituality in meaningful ways while honoring their students' religious diversity and identity. They enable students to wrestle with the spiritual and moral aspects of life.

Third, Christians have led efforts to provide government-funded schools of choice, especially in western Canada. All four Western Canadian provinces today channel some tax revenues to religious schools. In British Columbia, about 8 percent of all students attend non-public religious schools. In Alberta and Saskatchewan, some religiously based schools have become alternatives in the public system. For instance, nine Protestant

30. Tymchak, *School Plus*.

Christian Logos Schools operate in Edmonton as wings of public schools. These schools meet provincial curriculum requirements, but are distinctly Christian in orientation and ethos. The Edmonton Public Schools recognize that working together in a pluralistic society means allowing diverse schools to thrive, including Christian ones. In this way, Christians are contributing positively to educating students according to a Christian worldview, while at the same time promoting the overall quality of education in a community.

A democratic, pluralistic society can flourish only if it upholds a number of key principles. These include respect for all persons and their dignity, truthfulness in all dealings, responsibility towards self and others, and justice and compassion for the disadvantaged. Significantly, these were the principles that led Christians to found and operate schools and school systems in various parts of the world, including North America. These are still the principles propounded by Christians today who try to contribute to the welfare of society by being involved in education. By continuing to insist on these basic values, Christian educators will continue to have an impact on schooling.

Questions for Reflection

1. Think about the cultural context of the people of Israel in biblical times. Why would they have put so much emphasis on education? Can you give other examples from the Bible where the importance of education is stressed?
2. Unlike the Protestant Reformers and their followers, the Catholic Church in Europe emphasized education for boys only. And even as late as the first half of the twentieth century, education in Catholic Quebec lagged behind that of mainly Protestant English-speaking Canada. What were the religious and cultural reasons for such differences?
3. John Amos Comenius has been called "the father of modern education." Egerton Ryerson has similarly been called "the father of English-speaking Canadian schools." There is no doubt that these men had a formidable impact on education. But they also had their shortcomings. Check some online biographies of Comenius and/or Ryerson and develop an argument whether or not their "father" descriptions are warranted.
4. The description of the development of education in Canada is described as a "case study that has its parallels in other English-speaking nations." Investigate how the development of education in Canadian

was similar to and different from that in another English-speaking country (use your own country if you're not from Canada).

5. This chapter describes how a number of Christian leaders and their followers have had a significantly positive effect on the development schooling. However, it's possible to tell a different story. For instance, for many centuries the Catholic Church prevented girls from going to school, and more recently various churches have been involved in cultural and other abuse as they participated in educating indigenous children. Indeed, the initial Canadian residential school model was fully supported by Egerton Ryerson. And in the United States for several decades after 1960, many "Christian" private schools were established in order to maintain the segregation of Caucasian and African-American children. Should Christians defend the positive influence of their heritage while acknowledging its shortcomings? Why or why not?

Recommended Reading

I give a few websites below that give some additional information to the topics described in this chapter. They are introductory ones, but with some useful links. For more scholarly readings, it is best to search for books and journal articles on university library websites.

For education in Bible times, see http://www.biblestudytools.com/dictionaries/bakers-evangelical-dictionary/education-in-bible-times.html.

The website http://voices.yahoo.com/christian-education-early-church-4171245.html gives a brief introduction to educators in the early church as well as a number of useful links.

For helpful introductory websites on the educational influence of Martin Luther, John Calvin, and John Amos Comenius, respectively, see http://voices.yahoo.com/christian-education-early-church-4171245.html, http://equip.pcacep.org/john-calvin-the-reformer-and-educator.html, and http://www.froebelweb.org/web7005.html.

For a fairly short but balanced biography of Egerton Ryerson see http://www.biographi.ca/009004-119.01-e.php?id_nbr=5817.

You can find a brief introduction to the history of education in Canada with some useful links at http://www.thecanadianencyclopedia.com/articles/history-of-education.

Bibliography

Brown, Kathleen. *Schooling in the Clearings: Stanstead 1800–1850*. Stanstead, Quebec: Stanstead Historical Society, 2001.

Cubberley, Ellwood. *The History of Education*. Cambridge, MA: Houghton Mifflin, 1920; 1948.

Curtis, B. *Building the Educational State: Canada West, 1836–1871*. London, ON: Althouse; Philadelphia: Falmer, 1988.

Gangel, Kenneth, and Benson, Warren. *Christian Education: Its History and Philosophy*. Chicago: Moody, 1983.

Guldemond, A. *Ontario's Educative Prejudice: A Critical Exposition of the History and Philosophy of Education in Ontario*. Toronto: CJL Foundation, 1974.

Gutek, Gerald. *The History of the Western Educational Experience*. 2nd ed. Prospect Heights, IL: Waveland, 1995.

Kienel, P. *A History of Christian School Education*. Vol. 1. Colorado Springs, CO: Association of Christian Schools International, 1998.

Lockerbie, Bruce. L. *A Passion for Learning: The History of Christian Thought on Education*. Chicago: Moody, 1994.

Luther, Martin. "A Sermon on Keeping Children in School." 1524. Martin Luther's Writings: Sermons, Commentary & Other Works. Online: http://www.godrules.net/library/luther/NEW1luther_d12.htm.

Mann, Horace. *The Republic and the School*. Edited by L. Cremin. New York: Teachers College, Columbia University, 1957.

Ryerson, Egerton. *Report on a System of Public Elementary Instruction for Upper Canada*. Montreal: Lovell and Gibson, 1847.

Schmidt, Alvin. *Under the Influence: How Christianity Transformed Civilization*. Grand Rapids: Zondervan, 2001.

Sheehan, N. "Indoctrination: Moral Education in the Early Prairie School House." In *Shaping the Schools of the Canadian West*, edited by D. Jones, N. Sheehan, and R. Stamp, 222–34. Calgary: Detselig Enterprises, 1979.

Tomkins, G. *Common Countenance: Stability and Change in the Canadian Curriculum*. Scarborough, ON: Prentice-Hall Canada, 1986.

Tymchak, Michael, and Saskatchewan Instructional Development Unit. *School Plus: A Vision for Children and Youth*. Final report to the Minister of Education. Saskatoon: Government of Saskatchewan, 2001.

Van Brummelen, Harro. "Faith on the Wane: A Documentary Analysis of Shifting Worldviews in Canadian Textbooks." *Journal of Research on Christian Education* 3/1 (1994) 51–77.

Watras, J. *The Foundations of Educational Curriculum and Diversity: 1565 to the Present*. Boston: Allyn and Bacon, 2002.

Wilson, J., R. Stamp, and L. Audet, editors. *Canadian Education: A History*. Scarborough, ON: Prentice-Hall Canada, 1970.

2

Christian Educators Who Made an Impact

Comenius and His "School as a Forging Place of Humanity"

Jan Hábl

Introduction: Modernity, Postmodernity, and the Problem of Humanity

Humaneness is a precious commodity. It is more precious the more we are aware of its lack. Since the time of the Enlightenment people have believed that humaneness would follow the progress of knowledge, that the right *scientia* would secure the right *conscientia*. The one who knows what is right will do what is right. Historical experience, however, has proven that human beings are more complicated than that.

There is no doubt that certain areas of human potential have made unprecedented progress. Technologies have provided extraordinary power and overabundance—especially to the Western part of the world. On the other hand, our technocratic society faces gigantic ecological, economical, political, social, and other problems; millions of people are living in poverty on the edge of society, starving and lacking foundational care. "The technocratic optimism of the 50s and 60s is being re-evaluated today," observes Jarmila Skalková. "It appears that science and technology, as they have functioned in the resulting society, bring about a number of antihuman symptoms: objectification of human beings, one-sided development and neglect of spiritual needs. The key problematic motifs are the alienation of personality under the pressure of bureaucratic structures, and a mass consumerist culture."[1] In the same way, Zdenek Helus comments on our era from the sociological point of view, observing that it is a "period of great disruption" in which we are disturbed by realities such as the conflict of civilizations, potentials for global self-destruction, uncontrolled demographic explosions, the decline of moral literacy, a dramatic decrease in social capital, political and religious extremism, etc.[2] The moral aspect of the problem is underlined by statements such as the one by Gilles Lipovetsky: "the 21st Century will either be ethical or it will not be at all."[3] Similarly, Jan Sokol speaks about human beings as an "endangered species."[4]

There are some who still believe that the current crisis of humanity is a temporal and provisional thing.[5] Its overcoming is expected as soon as some new, technically better method is generated and implemented—whether political, economic, structural, educational or other. The optimistic spirit of modernity, however, is gradually yielding to postmodern skepticism. The new generation does not believe that any scientific, business, or economic, let alone political, solution exists that would ensure a better existence than what their parents had. The progress of humanity has been, for the postmodern individual, utterly lost in romantic illusions. Truth is an empty concept that means whatever anyone wants it to mean. Objective knowledge is irrelevant. Law and justice have been left to the mercy of interpretation. And schools have become tools of indoctrination, for their so-called preparation for life is—deconstructed with postmodern hermeneutics—nothing but a functional molding of individuals to be able to accept and play well their socially determined role, according to the agenda of modernity.[6]

1. Skalková, *Humanization of Education*, 46–47.
2. Cf. Helus, "Culture of Education."
3. Lipovetsky, *Twilight of Obligation*, 11.
4. Sokol, *Philosophical Anthropology*, 15.
5. Cf. Prázný, "Komenský."
6. In this work I will not deal with the specifics of modern and postmodern philosophy and culture, but rather rely on authors who have studied this area in greater detail, such as: Eagleton, *The Illusions of Postmodernism*; Erickson, *Truth or Consequences*; Geer, *Mapping Postmodernism*; Grenz, *A Primer on Postmodernism*; Greer and Lewis, *Brief History*; Harvey, *The Condition of Postmodernity*; Lyotard, *The Postmodern Condition*; Murphy, *Beyond Liberalism*; Murphy and McClendon, "Distinguishing Modern

Is there any alternative? A meaningful understanding of humanity? A meaningful way of educating a human being that would help the individual to become truly humane? Schools are often expected to play a significant role in developing "authentic humanity," but what does it mean to be human in the first place? To answer these questions, I want to turn to the work of Jan Amos Comenius. Why Comenius, a premodern thinker of the seventeenth century? His anthropology as well as his pedagogy offers something modern philosophy has lost. In contrast to the typical modern self-imposed restriction on metaphysics, Comenius's philosophy of education assumes it. In fact, he believes that a proper education is the key means of restoring humanity. Despite an antiquated language and premodern philosophical apparatus, his work brings fresh insights to the contemporary dehumanizing situation.

Biographical Context of Comenius's Work

Comenius was born on March 28, 1592, in Moravia. His family belonged to the Unitas Fratrum (Unity of Brethren), which was a branch of the Czech (and Moravian) Reformation movement begun in 1457. Inspired by the ideas of Petr Chelčický (c. 1380–c. 1460) and Jan Hus (c. 1369–1415) the Unity strove for radical piety and a return to Christ-like simplicity of life. It was their radicalism and separatism that caused much persecution of the Brethren right from the beginning of their existence. Their characteristic non-compromising desire for spiritual purity also included, in their early periods, a rejection of magisterial power, oath taking, and war. They also avoided worldly education and vocations such as commerce, which they considered a hindrance to a consistent following of the Lord. Due to their interaction with the Reformation ideas of the time, the community gradually developed into a Protestant denomination, standing theologically between Lutheranism and Calvinism.

Comenius's life was marked by a series of particularly difficult afflictions, which significantly shaped both his theology and his pedagogy. At the age of twelve (in 1604) Comenius lost his parents and two sisters, probably from the plague, and had to live with one of his other sisters and her family. When only thirteen years old Comenius experienced firsthand the destructiveness of war; as a consequence of the religious conflict between the Hungarians (Calvinists) and the Habsburgs (Roman Catholics) he lost all his inherited possessions, as well as his guardian family. His church community

and Postmodern Theologies"; Murphy, *Anglo-American Postmoderniity*; Wright, *Religion, Education and Post-Modernity*.

soon recognized his natural talent and sent him to Přerov Gymnasium—one of the best high schools in the country at the time. Later Comenius was sent to the reformed universities in Herborn and Heidelberg, where he encountered some of the most influential ideas of the time (Alstead's encyclopediasm, Piscator's irenism, Ratichius's educational reforms, etc.). Two years after returning from his studies he was ordained as a minister, and his first pastoral appointment was to the church at Fulnek in Northern Moravia. By this time the Brethren theologians had determined that there is no biblical reason for their pastors not to marry, so Comenius's young wife Magdalene accompanied him.

The beginning of the Thirty Year's War in 1618 brought about another series of life afflictions for Comenius. His homeland was devastated by various troops of the Habsburg (Roman Catholic) armies. Being a cleric of the Protestant church, Comenius was forced to leave both his family and his community, and hide in various locations in Northern Moravia. By 1623 he had lost virtually everything: his house was destroyed, his congregation dispersed, his library was burned by the Jesuits, and his young wife, having just delivered their second child, died of the plague along with the two babies. For the next five years Comenius led an insecure life, until the final expulsion of all Protestants from the country. The Brethren found refuge for a short while in Leszno, Poland. Comenius remarried, but his second wife also died, leaving him with four children. His third wife outlived him. In Leszno he became a co-rector of the Brethren's school and later the bishop (the last one) of the denomination. It was during this period that most of his educational works were written. Comenius's fruitful, twenty-eight-year-long Leszno period (1628–1656) was interrupted by three sojourns to other countries, where he was invited to work on educational reforms as his reputation as an outstanding educator spread across Europe. The first invitation came from England (1641–1642), the second from Sweden (1642–1648), and the third from (what is today) Hungary (1650–1654). Comenius even received an invitation to work as rector of the newly founded Harvard College in America. The Northern Wars in 1655 between the Protestant Swedish King Charles X Gustav and the Roman Catholic Polish King John II Casimir proved to be fatal for Comenius and his denomination. The Lezsno Brethren community naturally sided with Swedish party, which the Polish Catholic majority considered to be a betrayal of Poland. As soon as the city of Lezsno was no longer protected by the Swedish troops, the Polish partisans invaded it and burned it. Comenius and his family barely escaped with their lives, lost all their property, and were forced into exile once again. Particularly painful for Comenius was the loss of certain manuscripts on which he had worked for more than forty years. From Leszno he took refuge in Amsterdam in the Netherlands, where he died in 1670.

School as Humanitatis Officinae[7]

Comenius's contribution to education is enormous. He attempted to write about two hundred books related to education. To outline his philosophy of education I will focus on three main areas that represent the most significant contributions: 1) his revolutionary approach to language learning and teaching, 2) his emphasis on wholeness and universality in education, and 3) the concept of following nature in education.

Language Teaching/Learning

Comenius himself was surprised by the international fame brought about by the publication of his Latin textbook, *Janua linguarum reserata* (The Gate of Tongues Unlocked) in 1633. He quickly accompanied it with two additional language textbooks: *Vestibulum* for the elementary level, and *Atrium* for the advanced. The fame of these textbooks was so great that it soon reached the royal courts; Douphin the Great, son of Ludwig XIV, and Swedish Queen Kristina Augusta, for instance, learned Latin from them. Amazingly, even Jesuits, whose pedagogical approaches were so antagonistic to Comenius's pedagogical universalism, could not deny the effectiveness of his method and used his *Janua* in their schools.[8] To understand its success, it is necessary to know that the language teaching methodology of Comenius's time

7. Comenius first used this term in the *Czech Didactic* ("dílna lidskosti"). Later he reworked the *Czech Didactic* into the *Great Didactic*, published in Latin. For the English translation I will rely partly on Keating's translation of the *Great Didactic* (see bibliography), and partly on my own translation of the *Czech Didactic*. Keating translates the term *humanitatis officinae* sometimes as the "forge of humanity," sometimes as the "workshop of humanity." The differences between the *Czech Didactic* and the *Great Didactic* are very instructive. The Czech version was written for Czech readers who knew nothing about the subject, while the *Great Didactic* was written for an educated and international audience. The two books are almost identical in structure, but there are differences in emphases and formulations. Since the two books complement each other well, I will draw on both of them. Parenthetical citations to them will be abbreviated in the following manner: *Czech Didactic*, chapter I, paragraph 2 as *CD* I.2; and *Great Didactic*, chapter III, paragraph 4 as *GD* III.4.

8. The ambivalent relationship with the Jesuits would be almost amusing were it not for the tragic circumstances. At the very time when the Jesuits demanded Comenius's death for heresy (they burned his library in Fulnek in 1621), they published and used his textbook in their schools.

relied mainly on rote memorization and repetition. Boys were forced to recite long pieces of classical antique writings, for example, without any understanding of the sounds they were uttering; the meaning was "locked" to them. The process was long, painfull, and often completely unsuccessful, the learners simply never grasped the foreign language. Comenius's lament in the *Great Didactic* shows the point: "it is men we are forming and not parrots" (*GD* XXII.3).

In contrast to that spiritless recitation, Comenius's method was based on the *pansophic*[9] idea of an encyclopedic organization of material and the interconnection of real things, sense experience, and words. The key principles can be summarized in several maxims: 1) foreign languages ought to be learned through the mother tongue; 2) the ideas ought to be obtained through objects rather than words; 3) proceed from the familiar to the unfamiliar; 4) phasing and progression of teaching must be appropriate to the learner's development; 5) the learner ought to be equipped with a universal compendium of knowledge, that is, knowledge of all important aspects of his world (physical, social, religious, moral, etc.); 6) make the learning process a pleasure by the proper choice of learning matter, and also by the proper (nonviolent) methodological treatment of the matter.[10] The *Janua* was followed by a series of other textbooks that made language learning even more user friendly. Perhaps the most famous is *Orbis Sensualium Pictus* (The Visible World in Pictures), the first illustrated language textbook.

M. W. Keating comments on Comenius's language-learning revolution by saying that he "rescued the boys of his generation from the sterile study of words and introduced them to the world of mechanics, politics, and morality."[11] Similarly, Daniel Murphy praises his approach: "Seldom in the history of language teaching has it been so closely related to the personal and social environment of the learner as it was in these new texts, which probably explains their survival more than three centuries after their creation . . ."[12]

Interestingly, Comenius gradually became frustrated by the side effects of the fame. He kept receiving invitations from various countries asking him to help with didactic reforms, but he saw his calling elsewhere. He sought after greater goals: not merely the reformation of schools and learning methods, but the restoration of all human affairs.

9. For more on the idea of *pansophy* see below.

10. For Comenius's own summary of principles of language learning/teaching see *GD* XII.

11. Comenius/Keating, 24.

12. Murphy, *Comenius*, 195.

Holistic Approach to Education

The notion of "wholeness" or "universality" is an integral part of Comenius's pansophic approach to education. He often expressed it in the motto *omnes, omnia, omneno*, which means that all people ought to learn, in all possible ways, all things. Let's consider *omnia* first. When saying "all things" Comenius recognizes that "a perfect knowledge of all sciences and arts . . . is neither useful nor possible for any human being" (*CD* X.1). Wholeness in this context means the learning of "the foundations, reasons, and goals of all the important things," which enables human beings to "fulfill the essence" that is given them by God.[13] In the *Czech Didactic*, Comenius elaborates on this theme, and relates the content of education to the previously set goals: a) the goal of rationality refers to the knowledge of created beings (that which is); b) the goal of virtuousness refers to the knowledge of morality (that which ought to be); c) the goal of godliness refers to the knowledge of God's grace (that which is to be enjoyed). These three areas of knowledge then constitute the content of education, which enables humans to understand why they were brought to life: to serve God, other creatures, and themselves (*CD* X).

When saying *omneno*, that is, teaching/learning by "all possible ways," Comenius refers to the noetic as well as methodological aspect of education. He often expresses it in the triad *theoria/praxis/chrésis* (wise use), pointing to the fact that knowledge without virtue and piety is never complete, for knowledge—as well as anything else—might be both used and abused. A person who is well *informed* but not morally *formed* is merely a "useless encumbrance on the earth," according to Comenius—even a "misery," to oneself as well as to others (cf. *GD* XXIII). For the greater the knowledge, the worse it is when it's used for evil. Therefore Comenius contended that an educated but immoral humanity goes backwards rather than forwards, degenerating. On the other hand, his "forging-place of humanity" deliberately aims for regeneration, that is, for the restoration of every dimension of humanity—reason, character, and spirit.

The idea that morality as well as piety is both teachable and learnable might be surprising to a contemporary educator (and not only to Christian educators). After all, is not authentic piety (together with morality) a direct result of God's saving grace? What was implicit in the early *Didactic* is made explicit in the later *Pampaedia*. Here Comenius presents his argument for the necessity of leading students towards morality and courtesy, and the following paragraph—dealing with "instilling piety"—begins with the words, "For it is evident . . . that also piety is teachable . . ."[14] He further recognizes

13. Cf. Comenius, "Pampaedia," 1–12.

14. Ibid., 47.

that regeneration is the necessary starting point given by the grace of God. But grace does not "abolish" nature; on the contrary, grace "restores" and "perfects" it, argues Comenius.[15] Therefore, it is legitimate to use natural instruments when leading towards morality and piety. And to Comenius it is evident that nature teaches that morality and piety will be best instilled by:

a. providing a good and living example to children, for imitation is one of the key elements of human learning;

b. providing an adequate explanation of every rule or principle that is to be obeyed, for it is good for human action to know and understand why we do what we do;

c. providing an opportunity for everyday practice, because morality and piety are not only a matter of knowing, but also of doing.[16]

The whole process must never be "violent" or "coarse"; on the contrary, it must be "gentle," "free," and "smooth" (cf. III.46, 47). For that is the way God himself relates to people; he brings no one to himself violently, against his or her will.[17]

In Comenius's conceptualization, *omnes* refers to all people indeed. Education for everyone was a revolutionary idea in his time, and Comenius, being aware of this, anticipated his opponents' objections:

> Someone might say: For what [purpose] should workmen, peasants, porters, or even women be educated? My answer is: If this general education is properly instituted, everyone will have enough appropriate material for thinking, desiring, exertion, and acting. Secondly, everyone will know how to conduct all the behaviours and longings of life without crossing the enclosures one has to pass through. Moreover, even in the midst of labour, all people will be lifted through meditation on the words and deeds of God. . . . In brief, they will learn to see God everywhere, to praise him for everything, to embrace him always, and thus live better in this life of sorrows. (*CD* IX.8)

Elsewhere Comenius adds to his theological argument other material that seems to be based simply on his experience as an educator: "if a human being is to become a human being, he or she needs to be educated toward humanity."[18] Without proper education, he or she becomes "the most wild

15. For more details on the subject of regeneration see ch. 7 in *Mundus spiritualis*.

16. Notice that in both paragraphs (on morality and on piety) Comenius follows the same threefold structure of instruction—example, understanding, practice.

17. This thought comes from *Mundus spiritualis*, ch. 7, 2.

18. In the Latin version Comenius uses the term: *formatio hominis* (*GD*, VI.1).

of all creatures." Therefore, it is necessary to educate all people, whether smart or dull, rich or poor, boys or girls, rulers or serfs (*GD* VI.7–9). The need for the inclusion of all people in the "project" of the restoration of human affairs, Comenius also sees reflected in the mutual interdependence of each individual unit of humankind—whether a person, a city, or a nation. "We are all together on one big theatre stage of the world, and everything that happens here touches us all," states Comenius figuratively in one of his late writings.[19] The value of this idea cannot be overestimated, for the recognition of the fact that the harmony of the individual cannot be attained without the harmony of the whole has enormous implications for every aspect of human life.

To accomplish his holistic goals Comenius designed a complex system of schools based on both horizontal unity in respect to curricula at a given educational level, and vertical unity in the hierarchy of the stages of education. In the *Great Didactic* he distinguishes four major developmental stages of youth and proposes four types of schools:

1. the nursery school, up to the age of six;
2. the "comprehensive" or basic school, from age six to twelve;
3. the grammar or secondary (Latin) school, to end at age eighteen;
4. academia, from eighteen to twenty four.

In *Pampaedia* he later adds four more stages, with the explanation that the whole of life provides opportunities for conscious learning:

5. the school of youth;
6. the school of maturity;
7. the school of old age;
8. the school of dying.

However obscure the "school of dying" may sound, Comenius explains that it is the greatest sign of wisdom to "prepare for meeting with the Creator." Anytime before old age one "could" die, but when reaching the old age one knows he or she "must" die. This fact provides a good educational opportunity to "turn away from the ephemeral and adhere to the eternal."[20] In a time when education had neither stable institutions nor general programs of study, such a systematic and complex proposal was quite unique.

19. *Unnum neccesarium*. Taken from Molnár and Rejchrtová, *J. A. Komenský*, 294.

20. *Consultatio*, 135.

Educating According to Nature

Comenius was the first person to formulate the idea of "education according to nature." However his education was very different from the popular approaches of later thinkers such as Rousseau, because his understanding of nature (both that of the world and of the human being) was different. Comenius presented the foundations of his anthropology and cosmology in his early *Didactics* (*Great* and *Czech*). Here he explains that:

1. Human beings are "the greatest, strangest, and most glorious of all creation" (*CD* I.2–4).
   a. Human beings are the greatest, because only humans possess all the attributes of being: life, senses, and reason. E.g., a stone has being but does not possess life; plants and trees are given life, and even the ability to multiply, but do not sense things; all the animals, beasts, birds, fish, reptiles, etc. possess life and the senses but not reason (*CD* I.2).
   b. Human beings are the strangest of all creatures, for only in them "is the heavenly merged with the earthly; the visible with the invisible, the mortal with the immortal. To embed a rational, immortal, and eternal soul into a piece of clay and make it to be one personality, that is a mighty act of God's wisdom and artistry" (*CD* I.3). It was only the human being to whom God related personally (*nexus hypostaticus*) and thus united his nature with human nature (*GD* I.3).
   c. The greatest glory of human beings lies in the fact God himself in Jesus Christ became a human being in order to "recreate what has been corrupted." No other creature in the whole universe has been so gloriously honored by the Creator (*CD* I.4).
2. The ultimate goal of human life is not in this life (*CD* II). This is made known to people in the Scriptures, but also it is observable in human nature and life:
   a. The composition of our nature shows that what we have in our lives is never sufficient. For human beings have a threefold life in themselves: vegetative, in common with plants; animal, in common with beasts; and spiritual or intellectual, which is specific for people. From the fact that we tend to grow and develop toward perfection on all these levels, though we reach perfection on none of these levels, Comenius concludes that "there must be something greater cherished for us" (*CD* II.2).

b. "All our actions and our affections in this life show that we do not attain our ultimate end here" (*GD* II.5). "Everything that happens with us in this life happens on levels, onto which we ascend higher and on which we always see yet higher levels. . . . Similarly, our efforts are first smallish, thin, and feeble, but gradually they grow greater and reach further. But as long as we are alive . . . we always have something to do, something to desire, and something to strive for. Nevertheless, we can never fully satisfy or fulfil our efforts in this life" (*CD* II.3).

3. Earthly life is but a preparation for eternal life. Comenius sees the evidence of this in three things:

   a. Human beings. "If we examine ourselves, we see that our faculties grow in such a manner that what goes before paves the way for what comes after. For example, our first life is in our mother's womb. But for the sake of what does it exist? Of the life itself? Not at all. . . . In the same way, this life on earth is nothing but a preparation for eternity" (*GD* III.2).

   b. The world. "When we observe the world from any point of view, we can see it has been created for the purpose of the multiplication, edification, and education of humankind. . . . This world is but a seedbed, nourishment, and school, from which we are to proceed to the eternal academy" (*CD* III.3).

   c. The Scripture. "Although reason shows it, the Holy Scripture affirms most powerfully that God, having created the world and everything in it, made man and woman a steward of it and commanded him and her to multiply and to replenish the earth and subdue it. Hence the world is here for man and woman. God speaks about this clearly in Hosea, that the heavens are for the earth, the earth then for corn, wine, oil, etc., and those things are for people (Hos. 2:21,22). All things, therefore, are for humans, even time itself. . . . After all, the Scripture speaks about this world almost always as about preparation and training, a way, a journey, a gate, an expectation; and we are called pilgrims, visitors, arrivers, and expectant ones" (*CD* III.7).[21]

4. The ultimate goal of every human being is "eternal happiness with God" (*GD* IV.1). To reach this, a human being needs to fulfill his or her human vocation, which Comenius derives from the Scriptures,

21. To back his argument, Comenius gives the following biblical references: Gen 47:9; Ps 39:13; Job 7:1–2; Luke 12:34.

specifically from the account of the creation of human beings (Gen 1:26). There are, according to Comenius, three main tasks given to people as a life assignment:

a. To be a rational being, which means "to be an observer of all things, the one who names all things, and the one who learns all things. In other words, humans are to know, to call, and to understand all the known things of the world" (*CD* IV.3).

b. To be a master of all creation. It consists in "subjecting everything to his own use by contriving that its legitimate end be suitably fulfilled; in conducting himself royally, that is, gravely and righteously . . ." In other words, to govern the creation requires first of all to govern virtuously one's own "movements and actions, external and internal . . ." (*GD* IV.4).

c. To be the image of God. That is, "to constantly turn one's heart, desires, and efforts toward God, both externally and internally . . . and thus reflect the perfection which lies in human origin" (*CD* IV.9).

In the following chapter, Comenius further explicates the three tasks in order to show they are rooted in human nature. Human nature has a "natural" tendency toward *learning*, *virtue*, and *piety*. In the explanation, Comenius makes clear that by nature he understands "not the corruption which has laid hold of all men since the Fall . . . , but our first and original condition, to which, as to a starting-point, we must be recalled" (*GD* V.1). To support his view, he quotes Ludwig Vives, a recognized authority of the time, along with Seneca. Vives says: "What else is a Christian, but a man restored to his own nature." This is remarkably similar to Seneca: "That is wisdom, to return to nature and to the position from which universal error has driven us" (*GD* V.1). To strengthen his argument, Comenius relates naturalness with the doctrine of common grace (*universalis providentia Dei*; *GD* V.2).[22] The sign of God's wisdom, which secures the continual functioning of everything, is that

> he does not do anything in vain, that is, without a specific goal, nor without the specific means needed for achieving the goal. Whatever is, is for some purpose, and in order to reach the goal, it is furnished with the necessary instruments, even with some kind of impetus, that make things flow to their goals not against their nature, but rather spontaneously and gently. (*CD* V.2)

22. For the latest Latin edition, see also *Didactica magna*, 60.

It is similar with the human being, according to Comenius, who "is naturally fitted for the understanding of facts, for existence in harmony with the moral law, and above all things for the love of God" (*GD* V.2). Comenius acknowledges several paragraphs later that the "natural desire for God, as the highest good, has been corrupted by the Fall and has gone astray, so that no man, of his strength alone, could return to the right way," but God has his instruments of "Word and Spirit" by which he "illumines" his own. And, therefore, "while we are seeking for the remedies of corruption, let none cast corruption in our teeth," states Comenius, anticipating an objection, and continues: "Did not God, soon after the Fall, and after the exile . . . sow in our hearts the seeds of fresh grace by the promise of his blessed offspring?" (*GD* V.21–22).[23]

The interrelation of pedagogy, anthropology, theology, and cosmology in Comenius's thinking shows that he pursued high philosophical goals. It was a conscious and serious endeavor which in his later works he called *pansophy*, a special notion of universal wisdom. Assuming the universe is a harmonic unity created by one Creator, Comenius saw a fundamental parallelism between the cosmos (nature), the microcosmos (human nature), and revelation (Scripture). Bringing human nature into harmony with nature and Scripture is the real essence of education. It is the "art" (*ars*) of "forging" such humanity in which the "*nexus hypostaticus*" (the personal relationship) to God is restored.

Conclusion

It is evident that Comenius's anthropology, as well as his overall philosophy of education, is thoroughly grounded—both metaphysically and theologically. Comenius takes for granted that a human being is not made "only for himself, but for God and his fellow man." Likewise, human nature is not defined (even by an excellent observer) empirically, but theologically: man is the most perfect and excellent of all creation because he was made in the image of God, but he is also a sinner because he has denied that image. Out of this arises the need for education—human nature is broken and cannot by its own efforts become good; on the contrary, it has a tendency "to become

23. The paragraph explaining what is meant by *human nature* was added only in the *Great Didactic*. Perhaps some of his colleagues or critics pointed out to Comenius that the concept of "natural tendency" needs such clarification. It seems that part of Comenius's argument attempts to respond to some implications of the Calvinist doctrine of *total depravity*, which is the first component of the TULIP acronym (Total depravity, Unconditional election, Limited atonement, Irresistible grace, Perseverance of the saints).

obstructed by empty, fruitless and vile things." Comenius's education is thus *educatio* in the original sense of the word: *e-ducare*, a leading out of, or away from, the hindrances of one's sinful self.[24] Without any exaggeration, for Comenius education plays a soteriological role: it is a God-given means for the salvation of mankind.

Such assumptions and goals are understandably foreign to the point of view of secular modernity. Therefore most of the modern (especially Czech) Comeniological research has been affected by the secular tenets of modernity, and has had a tendency to ignore those assumptions and goals as merely a "residual of his time" or as a theoretical "wasteland" without much sense.[25] There were of course notable exceptions like Jan Patočka, Jan B. Čapek, Dagmar Čapková and Radim Palouš, who opposed the Marxist ideology and strove to understand Comenius in his thought integrity, but the mainstream of Communist Comeniology did its best to "save" Comenius from the metaphysical and medieval "slush" (*bahno*).[26] Comenius has been linked for example with social reformers and revolutionaries such as John Lilburne the Leveller, John Bellers the Quaker, and Robert Owen the Socialist. Thus the Communist prism prevented the interpreters from appreciating Comenius's work in its fullness. Jan Patočka, for example, bravely stated[27] (in 1957!—that is, during one of the most difficult periods under the totalitarian regime) that the Communist interpreters, such as Otakar Chlup, Robert Alt, and Archbishop Alexejovič Krasnovskij, "emphasize Comenius's relationship to Bacon's inductive realism and assume that this relationship affects his education. However, they usually do not provide sufficient warrant for their theses, but simply affirm that Comenius belongs to the materialistic and sensualistic traditions."[28] Similarly, as early as 1966 John Sadler identified the reductionist problems of the Communist interpretation:

24. Cf. R. Paluoš's notion of *educatio* in *Time of Education*, 63ff., or Wright, *Religion*, 130–31.

25. Cf. Popelová, *Comenius's Way*, 143.

26. Cf. Tichý, *Building the Socialist School*, 9.

27. Patočka was persecuted by the Czech totalitarian regime for his non-conformist views. It is quite instructive to read M. Bečková's review of Comeniological research (*Development of Comenius Research*, 143–50), where she lists extensively all the authors dealing with the subject since the War, but Patočka's studies, clearly not fitting to the socialist ideology, are not mentioned at all. It is a matter of fact that Patočka's scholarly, honest and excellent studies were banned and today are available to us only because certain brave people hid and protected them from the well-known STB (State Secret Police) who strove to destroy them. In Radim Palouš's study, I saw the cabinet with the secret case where the original manuscripts were kept.

28. Patočka, *Cusanus and Comenius*, 168; and Patočka, *Comenius's Spiritual Biography*, 18.

"[Comenius's] educational methodology is seen as an expression of his educational philosophy and as something which could be detached without great loss from its religious framework."[29] What is interesting (and somewhat frustrating) is the fact that this interpretation still prevails in Czech schools today.[30]

However, I believe that the crisis of the modern paradigm (especially its secular version) that we have witnessed for some time opens up new interpretational horizons in relation to pre-modern intellectual concepts.[31] Not everything that is old is necessarily obsolete.[32] Comenius's concept of education is indisputably old and non-modern, but in the context of the current state of "modern" humanity the question must be raised as to whether this isn't its greatest strength.

Response Questions

1. How does the contemporary crisis of humanity relate to the modern self-imposed restriction on metaphysics?
2. What is the cause of the success of Comenius's language-learning method?
3. Why Comenius did emphasize the wholeness of man in education?
4. How did Comenius understand nature and what did he mean by "educating according to nature"?

29. Sadler, *J. A. Comenius*, 35.

30. This is based on my own experience as a university professor of education. Year after year, when taking final state exams, students (future teachers) tend to repeat the "traditional" thesis of the reductionist interpretation that they were exposed to.

31. Stephen Toulmin (*Cosmopolis*, 167) illustrates the crisis of modernity with the help of a picture. He suggests the trajectory of modern philosophy is like the shape of the Greek letter Omega: Ω. It means that even with the achievements in experimental and technical areas, the philosophic questions of the meaning of life and the final order of things still remain, unsolved. After roughly 300 years we have returned to the beginning, never having gotten very far.

32. Lewis (*Surprised by Joy*, 207) captured this attitude in a wonderful way in his notion of *chronological snobbery*. He defines it as: "the uncritical acceptance of the intellectual climate common to our own age and the assumption that whatever has gone out of date is on that account discredited. You must find why it went out of date."

Recommend Readings

Comenius, John Amos. *The Great Didactic* [*Didactica Magna*]. Translated by M. W. Keating. New York: Russell & Russell, 1967. Original work published 1657. Online: http://core.roehampton.ac.uk/digital/froarc/comgre/.

Hábl, Jan. *Lesson in Humanity from the Life and Work of Jan Amos Comenius*. Bonn: Culture and Science, 2011.

Murphy, D. *Comenius: A Critical Reassessment of his Life and Work*. Portland, OR: Irish Academy Press, 1995.

Piaget, Jean. *Jan Amos Comenius*. 1993. UNESCO, International Bureau of Education, vol. XXIII, no. 1/2. Online: http://www.ibe.unesco.org/publications/ThinkersPdf/comeniuse.pdf.

Sadler, John Edward. *J. A. Comenius and the Concept of Universal Education*. London: Allen & Unwin, 1966.

Bibliography

Bečková, M. "On the Development of Comenius Research in Czechoslovakia since the War." In *Symposium Comenianum 1982*. Uherský Brod, 1984.

Comenius, John Amos. *Didaktika česká [Czech Didactic]*. 4th ed. Prague: Národní knihtiskárna I. L. Kober, 1926.

———. *Didactica magna [The Great Didactic]*. In *DJAK XV*. Prague: Academia, 1986.

———. *Didaktika velká [The Great Didactic]*. Prague, 1905.

———. *The Great Didactic* [*Didactica Magna*]. Translated by M. W. Keating. New York: Russell & Russell, 1967. Original work published 1657. Online: http://core.roehampton.ac.uk/digital/froarc/comgre/.

———. *Informatorium školy mateřské*. Prague: SPN, 1964.

———. "Pampaedia." In *Obecná porada o nápravě věcí lidských* [*General Consultation concerning the Improvement of Human Affairs*]. Vol. 3. Prague: Svoboda, 1992.

Eagleton, T. *The Illusions of Postmodernism*. Oxford: Blackwell, 1996.

Erickson, M. J. *Truth or Consequences: The Promise and Perils of Postmodernism*. Downers Grove, IL: InterVarsity, 2001.

Floss, P. *Poselství J. A. Komenského současné Evropě* [*The Legacy of J. A. Comenius to Contemporary Europe*]. Brno: Soliton, 2005.

Geer, R. C. *Mapping Postmodernism*. Downers Grove, IL: InterVarsity, 2003.

Greer, T. H., and G. A. Lewis. *A Brief History of the Western World*. 7th ed. Fort Worth, TX: Harcourt Brace, 1997.

Grenz, S. J. *A Primer on Postmodernism*. Grand Rapids: Eerdmans, 1996.

Harvey, D. *The Condition of Postmodernity*. Oxford: Blackwell, 1990.

Helus, Z. "Culture of Education at the Beginning of the New Millenium: Current Educational Challenges." In *Jan Amos Komenský: Odkaz kultuř e vzdě lávání* [*Jan Amos Comenius: the Cultural Legacy of Education*], edited by S. Chocholová, M. Pánková, and M. Steiner. Prague: Academia, 2009.

Lewis, C. S. *Surprised by Joy*. New York: Harcourt Brace, 1955.

Lipovetsky, G. *Soumrak povinnosti: Bezbolestná etika nových demokratických časů* [*Twilight of Obligation: A Non-Painful Ethics in New Democratic Times*]. Prague: Prostor, 1999.

Lyotard, J. F. *The Postmodern Condition: A Report on Knowledge*. Minneapolis: University of Minnesota Press, 1984.

Molnár, A., and N. Rejchrtová. *J. A. Komenský o sobě* [*J. A. Comenius About Himself*]. Prague: Odeon, 1987.

Murphy, D. *Comenius: A Critical Reassessment of his Life and Work*. Portland, OR: Irish Academy Press, 1995.

Murphy, N. *Beyond Liberalism and Fundamentalism: How Modern and Postmodern Philosophy Set the Theological Agenda*. Valley Forge, PA: Trinity, 1996.

———. *Theology in a Postmodern Age*. Prague: IBTS, 2003.

Murphy, N., and J. W. McClendon Jr. "Distinguishing Modern and Postmodern Theologies." *Modern Theology* 5/3 (April 1989) 191–214.

Palouš, R. *Čas výchovy* [*Time of Education*]. Prague: SPN 1991.

———. *J. A. Komenský—náboženský myslitel* [*J. A. Komenský—Religious Thinker*]. In *SCetH* 51, XXIV. 1994.

———. *Komenského Boží Svět* [*The World of Comenius's God*]. Prague: SPN, 1992.

Patočka, J. "Cusanus a Komenský" [Cusanus and Comenius]. In *Komeniologické studie* I. Prague: Oikoymenh, 1997.

———. "Komenského duchovní biografie" [Comenius's Spiritual Biography]. In *Komeniologické studie* III. Prague: Oikoymenh, 2003.

———. "Lidskost Komenského" [Comenius's Humanity]. In *Komeniologické studie* III. Prague: Oikoymenh, 2003.

———. "O nový pohled na Komenského" [On a New Perspective on Comenius]. In *Komeniologické studie* I. Prague: Oikoymenh, 1997.

Popelová, J. *Komenského cesta kvšenápravě* [*Comenius's Way to Universal Reform*]. Prague: SPN, 1958.

Prázný, A. "Komenský—myslitel krize" [Comenius—Crisis Thinker]. *Pedagogika* 3 (2008) 236–40.

Rýdl, K. "Didaktické perspektivy inovujících procesů vrámci humanizace výchovy a vzdělávání" [Didactic Perspectives on the Innovative Processes with Regard to the Humanisation of Education]. In *Historie a perspektivy didaktického myšlení* [*History and Perspectives of Didactic Thought*], edited by A. Vališová. Prague: Karolinum, 2004.

Sadler, John Edward. *J. A. Comenius and the Concept of Universal Education*. London: Allen & Unwin, 1966.

Skalková, J. *Humanizace vzdělávání a výchovy jako soudobý pedagogický problem* [*The Humanization of Education as a Contemporary Pedagogical Problem*]. Ústí nad Labem: Univerzita J. E. Purkyne, 1993.

Sokol, J. *Filosofická antropologie: Člověk jako osoba* [*Philosophical Anthropology: Human Being as Person*]. Prague: Portál, 2002.

Tichý, F. R. "*S J. A. Komenským do budování socialistické školy*" [*Building the Socialist School with J. A. Comenius*]. In *Jan Amos Komenský, Didaktické spisy* [*Jan Amos Comenius, Didactic Writings*], edited by F. R. . Prague: SPN, 1951.

Toulmin, S. *Cosmopolis: The Hidden Agenda of Modernity*, Chicago: University of Chicago Press, 1990.

Wright, A. *Religion, Education, and Post-Modernity*. New York: RoutledgeFalmer, 2004.

3

Christian Women and Their Influence on Education

The Contributions of Mary Wollstonecraft, Jane Addams, Lois LeBar, and Nel Noddings

Allyson Jule

The influence of women on education has been significant. That said, their contributions are often overlooked, and particularly so when a deep faith commitment has intersected with their development of theoretical and philosophical ideas. Women educators have long played an indispensable role both in developing and in caring for individual students and classrooms as well as in forming new ideas and educational philosophies. Yet many contemporary philosophers of education ignore women's influences in the theory of education and its implications for classroom praxis. This chapter highlights key ideas of four notable women, all of whom align their ideas, in some way, with the Christian faith. Their theories and ideas emerge from the Christian ideals of justice, mercy, and love. The women introduced here are Mary Wollstonecraft (1759–1797) and Jane Addams (1860–1935), as significant early influences in establishing a just and equitable education for all, as well as the more recent Lois LeBar

(1907–1998), and Nel Noddings (1929–), who have viewed educational contexts as key locations for the development of moral character.

The social contract, as constructed by European Enlightenment philosophers, was founded upon a sexual contract based on an assumption of a distinction between public and private spheres.[1] Western philosophical tradition asserted that the public/private divide was the natural order and aligned with one's sex. It was assumed that women's "God-given" concerns were for family and, thus, excluded their participation in public roles.[2] Feminist and postcolonial scholars have been particularly attuned to the need to challenge this public/private divide. The awareness of the contribution of women within the field of education has grown because the private sphere is now better understood as a critical site for the development of society and because women have much to offer public discussions and philosophical theories.

Even with advances of women in positions of educational leadership and scholarship, there remains an implicit understanding, deep in Western thought, that women perform nurturing roles and are more concerned with private matters, while men function better as leaders and thinkers and instigators of change. Over the past half-century, a whole generation of studies have explored gender differentials, such as educational attainment and teacher salaries and/or why imbalances persist despite the rise of feminist thought.[3] One likely explanation may well be the nature of the teaching task itself and the view of it as a nurturing one, something particularly "feminine" and well suited to women and functioning in more private ways, while the nature of philosophical work is viewed as something "masculine," including the thinking of deep thoughts and creating big-picture ideas.

Christian Scripture and dogma have often been used to justify and legitimize subservient roles for women and authoritative roles for of men in all sorts of contexts. Women, both in society and in the church, have long functioned mainly in supporting roles within a patriarchal hierarchical ordering of relationships and tasks. Explicitly or implicitly, many Christian communities view relations as based on male leadership (in the public domain) and female support (in the private domain). In discussing Christian women's influence in education (or in other contexts), there is acknowledgement of the lingering contradictions and/or injustices within some Christian communities regarding the role of women. As such, this focus on

1. Llewellyn, *Democracy's Angels*, 4.

2. Ibid., 5.

3. Ibid., 78.

the influences of Christian women on education is impressive in light of the mainly male world of educational thinkers.

The female educational thinkers discussed here stand out as having influenced the best of what modern education has and can yet become, particularly concerning the advancement of education for women, the necessity of women's engagement in civic society, the demand for intellectual engagement with material, and in the development of a "caring" place within educational establishments. Of course there are many more, but focusing on these key women serves as a way to see some women's influence on education, highlighting their particular contributions to educational philosophy.

Mary Wollstonecraft

England's Mary Wollstonecraft (1759–1797) was an early proponent of women's right to an education—and an education at the same level and with the same rigor as offered to men. Her most significant book is *A Vindication of the Rights of Woman*, written in 1792, which argued against Jean-Jacques Rousseau's *Emile*, published in French in 1762—thirty years earlier.[4] She quite rightly considered Rousseau's ideas degrading to women. His political and philosophical questions rested on the relationship between the individual as a rational being, but this order was firmly entrenched in distinctive sex-based roles with men as the rational beings capable of leading society and women as dependent and emotional. These differences justified a dramatically different education for men and women. Rousseau himself considered *Emile* his most significant work, and many regard it as the first articulated philosophy on education in Western culture.[5] At its base is the view of "innate human goodness."[6] However, his view of equality for all people because of "what they have in common" did not extend to women. Instead, the character of Emile views his female counterpart, Sophie, as an adulterous burden and one not to be trusted or ever relied upon too seriously. Rousseau understood this unreliability in women as a result of their natural inferiority.

A Vindication of the Rights of Woman is one long rejection of Rousseau's definition of a woman's inferior nature and the education he would give her—a separate, private and less intellectual education. Wollstonecraft rejected this view. Instead, "The best education is one in which both sexes in

4. Martin, *Reclaiming a Conversation*, 71.

5. Rousseau, *Confessions*, 529–30.

6. Martin, *Reclaiming a Conversation*, 72.

school are educated together."[7] Wollstonecraft requested to "educate women like men"[8] because she believed that the more similar the education, then the more powerful one could be. Many agreed, but few philosophers actually read Wollstonecraft. Not until recent feminist scholarship emerging in the twentieth century reviewed her work did it garner the attention of educational thinkers. Wollstonecraft was an eighteenth-century rationalist. As with other Enlightenment thinkers, Wollstonecraft viewed reason as the starting point: all human beings have rights because they are rational. Reason itself is God-given, and the intellect and the capacity to reason are not related to one's sex but to experience and education.

Wollstonecraft argued that women are not "naturally inferior" to men but that they may appear to be so because they lacked the quality of education that was offered to men. She believed that both men and women are born with both "innate human goodness" and rationality. Because of this, society can and must be based on the dignity of all citizens regardless of gender roles. Wollstonecraft argued that education for women is central for an enlightened society. While Rousseau is credited with envisioning an ideal education based on the assumption that all *men* are rational, Wollstonecraft demanded that this right be extended to women. Jane Roland Martin says, "No writer has made it clearer than Mary Wollstonecraft what it will cost [a woman] to keep her 'femininity.'"[9] The cost, of course, is an education and the development of her mind and intellect. Wollstonecraft rejected this cost entirely; she rejected an education based on female dependency. Instead, she believed a woman must be intelligent in her own right. This edict is partly based on her observation that a woman cannot assume her husband will be intelligent at all. She said, "Husbands are often overgrown children . . . and if the blind lead the blind, one need not come from heaven to tell us the consequences."[10] For Wollstonecraft, Rousseau's view of a woman's education would leave her unfit to be a mother. Wollstonecraft said, "Meek wives are, in general, foolish mothers."[11] By today's standards, her views may be considered regressive to some in that she considered the education of women important since that would make them better wives and mothers. Later in her life she opened up the idea of women's capacity for independent living and leadership. Even so, for her time and place, her views were extraordinary, disruptive, controversial, and visionary.

7. Ibid., 82.

8. Ibid., 84.

9. Ibid., 70.

10. Wollstonecraft, *A Vindication*, 22.

11. Ibid., 152.

Wollstonecraft's personal life was as unorthodox as her ideas. She experienced two high-profile and controversial love affairs. She married quite late and died that same year at the age of thirty-eight because of complications during childbirth (of her daughter, Mary Shelley, the author of *Frankenstein*).[12] The life of Mary Wollstonecraft is intimately connected to her emerging ideas of freedom as understood within Enlightenment thinking. She lived an unconventional life and was shunned by many who saw her and her ideas as scandalous and even reckless.[13] Even so, she was a passionate woman, as witnessed in her writings, and she opened up the idea of a full and thorough education for women. Wollstonecraft was not the first one to claim the equality of men and women, but for her to tackle a philosophical giant like Rousseau took a great deal of courage and determination.

William Godwin (her husband) wrote *Memoirs of Mary Wollstonecraft* in 1798, in which he explained that Wollstonecraft viewed God as perfect and good equated to rational and wise.[14] She viewed humanity as constantly attempting to improve itself to achieve a more God-like state. Hence, her educational ideas were based on the view that all citizens deserve the necessary tools to improve themselves; assisting women to do so is simply "true to God's wishes."[15] Her sense of justice for women emerges from Christian doctrine. Wollstonecraft's articulation of the fundamental idea of educating women was a supreme gift to an emerging modern society.

Jane Addams

Jane Addams (1860–1935) was a deeply religious American woman. Like Wollstonecraft, her ideas concerning the education of girls and young women were progressive and ahead of their time. Like Wollstonecraft, Addams was a rebel and a revolutionary. She too found herself living in a chaotic and unfair world, and she used her energies to improve social justice for those less fortunate. For her, this meant new immigrants in particular. She was born to a wealthy American family, one of great privilege and prestige but one with narrowly defined and very contrived roles for wealthy women. Her emerging democratic and Christian ideals propelled her to leave home as a young woman. Instead, she went to live in a working-class neighborhood in inner-city Chicago, where she established Hull House, a community center

12. Solomon, *In the Company*, 10–11.
13. Godwin, *Memoirs*.
14. Ferguson and Todd, *Mary Wollstonecraft*, 121.
15. Wollstonecraft, 21.

for new immigrants and the working poor.[16] She was a pivotal figure in the emerging American women's suffrage movement, but she also championed the end to child labor and promoted civil rights for all citizens. She cared deeply about those living in poverty. In 1915 she founded the Women's International League for Peace and Freedom, going on to receive the Nobel Peace Prize in 1931 for this work in securing the rights of women.

Addams was baptized in the Presbyterian Church at the age of twenty-six and remained a member her entire life. She wrote about how central her faith was to her ideas on social justice, and her interest in education emerged from her work at Hull House. There she came to see the education of immigrant children as necessary in the Americanization process, stressing the role of the state in creating safe and vibrant communities with citizens who were both educated and engaged. She tested her progressive ideas by establishing various boys' and girls' clubs, language/ESL classes, community reading groups, and local playgrounds.

Her work was based on her "ethical principles," which she articulated as "to teach by example, to practice cooperation, and to practice social democracy."[17] She contributed greatly to the feminist cause of her time, stirred by John Stuart Mill's *The Subjection of Women*, published in 1869 (some seventy-five years after Wollstonecraft's *Vindication*), which made her seriously question the social pressures on a women to marry and bear children. She believed that all women (regardless of their marital status) could and should exercise their civic duty and be involved in local and municipal affairs, calling such work "civic housekeeping."[18] She saw system-directed change as critical to keeping new immigrant families safe and communities thriving. She was an advisor to many presidents throughout her life, including Roosevelt. She also served for many years on Chicago's Board of Education and instigated many progressive educational policies concerning public education. In 1910 she became the first female president of the National Conference of Charities and Corrections. She is perhaps known best as a pioneer in the field of social work, placing education is at the center of a free and fair society. She never married and died of natural causes at the age of seventy-five.

Addams wrote two significant books, both concerned education: *Twenty Years at Hull House* (1910) and *The Second Twenty Years at Hull House* (1930). In both texts, she outlines gender constructions as related to society's ills (including the problems of prostitution and other sexual

16. Knight, *Spirit in Action*, 169.

17. Ibid., 182.

18. Linn, *A Biography*, 24.

behaviors) that she believed stemmed from poverty, lack of education, and lack of community involvement. She taught some courses at the University of Chicago, but only on a contract basis because her primary task, as she saw it, was to teach within the local community context among the working poor.[19]

Her social activism was clearly based on her views that Christians in particular should be more engaged with the world. She was a part of the Christian social gospel movement, which was popular at the time. By her own accounts, her religious faith was a central motive in her establishing Hull House. She believed that deep Christian belief must and would contribute to social justice and that education should be structured so that its day-to-day practice would in turn promote justice.

Lois LeBar

Lois LeBar (1907–1998) was an American professor of Christian education at Wheaton College in Illinois from 1945 to 1975. Her best-known book is *Education That Is Christian* (1959), which became a classic bestseller within the growing evangelical world of American Christian education in the mid- to late-twentieth century. Her book laid out her philosophy of Christian teaching and curriculum development based on her view of Jesus Christ as the master teacher.

LeBar was born in a small town in New York State where her father was a hardware salesman and her mother was a teacher in the one-room schoolhouse. Later in her life, LeBar would claim that it was her mother's deep personal faith that set an example for her of the Christian life. From an early age, she helped her mother with planning classroom lessons, and she began teaching Sunday School at the Methodist church at the age of twelve. In her writings, she explained that her early church involvement exposed her to moralism and a sense that Christianity involved adherence to a prescribed ethical code. By her own admission, her early experiences with Christianity were legalistic and anchored in self-reliance and obedience to social rules. But this orientation would soon change.[20]

After attending Normal School in New York, she began her teaching career in a grade one classroom; she was also engaged to be married. Around this time, however, LeBar and her sister became "born again" Christians and, through a series of Bible studies, LeBar embraced "Jesus Christ as her personal Savior" and promptly called off her engagement. Her conversion

19. Knight, *Citizen*, 24.

20. Setran, "Fifty Years of Lois LeBar," 5.

to evangelicalism prompted in her a deeper desire for Christian service and Bible teaching. Both sisters would leave their jobs (during the Depression) to enroll at Moody Bible School in Chicago in 1931. While studying in the Christian education program at this conservative evangelical institution, LeBar became familiar with the evangelical scholars of the time. Because of her background in teaching, she began writing lesson plans as Bible studies and began writing curricula for the Bible classes. By 1935, she was hired as a special instructor of children's work, a position she held for several years. She initially studied psychology at what is now Roosevelt University (also in Chicago), where she explored the importance of organized subject matter and the needs and impulses of the learners even and perhaps especially biblical instruction. Her later ideas were based on active learning, something she saw as in line with the teaching style of Jesus as observed in the Gospels. Her chief ideas concerned developmental readiness and the role of the teacher as guide. She would go on to complete her graduate degrees (both in religious education) at Wheaton College and New York University.[21]

Her ideas developed into a philosophy of education that emphasized student discovery alongside the application of biblical principles. She was influenced by her professors at Moody and Wheaton who used small-group inductive analysis and problem solving; such methods became her own. She developed much Sunday School curricula and developed a reputation as a master of curriculum development.

One of her lingering frustrations was the lack of strong theoretical books from an evangelical perspective, and her many books and papers seemed to stem from this frustration. She criticized evangelical education as "poor lay preaching"—proclaiming the Word but with no appreciation for the needs and life stage of the learners.[22] She felt this lack was due in part to the reliance on secular educational theories, which were concerned with organization of subject matter and the relationship of old to new. LeBar saw it all a different way. Instead, she believed a philosophy of Christian education could be rooted in a series of mutually reinforcing principles of growth as a Christian, what she called the "inner factors." This process required the engagement of emotions, will, and the power of perceived needs. Teachers should begin with student needs in order to elicit interest and motivation for learning. At the root of student needs rests their own longings for a meaningful Christian life. With motivation moving this direction (student needs first), students would come to recognize their own spiritual needs and direction.

21. Setran, "Spiritual and Intellectual Formation."

22. LeBar, *Education*, 26.

LeBar can be seen in many ways as a connecting force between the modernization of American education, as experienced throughout the twentieth century, and the conservatism of the evangelical subculture that emerged with a particular force in the 1970s and 1980s. She had grown up in the church and attended a traditional and conservative Bible Schools, and she continued to teach in evangelical settings; however, she also taught in public schools and received her PhD from a progressive university. She studied psychology and made its chief ideas relevant to religious education.[23]

She died at the age of ninety; she never married. Several honors point to her significant contributions to the field of Christian education in particular and her philosophy of religious education as propelled by student needs meeting the Divine in a meaningful and intelligent way.[24]

Nel Noddings

Nel Noddings (1929–) is an American feminist best known for her philosophy of education. She wrote *Caring: A Feminine Approach to Ethics and Moral Education* (1984), which first described what she saw as an "ethics of care" necessary in the educational experience. [25] Her "ethics of care" is relational, and its concern is for genuinely caring relationships between teachers and students, students and students, and teachers and teachers. She saw caring as "rooted in receptivity, relatedness, and responsiveness."[26] Her philosophy is centered on her view of caring as the critical posture needed in schools if educational communities are to be vibrant places of learning.[27]

Noddings spent seventeen years as an elementary and high school teacher of mathematics before earning her PhD from Stanford and beginning her life's work in developing a philosophy of education based on the notion of caring. She joined the faculty at Stanford in 1977 and received many awards for teaching excellence over the years. She retired in 1998 but remains active in her writing and in the engagement with her ideas with a wide audience. She is a high-profile guest lecturer and conference presenter.

Noddings has ten children (some adopted) and was happily married for over sixty years until her husband's death. She has described her close family relationships as key to the development of her philosophical ideas. Noddings suggests the main requirements for caring including the

23. Setran, "Lois E. LeBar."

24. Ibid.

25. Noddings, *Caring*, 11–12.

26. Ibid., 2.

27. Flinders, "Nel Noddings," 211.

carer (the one caring) as exhibiting "engrossment," prompting the one being "cared for" and "cared about" to respond in some way; caring is relational.[28] Her use of the term "engrossment" refers to a concern for someone for the purposes of understanding that person so that the "care" is always based on another's need. This directionality is necessary to creating responsive relationships.[29]

Attention to the needs of others is needed to understand the position of "the other," but this in and of itself does not constitute caring (i.e., one could see need but not care, or care but not see need). Nodding's philosophy requires all elements of caring to be present and nurtured in schools and classrooms and between all participants. This, in turn, can create more empathetic societies. Noddings sees a kind of "motivational displacement" as critical for the one caring (students and/or teachers) to respond to the needs of the cared for (students and/or teachers). Noddings believes that caring requires recognition if caring is to be "completed in the other."[30]

One possible problem with Noddings's theory is that it appears to be based on unequal relationships (more like giver and taker): is the one caring more powerful than the one being cared for? If teachers are more powerful than their students, is the "caring" authentic or just part of the job? Teachers are expected to respond to the needs of their students and can adjust teaching methods and curriculum to work closely with students, so can their "caring" ever be entirely authentic? But Noddings is identifying something more. Her ideas are extensively explained in her many books and articles. Ultimately, she believes that the education system can be about a genuinely caring one where there is authentic attachment and warmth extended and accepted by all participants. She argues against a notion to keep emotions out of the classroom. Instead, she sees an ethic of care model as centered around lots of emotion as part of dynamic interactions within a community. She says,

> We will not find the solution to problems of violence, alienation, ignorance, and unhappiness in increasing our security, imposing more tests, punishing schools for their failure to produce... or demanding that teachers be knowledgeable in the subjects they teach. Instead, we must allow teachers and students to interact as whole persons, and we must develop policies that treat the school as a whole community.[31]

28. Tong, "Nel Noddings's Relational Ethics," 208.
29. Hoagland, "Some Concerns," 246.
30. Noddings, *Philosophy of Education*, 4.
31. Ibid., "What Does It Mean," 13.

Noddings has also written extensively about religious belief and un- the absence of it in public education. Her Christian background (Baptist), however, has clearly had an impact on her view of morality and care. She sees religious and spiritual literacy as fundamental to an educated person. For Noddings, "If one is going to be a believer, one ought to be an intelligent believer";[32] there should be religious education so that students know what they've accepted as faith and why they have accepted it (or what they don't accept and why). She sees moral education as necessary in schools. She criticizes many educators for being ignorant of religion and sees belief as a central part of the human experience. Religious life, rituals, and belonging to religious communities are central to a full human experience. She sees an understanding of religion as part of critical thinking and something schools must teach. Importantly, Noddings sees feminism as not antagonistic to spirituality, citing many feminist philosophers as remaining in their traditional faiths. Instead, she sees feminism as critical in the "ethics of care." Her philosophy concerns the whole person as needing care, needing to give care to others, and needing a thoughtful experience with others as part of a genuine spiritual journey.

Conclusion

The purpose here has been to highlight women who have been influential in education at a more public level than as classroom teachers. Seemingly, most books on the philosophy of education include almost exclusively the work of males. This is partly due to women not being recognized during their own time (as in the case of Mary Wollstonecraft) or because the work of males has been made more easily accessible. Perhaps, though, it is due to a particular tradition within early Western thought and/or within Christian tradition itself that has failed to see the contributions of those born female as equally relevant as the contributions of those born male. Moreover, the analytic movement that dominated the philosophy of education in the mid to late twentieth century narrowed its scope to clear, logical argumentation and language analysis, often steering away from those (often women) more interested in broader approaches to educational issues.

In *Vindication*, Wollstonecraft makes clear the disastrous consequences for men when there is an unjust education for women. As long as men and women inhabit the same society, both sexes will be affected by the education and development of the other. Israel Scheffler says, "The arguments and conceptions of past thinkers retain a fundamental relevance for contemporary

32. Tong, "Nel Noddings's Relational Ethics," 209.

philosophy even as it struggles to find new ways for itself."[33] Philosophical ideas put forth by women of the Christian faith and those most influenced by their Christian heritage are fundamentally relevant to education. When past and present philosophical conversations about women's education and/or notable women in education are missing, it follows that "tasks, functions, institutions, and traits of character" will be associated with men and male characteristics.[34] There is great harm done to both sexes if we do not study the ideas of great thinkers of the past, a group that includes many women such as Wollstonecraft, Addams, LeBar, and Noddings.

As educators, we need to consider what women have had to say about the role of education, in particular the role of community and the provision of a rigorous education for girls as is more often offered to boys; the necessary engagement of Christians to attend to the communities in which they live and create safe spaces for all; to apply biblical principles of love, peace, justice, and integrity in classroom pedagogy and in curriculum development or the need to exhibit an "ethics of care" philosophical position as educators. If rationality and intelligence are linked with the productive processes of education, it is critical that women be included as rational and intelligent and also able to influence ideas and propel educational philosophical thought.

The field of educational philosophy is in a unique position to expose a lingering hidden curriculum. This hidden curriculum is one that too often sidelines the tasks, traits, functions, and fundamental influences of women. Women in educational philosophy have offered some critical positions: a demand for inclusion (Wollstonecraft), community engagement with social justice (Addams), American evangelicalism and the necessity of Scripture in a solid education (LeBar), and the need for well-developed theories on the ethics of care in education (Noddings). The power of the Christian heritage at the root of these ideas is a testament to the necessity of Christian-based thinking, noting that the influence of women educators basing their work on a positive Christian framework has been profound.

Response Questions

1. Why have there been so few women recognized for their contributions to educational philosophy? What have been some of the cultural

33. Scheffler, *Of Human Potential*, 3.

34. Martin, *Educational Metamorphoses*, 6.

barriers for women working in the philosophy of education, and do these barriers still exist today?

2. This chapter introduces the reader to four notable Christian women in the area of educational philosophy. By Googling the names of these four women, can you find two or three other women who have contributed to educational thought? What were their contributions?
3. How important is it that the ideas and theories of women be part of the mainstream of philosophical thinkers? Why would it matter?

Recommended Reading

LeBar, Lois. *Education That Is Christian.* Wheaton, IL: Victor, 1989.

Lewis, Hunter, editor. "Introduction." In *The Essence of Jane Addams's 'Twenty Years at Hull House'.* Edinburg, VA: Axios, 2012.

Noddings, Nel. *Caring: A Feminine Approach to Ethics and Moral Education.* Berkeley: University of California Press, 1984.

Wollstonecraft, Mary. *A Vindication of the Rights of Women.* Edited by Carol Poston. New York: Norton, 1975.

Bibliography

Comenius, John Amos. *The Great Didactic of John Amos Comenius.* Translated by M. W. Keatings. Kila, MT: Kessinger, 1991.

Ferguson, Moira, and Janet Todd. *Mary Wollstonecraft.* Boston: Twayne-G. K. Hall, 1984.

Flinders, D. J. "Nel Noddings." In *Fifty Modern Thinkers on Education*, edited by Joy A. Palmer. London: Routledge, 2001.

Gangel, K., and W. Benson. *Christian Education: Its History and Philosophy.* Chicago: Moody, 1983.

Godwin, William. *Memoirs of Mary Wollstonecraft.* New York: Haskell House, 1969.

Hamington, Maurice. "Jane Addams." *The Stanford Encyclopedia of Philosophy*, 2010. Online: http://plato.stanford.edu/entries/addams-jane/.

Hoagland, Sara. "Some Concerns about Nel Noddings' Caring." *Hypatia* 5/1 (1990).

Johnson, Patricia Altenbernd. *On Wollstonecraft.* Wadsworth Philosophers Series. Belmont, CA: Wadsworth, 2000.

Joslin, Katherine. *Jane Addams: A Writer's Life.* Chicago: University of Illinois Press, 2004.

Knight, Louise W. *Jane Addams: Spirit in Action.* New York: Norton, 2010.

LeBar, Lois. *Education That Is Christian.* Wheaton, IL: Victor, 1959/1989.

Linn, James Weber. *Jane Addams: A Biography.* Urbana, IL: University of Illinois Press, 2000.

Llewellyn, Kristina R. *Democracy's Angels: The Work of Women Teachers.* Montreal and Kingston: McGill-Queen's University Press, 2012.

Martin, Jane Roland. *Educational Metamorphoses: Philosophical Reflections on Identity and Culture.* New York: Rowman and Littlefield, 2006.

———. *Reclaiming a Conversation: The Ideal of Educated Woman.* New Haven, CT: Yale University Press, 1985.

Noddings, Nel. *Caring: A Feminine Approach to Ethics and Moral Education.* Berkeley: University of California Press, 1984.

———. *Justice and Caring: The Search for Common Ground in Education.* New York: Teachers College Press, 1999.

———. *Philosophy of Education.* 2nd ed. Boulder, CO: Westview, 1995.

———. "What Does It Mean to Education the Whole Child?" *The Whole Child* 63/1 (September 2005) 8–13.

Rousseau, Jean-Jacques. *The Confessions.* Translated by J. M. Cohen. London: Penguin, 1953.

Scheffler, Israel. *Of Human Potential: An Essay in the Philosophy of Education.* London: Routledge, 1990.

Setran, David P. "Lois E. LeBar." Christian Educators of the 20th Century Project. Talbot School of Theology, Biola University. Online: http://www.talbot.edu/ce20/educators/protestant/lois_lebar/.

———. "Notes—Fifty Years of Lois LeBar's *Education That Is Christian.*" *Ministry by and for Those beyond the Age of 55*, Fall 2008.

———. "The Spiritual and Intellectual Formation of Lois E. LeBar and an Assessment of her Contributions to the Field of Christian Education." Masters thesis, Wheaton College, 1994.

Solomon, Barbara Miller. *In the Company of Educated Women.* New Haven, CT: Yale University Press, 1985.

Tong, Rosemarie. "Nel Noddings's Relational Ethics." In *Feminine and Feminist Ethics.* Belmont, CA: Wadsworth, 1993.

Weinrich, William. "Women in the History of the Church." In *Recovering Biblical Manhood and Womanhood*, edited by John Piper and Wayne Gruden. Wheaton, IL: Crossway, 2012.

Wollstonecraft, Mary. *A Vindication of the Rights of Women.* Edited by Carol Poston. New York: Norton, 1792/1975.

4

Christianity and Special Education

The Concern for the Blind and the Deaf

Matthew Etherington

Introduction

In the Greco-Roman world, the aim of education was geared exclusively for wealthy and healthy males. In contrast, Christianity aimed for a universal education that would include all children. Although church-run schools were by no means perfect, they did defy many ancient cultural practices inflicted on the less fortunate.[1] In particular, the Christian understanding of teaching children with special needs laid a foundation for a high view of human life to be protected and loved.[2]

The Greek view of both the uneducated and the sick was that they were inferior.[3] In *The Republic* Plato suggests that deformed children of both the superior and inferior be put away in some "mysterious unknown places, as they should be."[4] Aristotle characterized the deaf as "senseless, unreachable

1. Schmidt, *How Christianity Changed the World.*
2. Schaeffer and Koop, "Whatever Happened to the Human Race?"
3. Barker et al., *Adjustment to Physical Handicap and Illness.*
4. Plato, *Republic.*

and incapable of reason,"[5] and therefore friendship with them would be inconceivable.[6] The Egyptians also gave little reverence to the deaf. Deafness was understood by the ancients in terms of intellectual rather than sensory impairment, and often the deaf were politically marginalized.[7] De Land reports of one early Egyptian stating that "there is no use wasting words upon the dumb."[8]

In compliancy with the Roman law code of the Twelve Tables in the fifth century BC, Cicero expressed little devotion to children with deformities. He justified abortion and infanticide, giving the family absolute power to sell, kill, or mutilate sickly, burdensome, or deformed children.[9] The father possessed the power of life and death over his children and had the legal right to either kill his children or abandon them. [10] The ruling law of Romulus, recorded by Dionysius of Halicarnassus, demonstrates the disregard held by Roman law for children with disabilities. The law reads,

> In the first place, he obliged the inhabitants to bring up all their male children and the first-born of the females, and forbade them to destroy any children under three years of age unless they were maimed or monstrous from their very birth. These he did not forbid their parents to expose, provided they first showed them to their five nearest neighbors and these also approved.[11]

In fact, it was not until the fourth century that parents lost the power of death over their children.[12] The great numbers of infants who were abandoned by their parents were rescued, baptized, educated, and maintained by the early Christians.[13]

In the 1800s to 1920s people who were labeled "genetically defective" or "inferior" were hidden away, and displayed as mutants. Oppression has many faces. In 1880 discriminatory attitudes towards the deaf were evident at the notorious Milan Congress. A final decision was made at Milan by a small group of hearing instructors that the use of sign language should be

5. McGann, *Home Education for the Deaf and Dumb*, 9.

6. Reinders, *Receiving the Gift of Friendship.*

7. Yong, *Theology and Down Syndrome.*

8. DeLand, *Story of Lip Reading*, 7.

9. DeMause, *History of Childhood*; Schaeffer and Koop, *Whatever Happened to the Human Race?*

10. Saller, *Patriarchy, Property and Death*, 115.

11. Dionysius of Halicarnassus, *Roman Antiquities*, 1:357.

12. Winzer, "Confronting Difference."

13. Gibbon, *Decline and Fall of the Roman Empire*, quoted in Winzer, "Confronting Difference."

restricted in favor of oralism. As a result, deaf children were punished by teachers if they were found communicating using sign language.[14]

In the 1930s and 1940s the "genetically defective" were seen to pollute the German race and were institutionalized, sterilized, and in some cases exterminated. Many academic journals propounded this view. The racial hygiene journals "used graphics to criticize 'excessive' expenditures on disabled children (1500 Reichmarks/yr. for blind and deaf children) in a campaign that eventually led to the 'elimination' of the 'unfit' in hospital gas chambers."[15]

Persons with disabilities were completely rejected, while in some cultures they were treated as economic liabilities and reluctantly kept alive by their families. For example, in parts of pagan Africa deformed children were killed upon birth. Such a child was a "shame" to the whole family.[16] Among the Ashanti of central Ghana, "severely retarded children were often abandoned on riverbanks or near the sea so that such 'animal-like children' could return to what was believed to be their own kind."[17]

In AD 374, the Christian emperors Valentinian, Valens, and Gratian outlawed infanticide, declaring that a punishment of death would immediately follow anyone who killed an infant because of a deformity.[18] Christians opposed and condemned the culturally embedded practice of child abandonment and childhood soon came to be an honored state to be taken seriously.[19] And so early Christian doctrine presented a view that misfortune or disease was neither a disgrace nor a punishment for sin but, on the contrary, a means of purification and a way of grace.[20]

At the same time, disabilities such as deafness and blindness were given theological explanations. For example, "links between 'disability' and evil spirits were clearly established in the gospel narratives."[21] If Christian anthropology defined human beings by their capacity to reason, then obviously not all human beings would meet these conditions.[22] While biblical and theological views of disability sometimes led to a discriminatory and exclusive approach, it is important to note that perspectives that took an

14. Hitching, *Church and Deaf People.*
15. Proctor, "Nazi Science and Medicine," 18.
16. Dennis, *Social Evils of the Non-Christian World*, 69–70.
17. Munyi, "Past and Present Perceptions towards Disability."
18. Wiedemann, *Adult and Children in the Roman Empire.*
19. Cunningham, *Children and Childhood in Western Society since 1500.*
20. Barker et al., *Adjustment to Physical Handicap and Illness.*
21. Yong, *Theology and Down Syndrome*, 26, 38.
22. Reinders, *Receiving the Gift of Friendship.*

emancipatory and inclusive approach to disability issues were also found in the Bible and Christian theology and practiced by believers.[23] The Trinitarian argument offers an account of the relationship that God maintains with all human beings—man is born from man—therefore, those who fail to develop the capacities of reason are not excluded from God's loving-kindness, relationship, and salvation.[24]

God's plan for the restoration of the Israelites included bringing and gathering the blind and the lame (see Jer 31:8–9). Micah 4:6–7 says, "I will gather the lame . . . I will make the lame my remnant"; God will favor above all others the weak, the lame, and the outcasts. In Isaiah 29:18 we read that God includes the handicapped in his plans of salvation: "In that day the deaf will hear the words of the scroll, and out of gloom and darkness the eyes of the blind will see." And in Luke 14:21 we are told to "Go out quickly into the streets and alleys of the town and bring in the poor, the crippled, the blind and the lame" (NIV).[25]

Thomas Hopkins Gallaudet (1836), a Congregational minister, defined his role to care for the deaf within a missionary context.[26] Gallaudet made a public profession of his religious faith and became a member of the First Congregational Church of Hartford.[27] He saw himself entrusted by God as a private steward of the welfare of the deaf.[28] Using the vernacular of the day, Gallaudet observed that deaf people were "long neglected heathens, excluded from the hopes and knowledge of Christianity"[29] and "dwelling in a moral desert."[30] Gallaudet went on to establish the nation's first school for deaf people in Hartford, Connecticut, in 1817. Today Gallaudet University, named after Thomas Hopkins Gallaudet, is one of the premier academic institutions for deaf and hard-of-hearing people in the world today. Established in 1864 in Washington, DC, Gallaudet University is the world's only university with programs and services specifically designed to accommodate deaf and hard-of-hearing students.

On the whole it was widely accepted that individuals with disabilities were appreciated by the religious as blessed children of God who needed care and protection of the church (and society).[31] The historian Hugh Cun-

23. Otieno, "Biblical and Theological Perspectives on Disabilities."

24. Reinders, *Receiving the Gift of Friendship.*

25. Otieno, "Biblical and Theological Perspectives on Disabilities."

26. Winzer, "Confronting Difference."

27. Barnard, *Discourse*, 11.

28. Valentine, "Thomas Hopkins Gallaudet."

29. Ibid., 217.

30. Barnard, "Eulogy: Thomas Hopkins Gallaudet," 102.

31. Rotatori, Obiakor, Bakhen, *History of Special Education.*

ningham observes that the Christian belief in the need of every human being for salvation immediately implied a higher status for young children. In contrast to the Greeks and Romans, Christians acted on behalf of children and for their protection.[32] In his biography *Life of John Kitto*, Eadie quotes Kitto suggesting that some of the most eminent men and women of ancient times were subject to infirmities.[33] Moses stuttered; Leah had weak eyes; Jacob was lame; Isaac suffered from blindness; Zechariah was mute—yet they were nonetheless chiefs of the chosen race, and accepted of God.[34] Therefore, one's "limp" is no longer a pathological wound but a distinguished mark of a new identity.[35]

The Christian vision of the deaf and the blind held to an interpretation of life that acknowledged ultimate purpose and meaning: the deaf and the blind were persons of value made in God's image. This is still the view today. Christians believe disability does not define a person's identity and should not restrict God's purpose for life. Moltmann suggests, "If we compare the Greek ideal of a human being, bursting with health, strength and goodness with the Gospel picture of a human being we see that sickness or disability is actually the very definition of the true person."[36] Where sickness is, Christ is. Yet we are still so affected by the Greek ideal of perfection that we do not see people with disabilities as whole and therefore we do not judge accordingly.[37] And yet the truth of Christianity shows itself when it liberates people with disabilities and offers them deep respect and compassion. [38]

The Lord Gives Sight to the Blind (Psalm 146:8)

Two of the most common diseases mentioned in the Bible are blindness and deafness. In John, the story of the man born blind conflates blindness with the issue of sin. Jesus responds that sin did not cause the man's blindness; rather, the man was born blind so God's work would be revealed in him. In a profound way, the story indirectly rejects the view that people with disabilities cannot teach the non-disabled. The lesson of the blind man

32. Cunningham, *Children and Childhood in Western Society since 1500.*
33. Eadie, *Life of John Kitto.*
34. Ibid.
35. Young, *Theology and Down Syndrome*, 19–42.
36. Moltmann, *Power of the Powerless*, 145.
37. Hitching, *Church and Deaf People.*
38. Vanier, *Becoming Human*, 16.

demonstrates that we can only see the blind man as God sees him when we regard ourselves in the same light.[39]

One particular defiance of the poor treatment of children with special needs was Christianity's openness to receiving the deaf and the blind. How did Christians perceive those with special needs? Jesus told a parable that challenges our tendency to serve only the more proficient students. Jesus said that when we give a dinner we are not to ask our friends, family, the rich, or the well esteemed; rather, when we give a feast we should invite the poor, the maimed, the lame, and the blind (see Luke 14:12–13). For Christian educators, schools offered places for those with special needs. In his role as chaplain to the Retreat for the Insane at Hartford, Gallaudet reflected, in an 1842 report for the officers, a concern and a duty for those with special needs. He states,

> It is important to restore *the whole man* to the healthful exercise of his various functions, both of body and of mind. . . . I feel it a duty, therefore, which I owe to this unfortunate class of my fellow-beings . . . by the habitual and frequent personal intercourse which a judicious and kind Chaplain.[40]

Thomas Gallaudet[41] thus occupies a large and honorable place in the record of Christian compassion.

In the early 1920s, the Lutheran Church-Missouri Synod (LCMS) began mission and ministry work to assist blind people by providing Braille materials. In service and ministry to the blind, the Synod then looked to what else might be done. It noticed that state schools for the blind (during the middle of the twentieth century) were year-round residential schools, and so it urged congregations to get local families involved by inviting children from the schools to attend Sunday School and worship services and then to spend an afternoon at a family's home. These hands-on experiences helped form in the blind children an image of a loving, caring, forgiving God found in Jesus.[42]

Although the physician Samuel Gridley Howe was not from the clergy but from medicine, he also was committed to helping the blind to be independent and literate. He established the Perkins School for the Blind, later made famous by a student named Helen Keller. Howe could see the benefits

39. Reinders, *Receiving the Gift of Friendship.*

40. Gallaudet, "Report of the Chaplain."

41. To read the entire funeral tribute to Rev. Thomas Gallaudet given by Rev. Henry Codman Potter in 1902 go to http://anglicanhistory.org/usa/gallaudet/memorial1902.html.

42. Andrus, "Practical Principles of Ministry in a Local Congregation."

of Christianity and was committed to using the Bible to help the blind live lives that reflected Christian principles and morality.

In That Day Shall the Deaf Hear the Words of a Book (Isaiah 29:18; 35:5; Matthew 11:5)

Churches were not exempt from helping the deaf. They were actively involved in the social and literary requirements of the deaf.[43] A number of Christian leaders set about restoring the potential and worth of people who were deaf. Major early efforts to educate deaf children included Pedro Ponce de Leon, a Spanish Benedictine monk often credited as the first teacher for the deaf.[44] In the 1550s, Ponce de Leon established a school for the deaf at the San Salvador Monastery in Oña,[45] where he taught deaf students to speak and fingerspell. In 1755, French priest and father of sign language and deaf education Charles M. de L'Epee established the first school for the deaf in Paris, France.[46]

The American School for the Deaf, founded in 1817, notes the important role played by Christianity in the nineteenth century by according the deaf with universal literacy—which was by no means a shared goal in the world at the time.[47] Significantly, the particular missionary religious doctrines of the prevalent Protestant groups provided the means and motive for the attempt to educate deaf people. The Protestant ethic of self-reliance and the belief that religious salvation is possible through understanding the Bible determined the purposes of literacy, salvation, and the skills needed to earn a living. Achieving these goals required clarity and fluidity of communication; thus, these schools from the start were based on sign language.

Between 1840 and 1939, sixty-two societies and missions were established by Christians for the benefit of deaf people. The work was established by "clergymen or educated deaf men of strong religious principle."[48] The missioners provided activities such as church services and Bible reading but

43. Whildon, *Letters to Mrs. W. M. Voires.*

44. MacMillan and Hendrick, "Evolution and Legacies."

45. Lang, Cohen, and Fischgrund, *Moments of Truth*, 4.

46. Butterworth and Flodin, "History of Sign Language," 11.

47. The American Schools for the Deaf was the first permanent school for the deaf in the United States. For more details go to http://www.asd-1817.org/page.cfm?p=9.

48. Dimmock, "Sport and Leisure," 330.

also worked to help unemployed deaf people find work and always "attending to other spiritual and practical welfare needs."[49]

As previously noted, the work of Thomas Hopkins Gallaudet established an inclusive pedagogy for the deaf in schools.[50] Gallaudet understood his responsibility was for those less fortunate, thus the deaf were to be included fully in the events of the time. They were offered instruction in Christianity and allowed full participation in chapel. Therefore they would not be excluded like the "ignorant heathens" or "idiots" that John Carlin perceived the deaf to be in comments to Gallaudet, adding that "all deaf mutes . . . were ignorant heathens."[51] The motivation to provide deaf or hearing-impaired students with religious and moral instruction was commended as a means for the deaf to become literate and develop the skills to participate in reading the Scriptures themselves.[52]

A duty towards the deaf was therefore understood as a responsibility to God. Although service to the deaf was integral, love through example was paramount for teachers to demonstrate with their students. In 1949 a Baptist plan to serve the deaf was organized when eighteen interpreters and workers offered a service to the deaf. Baptist churches throughout the South took up the initiative.[53]

Criticisms have been leveled against the church—namely, that it had religious motivations for helping the deaf. It is important to note, however, that such charges aimed against the Christian church are both unrealistic and unfair. The church acted as an important force for social change, to include the deaf fully. Such inclusion signified not only their importance as citizens but their humanness as people loved and valued by God and his people. Moreover, in the United Kingdom, the Christian church founded most of the caring services and was committed to dealing with poverty among the deaf.[54]

Special Education and Academic Excellence Today

Christian education has always had a unique role to play for children with special needs. On the one hand, it has promoted inclusiveness and centers of academic excellence under the belief that all children can learn and all are

49. Hitching, *Church and Deaf People*, 21.

50. Winzer, *History of Special Education.*

51. "Ceremonies at the Completion of the Gallaudet Monument," 33.

52. Winzer, *History of Special Education.*

53. Wingfield, "Baptists Plan Service to the Deaf."

54. Parratt and Tipping, "State, Social Work and Deafness."

precious to God. On the other hand, in the pursuit of academic attainment, Christian schools face an ongoing dilemma. Teachers and parents can still hold to the old "your kids/my kids" mentality that sees inclusion of all children as a "one-size-fits-all approach."[55] In many countries around the world, however, Christian organizations continue to care for the blind and the deaf.

Since 1846, for example, St. Mary's School for Deaf Girls in Dublin, Ireland,[56] has operated as a primary and post-primary school exemplifying Catholic Christian values of truth, justice, and peace. The school provides a holistic education for children who are severely or proudly deaf.

In 1985 a group of concerned Christians in the Philippines founded the Christian Foundation for Persons with Disabilities (CFPD) and began serving hearing-impaired children when statistics revealed that out of the 2.7 million children who have disabilities in the Philippines only 1.97 percent are permitted to go to school.[57]

Such schools nurture the physical, emotional, intellectual, social, and spiritual nature of every child.

Conclusion

The Christian tradition does not conceive humanity solely in terms of a capacity to act rationally or purposively, but instead regards our source of value grounded in God's grace towards us in Christ. Therefore, a human being is more than their power to think and perform.[58] The Christian tradition holds the sacredness of the deaf and the blind but such thinking and living requires us all to die to the dominating self that pushes up to seek our own glory.

Christianity acted to protect blind and deaf people from society, to fight against the injustice heaped on them, and to liberate those who had been oppressed from a world that expects perfection. While secular motivations to establish institutions for the disabled were meant to protect society *from* the handicapped, Christian monasteries and hospices arose to save handicapped people from society.

History reports instances where church law denied church membership and participation in the rites to the deaf. Nonetheless, Christian

55. Anderson, "Hospitable Classrooms."

56. St. Mary's School for Deaf Girls is located at http://www.stmarysdeafgirls.ie/index.php.

57. The Christian Foundation for Persons with Disabilities is located at http://cfpdinc.org/who_we_are.html.

58. Vanier, *Becoming Human*, 86.

monasteries and hospices arose to save people with special needs from a society in which the early legal code of nearly every European country subjected them to unjust laws and practices: they were deprived the right of inheritance, forbidden to testify in court, and not allowed to make a deed or will.[59]

In the past and present, the Christian community has reflected Christ best when its believers have opened their lives to people with disabilities, when it has shared a desire to meet, share, and enter into dialogue with the blind and the deaf, and when it has united to pray together with a shared human brokenness.

Reflection Questions

1. What are the counterarguments that full inclusion of the deaf and blind in the classroom is more an ideological position than an adequate pedagogical reality?
2. What is the mission and purpose of disabled human beings, according to Christ? Does denomination make any difference to answering this question?
3. There are different understandings regarding what it means to be made in the image of God. Can you list them? What do you consider the most accurate understanding in regards to people with and without disabilities?
4. In John 9, Jesus is reported to have spoken about blindness as a kind of ignorance. What did Jesus mean by this, and can someone still "see" truth even when their eyes are shut?
5. Does your church and school make the necessary accommodations for the deaf and blind? If not, do you think the institution is being truly inclusive?

Recommended Reading

Reinders, Hans. *Receiving the Gift of Friendship: Profound Disability, Theological Anthropology, and Ethics*. Michigan: Eerdmans, 2008.

Vanier, Jean. *Becoming Human*, Toronto: House of Anansi Press, 2008.

Winzer, Margaret. *The History of Special Education: From Isolation to Integration*. Washington, DC: Gallaudet University Press, 1993.

Yong, Amos. *Theology and Down Syndrome*. Waco, TX: Baylor University Press, 2007.

59. Gaw, "Development of the Legal Status of the Deaf."

Bibliography

Allen, Edward E. "Louis Braille." Outlook for the Blind. *Journal of Visual Impairment & Blindness* 100/10 (October 2006) 583–84.

Anderson, David. "Hospitable Classrooms: Biblical Hospitality and Inclusive Education." *Journal of Education and Christian Belief* 15/1 (2011) 13–27.

Andrus, David. "Practical Principles of Ministry in a Local Congregation: Working with Those Who Are Blind or Visually Impaired." *Missio Apostolica* 18/2 (2010) 94–97.

Barnard, Henry. *A Discourse in Commemoration of the Life, Character, and Services of the Rev. Thomas H. Gallaudet, LL. D.* Hartford: Brockett & Hutchinson, 1852. U.S. National Library of Medicine, Digital Collections. Online: http://collections.nlm.nih.gov/catalog/nlm:nlmuid-60531070R-bk.

———. "Eulogy: Thomas Hopkins Gallaudet." *American Annals of the Deaf and Dumb* 4 (1852) 81–136.

Barker, R. G., B. A. Wright, L. Meyerson, and M. R. Gonick. *Adjustment to Physical Handicap and Illness: A Survey of the Social Psychology of Physique and Disability.* New York: earch,1953.

Butterworth, Rod, and Mickey Flodin. "History of Sign Language." In *The Perigee Visual Dictionary of Signing.* Rev. 3rd ed. New York: Berkeley, 1995.

"Ceremonies at the Completion of the Gallaudet Monument.". *American Annals of the Deaf and Dumb* 7 (1854) 19–54.

Cunningham, Hugh. *Children and Childhood in Western Society since 1500.* New York: Longman, 1995.

DeLand, F. *The Story of Lip Reading.* Washington, DC: Alexander Graham Bell Association for the Deaf, 1931.

DeMause, L. *The History of Childhood.* New York: Psychohistory Press, 1974.

Dennis, James. *Social Evils of the Non-Christian World.* New York: Revell, 1898.

Dimmock, A. "Sport and Leisure." *Gallaudet Encyclopedia of Deaf People and Deafness,* edited by John V. Van Cleve. New York: McGraw-Hill, 1987.

Dionysius of Halicarnassus. *The Roman Antiquities of Dionysius of Halicarnassus.* Translated by Earnest Cary. 1937. Online: http://penelope.uchicago.edu/Thayer/E/Roman/Texts/Dionysius_of_Halicarnassus/.

Eadie, John. *Life of John Kitto, D.D., F.S.A.* Edinburgh: Oliphant, 1857.

Gallaudet, Thomas H. "The Duty and Advantages of Affording Instruction to the Deaf and Dumb." In *The Deaf and Dumb, or, A Collection of Articles Relating to the Condition of Deaf Mutes, Their Education, and the Principal Asylums Devoted to Their Instruction,* by dwinohn217–31. Boston: Hitchcock, 1836.

———. "Report of the Chaplain" (1842). *Journal of Pastoral Care* 33/2 (1979) 136–38.

Gaw, A. "The Development of the Legal Status of the Deaf." *American Annals of the Deaf* 51 (1906) 269–423.

Gelb, S. A. "'Not Simply Bad and Incorrigible': Science, Morality, and Intellectual Deficiency." *History of Education Quarterly* 29 (1989) 359–80.

Hitching, Roger. *The Church and Deaf People.* Carlisle, Cumbria: Paternoster, 2003.

Lang, Harry, Oscar Cohen, and Joseph Fischgrund. *Moments of Truth: Robert Davila: The Story of a Deaf Leader.* New York : RIT, 2007.

MacMillian, Donald, and Irving Hendrick. "Evolution and Legacies." In *Integrating General and Special Education,* edited by John Goodlad and Thomas Lovitt, 23–48. New York: Macmillan, 1993.

McGann, J. B. *Home Education for the Deaf and Dumb: First Book of Lessons*. Toronto, 1888.

Moltmann, Jurgen. *The Power of the Powerless*. London: SCM, 1983.

Munyi, Wa Chomba. "Past and Present Perceptions towards Disability: A Historical Perspective." *Disability Studies Quarterly* 32/2 (2012). Online: http://dsq-sds.org/article/view/3197/3068.

Otieno, Pauline A. "Biblical and Theological Perspectives on Disability: Implications on the Rights of Persons with Disability in Kenya." *Disability Studies Quarterly* 29/4 (2009). Online: http://dsq-sds.org/article/view/988/1164.

Parratt, D, and B. Tipping. "The State, Social Work and Deafness." *Journal of the National Council of Social Workers with the Deaf* 4 (1986) 8–11.

Plato. *The Republic: The Complete and Unabridged Jowett Translation*. New York: Vintage, 1991.

Proctor, Robert. "Nazi Science and Medicine." *Science for the People* 14/2 (1982) 15–20. Online: http://socrates.berkeley.edu/~schwrtz/SftP/MagazineArchive/SftPv14n2s.pdf.

Reinders, Hans. *Receiving the Gift of Friendship: Profound Disability, Theological Anthropology, and Ethics*. Grand Rapids: Eerdmans, 2008.

Rotatori, Anthony, Festus Obiakor, Jeffrey Bakken. *History of Special Education*. Bingley: Emerald Group, 2011.

Saller, Richard. *Patriarchy, Property and Death in the Roman Family*. Cambridge: Cambridge University Press, 1997.

Schaeffer, F., and C. Koop. *Whatever Happened to the Human Race?* Old Tappan, NJ: Revell, 1976.

Schmidt, Alvin. *How Christianity Changed the World*. Grand Rapids: Zondervan, 2004.

Valentine, P. "Thomas Hopkins Gallaudet: Benevolent Paternalism and the Origins of the American Asylum." Paper presented at the First International Conference on the History of Deafness, Washington, DC, June.

Vanier, Jean. *Becoming Human*. Toronto: House of Anansi Press, 1998.

Whildon, P. J. *Letter to Mrs. W. M. Voires, May 24*. Rare Pamphlets. Washington, DC: Volta Bureau, 1926.

Wingfield, Marshall. "Baptists Plan Service to the Deaf." *Christian Century* 66/4 (1949) 122.

Wiedemann, Thomas. *Adults and Children in the Roman Empire*. London: Routledge; New Haven, CT: Yale University Press, 1989.

Winzer, Margaret. "Confronting Difference: An Excursion through the History of Special Education." In *The Sage Handbook of Special Education*. Thousand Oaks, CA: Sage, 2007.

———. *The History of Special Education: From Isolation to Integration*. Washington, DC: Gallaudet University Press, 1993.

Yong, Amos. *Theology and Down Syndrome: Reimagining Disability in Late Modernity*. Waco, TX: Baylor University Press, 2007.

5

Religion and the Science Classroom

Arnold E. Sikkema

Abstract

Religion is in the science classroom. It's already there for reasons of all sorts, and so it's not the teacher's choice *whether or not* to engage it, but *how*. Humans are irreducibly religious. Science is a human cultural activity, motivated in part by the desire to answer deep questions. Many questions science addresses today touch upon, or indeed dive into, matters that members of religious communities have considered (and still do consider) their territory. And so the manner in which teachers present such questions and the scientific approaches to their answers can alienate some of their students and thus be a roadblock to science education. It is incumbent upon teachers to become aware of the religious connections that science carries with it and to create pedagogical strategies correspondingly.

Science, Religion, and the Purpose of Education

Schools of all stripes often articulate a mission statement including the preparation of good citizens. This expects awareness of and engagement with culture, and some degree of enculturation and the inculcation of values. Education expects teachers to pass on to students what they will need to function well within society, to flourish, to be fruitful, to actively participate toward the common good. Education cannot simply present the full range of options to students; particular emphases and approaches are employed depending upon the political, economic, sociological, environmental, geographical, ethnic, and religious realities in which students and teachers find themselves.

How science is presented will differ across these spectra, but in some sense science spans, if not stands above, the diversity due to its distinctive empirical character. In fact, the scientific community encounters and interrogates a shared world in ways that are not subject as readily to ideological influence as other communities are. Predominant among the features of science responsible for this are its international community and public character; scientific research is a vast worldwide collaboration. Research teams consist of members hailing from and rooted in significantly diverse backgrounds.[1]

Religion is quite different from science in this respect. The unique expressions of faith and worship, and the degree to which personal faith is tolerated in the public sphere, show significant variations, as world religions are highly correlated with, though certainly not exclusively dependent upon, ethno-geographical context.

However, these differences between science and religion do not lend support to a popular metanarrative in Western culture, the mythology that claims scientific discovery is a systematic replacement of religious superstition. Over time, so this story goes, the irrational ideas of religious communities are beaten back into the dustbin of history and the backwaters of civilization, while the solid and proven demonstrations of science march forward relentlessly. Always just over the horizon is a "theory of everything" in which all human knowledge and experience are explained, if not explained away.

Nord stresses the importance of remembering that science has a "liberal-arts" reason for being in the curriculum.[2] To that end, he suggests that science textbooks should at least note that certain elements of modern science are considered controversial in many religious contexts, and encourages textbook authors and teachers to employ what he calls "the 5 percent rule," arguing that "in teaching any introductory course that addresses important matters of religious and philosophical controversy, at least 5 percent of the textbook should be devoted to locating the discipline at hand in our

1. This is well discussed in Meer, "Background Beliefs, Ideology, and Science."

2. Nord, "Religion and Science Courses."

ongoing conversation about how to make sense of the world."[3] Care must be taken in this approach, for setting the stage in this way might prejudicially taint the science being presented.[4]

Education is not simply the passing on of authoritative knowledge. Yet presentations of science are often received by students as dogma. Nord writes, "We typically teach science as one more disciplinary monologue that students must listen to uncritically. In fact, because science texts don't take seriously contending interpretations of nature, students typically come to accept the claims of science as a matter of faith in the scientific tradition rather than of critical reason."[5] Potvin and Charland criticize as woefully inadequate the educational approach that simply communicates information, such as learning the "facts" of science. This can simply result in the pitting of one authority (science) against another (religion). Instead, learning science must be accompanied by *learning about* science and *doing* science.[6]

The development of critical thinking skills is one of the highest goals of education. As just mentioned, science teaching is not always exemplary in this respect. However, opponents of recognizing the compatibility of science and religion in education, such as Mahner and Bunge,[7] tend to overplay the solid educational value of science as the key to all human knowledge and progress, while caricaturing religion as being the authoritarian propagation of blind irrationalities.[8] Many religious communities, however, have shown that critical thinking is also an important feature for them.[9] And so it can be well argued that science and religion are able to fruitfully engage one another even in K–12 education.

3. Ibid., 248.

4. Long, *Evolution and Religion*, 115–47.

5. Nord, "Religion and Science Courses," 243.

6. Potvin and Charland, "Implications of Two Competing Approaches."

7. Mahner and Bunge, "Is Religious Education Compatible with Science Education?"

8. For excellent critiques of Mahner and Bunge, see the other articles in that issue of the journal *Science & Education* (5/2, April 1996), viz. Settle, "Applying Scientific Openmindedness"; Lacey, "Relations between Science and Religion"; Turner, "Religion: Impediment or Saviour"; Poole, "For More and Better Religious Education"; Woolnough, "Fruitful Compatibility"; Wren-Lewis, "Babies and Bathwater."

9. This is brought out in a number of the critiques of Mahner and Bunge, especially Settle.

Why and How Religion Is in the Science Classroom

Student and teachers are humans, and therefore experience irreducibly all aspects of human existence. Wolterstorff emphasizes that a key goal of all education is to encourage flourishing, or *shalom*, in each of the four intertwined relationships every human has: with God, with oneself, with other humans, and with the environment.[10] The Christian worldview emphasizes God's good creation of humans and their relationships, the brokenness of these relationships due to sin, and the hope and promise of the redemption and restoration of these in and through Jesus Christ. Our encounter with the world is not separable from this set of relationships, and while education separates disciplines from one another, the attendant abstraction is not absolute. And thus religion is often somewhere in the background.[11]

For example, a student in the primary grades dealing with the death of a relative or pet will not be satisfied with simply a biological explanation of life and death, but will be caught up in the entire experience. Schleifer and Talwar dedicate nearly half of the chapters of their co-edited volume *Science and Religion in Education: How to Respond to Children's Questions* to this topic, pointing out the importance of speaking with bereaved students not only about what happens to the body ("science") but also about the relational, emotional, and belief context ("religion").[12] As humans, we recognize that despite the significant value of science, it cannot give the whole picture. For example, Riopel emphasizes that it is important to communicate the conclusions and methods of science, but it is as important to communicate that science cannot address everything, particularly on what he calls "Great Questions."[13]

Perhaps the most widely acknowledged example of the presence of religion in the science classroom is in the context of teaching biology. Within the discipline of biological science, evolutionary theory is undeniably the reigning paradigm; yet, as chronicled and analyzed by Long, its presentation is widely varied, and often completely absent, in public education in the United States.[14] Largely due to the influence of local and national religious communities and organizations, biology is immediately perceived by teachers, students, and parents as infringing upon deep questions of origin and

10. Wolterstorff, *Educating for Shalom*.

11. After Clouser, *Myth of Religious Neutrality*, I take religion to be a universal human foundational commitment, not necessarily articulated, whereby one regards something or someone as absolute, unquestioned, self-evident, self-existent.

12. Schleifer and Talwar, *Science and Religion in Education*.

13. Riopel, "Children, Science, and Beyond."

14. Long, *Evolution and Religion*.

purpose, and they respond in varying ways to the impression that "evolution is poison in the water [of] our apprehension of reality through the competing lenses of science, religion, and cultural life generally."[15] Roughly speaking, evolution is considered a threat by many members of religious communities because of their belief that their sacred Scriptures directly contradict the theories and results of modern science, including an ancient cosmos[16] as well as the common ancestry of all living things on earth.

The model of evolution versus religion is a popular rhetorical tool employed by both "scientific atheists" and "creation scientists." Occupants of these poles are ironically in full agreement in that they both insist that evolution and Christianity are incompatible. Richard Dawkins issues raucous cries that science has proven everything about the grand evolutionary narrative, from an uncaused Big Bang cleanly and naturalistically through to a purposeless humanity, accusing religious believers of being merely blind followers of irrational superstitions while being the root cause of the majority of the world's evils. Ken Ham's charismatic rhetoric claiming modern science as a direct conspiracy against God, the Bible, and morality is met by cheering and laughing evangelical Christians even as he labels all Christians who disagree with his version of young-earth creationism "compromisers."

While evolution is commonly perceived as the greatest threat science offers to religion, it is certainly not the only territory of engagement. Others include Big Bang cosmology and creation; laws of nature and miracles, prayer, and divine action; the mind-brain relation and the human soul; quantum randomness and divine providence.[17] The last two here bear only minimal relevance to K–12 education, as they relate to advanced scientific and theological concepts, but the first two can be fruitfully engaged before college or university.

Nuancing Polar Science-versus-Religion Claims

A primary reason that religion is in the science classroom is the popularity of these two figures and their pitting religion and science against one another. Students are not well served if we allow them to experience only

15. Ibid., 4.

16. Note that while an ancient cosmos is itself not a biological matter, it is certainly closely connected via the multiple intersections biology has with geology and astrophysics.

17. Excellent sources addressing these points include Barr, *Modern Physics and Ancient Faith*; Morris and Petcher, *Science and Grace*; Polkinghorne, *Belief in God*.

the two poles; one of the teacher's roles is to be a reliable guide to combat polarization.

A significant way forward in engaging both science and religion, and resolving the Ham/Dawkins dichotomy, is to carefully nuance the claims made at both poles. Essentially in agreement that science and religion (or at least Christianity) are utterly incompatible, both Ham and Dawkins make opposing fundamentalist claims. Ham claims that biblical texts contain all that is needed in order to condemn theories of modern science, and Dawkins thinks that modern science is universally competent to settle all questions and to render religion utterly invalid.

While few would count themselves in full agreement with these fundamentalist positions, each pole has a constellation of myths in its near orbit, partly seen as justification for or corollaries to the specific position itself.

Close to Dawkins's position are the following ideas that are popular within today's culture:

- Science is *the* source of *certain* knowledge.
- Science is purely objective or systematic.
- Science opposes/displaces/replaces religion.
- Science is a set of facts, or the art of fact collection.
- Science inexorably marches forward.
- The Big Bang (or evolution) is a "fact."
- Only physical things and processes are real.
- Each thing or person is a collection of atoms.
- The world is a machine/computer.

Close to Ham's position are the following notions that are popular within much of evangelical Christianity:

- Most scientists are anti-Christian in their work.
- Science is driven by ideology.
- Evolution (or the Big Bang, e.g.) is "just a theory, and not proven."
- Origins is the only area where science and Christianity impact.
- Genesis 1 is *the* story of *how* God created the world.
- Science really has nothing to say.
- Miracles are God's intervention into natural processes.
- The world will just be destroyed anyway.

Each of these points contains an element of truth, but also misses something significant. It is beyond the scope of this chapter to give a detailed critique of these points, but science education in any context—whether it's in a government school or an independent school (religious or secular)—will greatly benefit from the teacher developing, displaying, and inculcating certain habits of mind regarding the true character of science.[18] The proper place of science vis-à-vis culture in general and religion should be discussed, and some of the above myths could be addressed explicitly. The following features of science are central in this respect:

- Science is a cultural activity.
- Science is possible to use for good and for ill.
- Science is a complex web of theory and experiment.
- Science deepens our understanding of (created) reality.
- Science is not easily definable.
- Modern science was founded largely upon Christian convictions.

The reader might feel this last point is only for Christian education. But it is the clear conclusion of *secular* historians that, far from being an opponent of science, Christianity was a key to the rise of science for reasons such as the recognition of laws of nature coming from a law maker and the belief that nature is not divine.[19] And thus non-Christian teachers and teachers in non-Christians schools do their students a disservice in not unveiling this historical fact. It might also reduce the tension lurking in the classroom as a controversial topic is approached.

Christian teachers of science should bring out a number of additional themes connecting science and Christianity, such as:[20]

- Science is possible due to God's covenant faithfulness.
- Science deepens our knowledge of the Creator.
- Science enhances humanity's ability to carry out the cultural mandate.
- Science motivates us to participate in the redemptive work of Jesus Christ.
- God reveals himself in the "two books" of world and Word.

For this task, one can draw upon resources from ancient times to the present.

18. I began to develop these ideas in Sikkema, "Laws of Nature."

19. For details, see Cohen, *Scientific Revolution*; Harrison, *Cambridge Companion to Science and Religion*; Pearcey and Thaxton, *Soul of Science*.

20. These themes are drawn out in, e.g., Morris and Petcher, *Science and Grace*; Wolters, *Creation Regained*; Pearcey and Thaxton, *Soul of Science*.

Recognizing the Limits of Science

The religious claims made by some public spokespersons for science have contributed to religion being in the science classroom. When Richard Dawkins speaks, everything he says is regarded by the general public as being a claim of science.[21] An important goal of education is that students think critically about popular voices in culture. Figures such as Dawkins position themselves as scientists able to tackle the big questions of life, especially (but not only) origins questions.

In speaking about origins, however, it is important to distinguish between *origin* and *history*.[22] "Origin science" *per se* does not actually even exist, except as a limit upon what science can hope to achieve. Science clearly reaches a point where nothing more can be said that is in any way amenable to the methods of scientific investigation. Where does something come from in the final analysis? What is its absolute origin? How did it come to be in the first place? Why does it have the particular characteristics it has? These questions are more philosophical and theological than scientific. For the theist, these questions are answerable in the ultimate sense only with reference to the specific creative work of God, everything being contingent upon him.

In cosmology, the Big Bang theory does not actually address the origin of the universe *per se*, but only its early development. No one claims to know why the Big Bang occurred, what triggered it, or what conditions were present prior to it, either theoretically or observationally. Cosmologists clearly state that they cannot address anything in the first 10^{-43} seconds; beyond that, nothing is known. Now there certainly are speculative ideas that give alternative scenarios for the cosmos prior to the earliest moments within the reach of astrophysical cosmology (such as the multiverse), and there are ways of dealing with time that do not require an absolutely identifiable origin instant. But that does not even begin to engage the deeper matter of sheer existence; that is, nothing in science can give final answers to cosmic origins questions.

Similarly, biology (especially through paleontology and comparative genomics) may investigate the historical development of living things, but cannot hope to make much progress in scientific investigations of the actual origin of life due to the contingencies and singularities involved, much less the reason for life's existence.

21. It is ironic that Dawkins, and the other scientist atheists, despite their zeal for evolution(ism), may be contributing to anti-evolutionary thinking in the USA since they strongly link evolution to atheism. See Long, *Evolution and Religion*, 7, 167–76.

22. Some of this material is adapted from Sikkema, "Origin Science."

For the Christian, every origin story in history (the origin of the universe, or of stars and galaxies, the solar system, earth, life, humanity, or even each individual) can only be so by virtue of the cosmos being created by God with its divinely ordained lawfulness and coherence. This lawfulness and coherence is simply taken as a given without which science cannot function.[23] But God is also understood as revealed in Scripture as being personally involved in all events that occurred in history. Again, all is contingent upon him.

Tom Settle aptly notes, in his response to Mahner and Bunge, that "religions have no need to fear the growth of scientific knowledge, provided science is not confused . . . with its materialistic interpretation."[24] Evolution is often conflated with evolution*ism*.[25] On the one hand there is a biological theory of evolution, while on the other hand there is a philosophical and religious worldview of evolutionism. Evolutionism assumes that humanity is fully explained by science within a naturalistic theory of biological evolution. This is said to include human psychology, sociology, reason, morality, and religion. There is no place within this worldview for theological claims about humans, such as their being created in God's image, their covenantal relationship with God, their being recipients of divine revelation; no place for spiritual realities such as sin, grace, and purpose. But the biological theory of evolution does not settle, or even begin to address, questions of the origin or character of humanity as humanity. Nor does it touch upon the origin of life itself. It can only deal with the biology of organisms, including that of humans. Now the Christian worldview recognizes that being human is more than having a certain biology. There are indeed scholars who work on evolutionary psychology and evolutionary morality, but human psychology and morality are areas where not only Christians, but also other scholars[26] recognize that forms of knowledge besides the scientific are required. Especially (but not only) for the Christian, the doctrines of *imago Dei* and sin are simply not amenable to scientific studies; these are theological doctrines that, along with the framework of creation, fall, and redemption, have significant implications for the humanities.[27]

23. This is called "belief in God" in Poythress, *Redeeming Science*, 13–31, as he strikingly identifies the "divine" character of laws of nature.

24. Settle, "Applying Scientific Openmindedness," 125.

25. Some of this material is adapted from Jelsma et al., "Does Evolution Require New Theology?"

26. A recent solid dismantling of reductionism is Nagel, *Mind and Cosmos*. Nagel argues against the idea that materialistic naturalism can explain life, consciousness, rationality, and morality.

27. On "creation, fall, redemption," see especially Wolters, *Creation Regained*.

Evolution is often tied in with materialism. Harvard astronomer Owen Gingerich responds to this in the context of education by writing,

> Evolution as a materialist philosophy is ideology, and presenting it as such essentially raises it to the rank of final cause. Evolutionists who deny cosmic teleology and who, in placing their faith in a cosmic roulette, argue for the purposelessness of the universe are not articulating scientifically established fact; they are advocating their personal metaphysical stance. This posture, I believe, is something that should be legitimately resisted. It is just as wrong to present evolution in high school classrooms as a final cause as it is to fob off Intelligent Design as a substitute for an efficacious efficient cause.[28]

It is outside of the realm of science to handle questions of purpose, value, meaning, ethics, etc. Yet Steven Weinberg, Nobel laureate in physics, wrote, "The more the universe seems comprehensible, the more it also seems pointless."[29] Many regarded this as a scientific claim. It is important to remember, as Gingerich says, "this is a personal philosophical speculation that falls well beyond the purview of science."[30] Indeed, Weinberg acknowledged years later that "we are not going to be able to look to science for any help in deciding what we are to value. . . . [I]f we search in the discoveries of science for some point to our lives, we will not find it. . . . [S]cience can't provide us with values, neither can it invalidate them."[31]

Space precludes a full treatment of the limits of science, but let me close this section with just a few additional brief remarks.[32] Science ought to be presented as one of the various forms of knowledge humans have access to.[33] Religious perspectives can deepen and complement scientific ideas, as can art and literature.[34] The suggestion that science has disproven miracles ignores the facts that "laws of nature" are only descriptions and explanations of things and processes that we have empirical access to, while miracles are events of a divine revelatory nature not amenable to scientific investigation.

28. Gingerich, *God's Universe*, 75. It is noteworthy that the U.S. National Association of Biology Teachers removed the words "impersonal" and "unsupervised" from their definition of evolution in 1997.

29. Weinberg, *First Three Minutes*, 154.

30. Gingerich, *God's Universe*, 85.

31. Weinberg, *Facing Up*, 47.

32. See also Ratzsch, *Science and Its Limits*.

33. For an excellent critique of scientism, see Hutchinson, *Monopolizing Knowledge*.

34. Sidelining religion is paralleled with ignoring the arts in both Settle, "Applying Scientific Openmindedness," 133; and Poole, "For More and Better Religious Education," 173.

Finally, science does not speak of "believing in" or "proving"[35] theories, but of examining multiple converging lines of evidence, usually in the context of models, while displaying a critical realist stance.[36]

Recognizing the Limits of Religion

When science speaks about "origins," even when nuanced to "history" as I have done above, a significant portion of the Christian community sees this as an affront to the biblical story of creation of Genesis 1. However, there are rich resources within the Christian tradition, both historical and contemporary, that can be drawn upon to moderate this idea.

Consider that "Genesis 1 is *the* story of *how* God created the world" (identified above as a myth in the constellation of Ken Ham) ought to be nuanced in several ways, hinted at in the emphasis upon the words "the" and "how." First, the Christian Scriptures contain a large number of creation stories besides Genesis 1, key among these being Genesis 2; Job 38–40; Psalm 74:13–17; Psalm 104; John 1:1–5; and Colossians 1:15–17. Second, as suggested by many, Genesis does not so much tell *how* and *when* God made all things as it does *who* and *why*. (Related to this is Galileo's point in quoting Cardinal Baronius as saying that "the intention of the Holy Ghost is to teach us how one goes to heaven, not how heaven goes."[37])

Augustine advises Christians to take significant care in deciding exactly what the Scriptures mean when they touch upon matters also explored in the sciences, and in being properly informed about scientific matters:

> Usually, even a non-Christian knows something about the earth, the heavens, and the other elements of this world. . . . Now, it is a disgraceful and dangerous thing for an infidel to hear a Christian, presumably giving the meaning of Holy Scripture, talking nonsense on these topics. . . . If they find a Christian mistaken in a field which they themselves know well and hear him maintaining his foolish opinions about our books, how are they going to believe those books in matters concerning the resurrection of the dead, the hope of eternal life, and the kingdom of heaven . . . ?[38]

35. Settle, "Applying Scientific Openmindedness," 126.

36. One of the best presentations of critical realism in science is Polkinghorne, *Belief in God*.

37. Galileo, "Letter to Madame Christina."

38. Augustine, *On the Literal Meaning of Genesis*, 42–43 (para. 39).

The reader is encouraged to review the entire passage, as it remains highly relevant even after 1,600 years.

Calvin recognizes the limitations of Scripture in not giving details in the sciences: "He who would learn astronomy and other recondite arts, let him go elsewhere."[39] He endorses scientific work by unbelievers as a gift of God, and notes that the Scripture's purpose is not to give descriptions of the world of the form suitable to scientific analysis. And so if one finds a scientific result that seems to contradict what it appears Scripture teaches, it is important for the Christian to carefully assess whether Scripture actually teaches that or whether it is what Calvin describes as the author "accommodat[ing] his discourse to the received custom."[40]

Many contemporary scholars address the interpretation of Scripture in the context of our scientific age. Nord,[41] following Barbour,[42] outlines the diversity of views on how science and faith interact, going beyond the so-called matter of creation/evolution to include cosmology and psychology; the main categories summarized by Nord are biblical creationism, scientific naturalism, independence, and integration/dialogue. While views from literalistic to liberal exist, as a scientist and a theologically informed Christian, I have found Collins[43] and Walton[44] particularly valuable in terms of their perspectives on Genesis. Both of these Old Testament professors carefully and humbly engage Genesis in its historical, literary, linguistic, cultural, and religious context. They demonstrate quite convincingly that the Bible does not make claims of the sort many wish could answer today's scientific questions. The science student who accepts the Holy Bible (or even just the Old Testament) as God's Word should not be burdened by an anachronistic expectation that their scientific conclusions ought to concord with the prevailing cultural expressions of ancient times, while still being able to deeply appreciate theological truths clearly taught in Scripture especially when seen in context.

Conclusion

The teacher's approach to the encounter with religion in the science classroom should be one that opens doors. To prepare students for flourishing

39. Calvin, *Commentaries on Genesis*, 1:6.

40. Ibid., 1:5.

41. Nord, "Religion and Science Courses," 245–47.

42. Barbour, *Religion and Science*, 77–105.

43. Collins, *Science and Faith*.

44. Walton, *Lost World*.

in today's society, a teacher cannot simply present his or her own personal views, but should open to the student the diverse world of critical engagement of science and religion, helping them navigate the waters in ways dependent upon the particular school context. Students in schools that endorse young-earth creationism will be ill prepared for university, church, and cultural experiences if they have been shielded from legitimate encounters with Bible-believing evangelical Christians who have quite different views from themselves. Students in schools that pride themselves as being modern and secular will better equip their students by having them exposed to materials from thoughtful religious perspectives. In fact, Potvin and Charland suggest that explicitly discussing both Intelligent Design and standard evolutionary pictures might be a good example within pedagogical approaches toward a definition of science, and for students to learn what distinguishes it from, e.g., astrology and homeopathy.[45] As discussed above, and also by Long,[46] recognizing the limits of both science and religion is an important aspect of resolving the tensions.

Science and religion are often viewed as being in conflict, but the science teacher has good reasons for countering this myth in the classroom. As Plantinga says, the real conflict is not between science and religion, but between science and naturalism.[47] For if one wishes to claim that science is the only arbiter of truth, that claim itself could not be adjudicated by science.

Response Questions

1. What similarities and differences exist in how religion in the science classroom ought to be engaged among three categories: believing teachers in secular schools, unbelieving teachers in secular schools, and believing teachers in religious schools?
2. In matters of science and religion, it is common for pastors and teachers to be uncertain of or unclear in their own views. What pedagogical value might there be in sharing one's own unsettledness? Closely related to this: How comfortable are you in discussing the diversity of views on science and religion?
3. On matters of science and faith, many religious schools (and their supporting communities) will have either implicit or explicit views. How

45. Potvin and Charland, "Implications of Two Competing Approaches," 237–38.
46. Long, *Evolution and Religion*, 167–79.
47. Plantinga, *Where the Conflict Really Lies*.

can a more "open-minded" teacher appropriately address such matters with academic integrity and still respect those views?[48]

4. Is Nord's "5 percent rule" for the inclusion of science's connections with history, philosophy, and culture something you find constructive, and could you contribute to it as a textbook author or teacher?

Recommended Reading

Collins, C. John. *Science and Faith: Friends or Foes?* Wheaton, IL: Crossway, 2003.
Galileo Galilei. "Letter to Madame Christina of Lorraine, Grand Duchess of Tuscany." 1615. In *Discoveries and Opinions of Galileo*, edited and translated by Stillman Drake, 173–216. New York: Anchor-Doubleday, 1957. Online: http://inters.org/Galilei-Madame-Christina-Lorraine.
Nord, Warren A. "Religion and Science Courses." In *Does God Make a Difference?: Taking Religion Seriously in Our Schools and Universities*, 241–62. Oxford: Oxford University Press, 2010.
Polkinghorne, John. *Belief in God in an Age of Science*. New Haven, CT: Yale University Press, 1998.
Ratzsch, Del. *Science and Its Limits: The Natural Sciences in Christian Perspective*. 2nd ed. Downers Grove, IL: InterVarsity, 2000.
Settle, Tom. "Applying Scientific Openmindedness to Religion and Science Education." *Science & Education* 5 (1996) 125–41.

Valuable Online Resources

American Scientific Affiliation: www.asa3.org
BioLogos: www.biologos.org
Canadian Scientific & Christian Affiliation: www.csca.ca
National Center for Science Education: www.ncse.com
Understanding Science: www.understandingscience.org or undsci.berkeley.edu

Bibliography

Augustine. *De Genesi ad Litteram* (*On The Literal Meaning of Genesis*). Volume 1. Translated by John Hammond Taylor. Mahwah, NJ: Paulist, 1982.
Barbour, Ian G. *Religion and Science: Historical and Contemporary Issues*. San Francisco: HarperSanFrancisco, 1997.
Barr, Stephen M. *Modern Physics and Ancient Faith*. Notre Dame, IN: University of Notre Dame Press, 2003.

48. For background and examples, see Long, *Evolution and Religion*, 115–47.

Calvin, John. *Commentaries on the First Book of Moses Commonly Called Genesis*. 1554. Translated by John King. 1847. Online: http://www.ccel.org/ccel/calvin/calcom01.html.

Collins, C. John. *Science and Faith: Friends or Foes?* Wheaton, IL: Crossway, 2003.

Clouser, Roy A. *The Myth of Religious Neutrality: An Essay on the Hidden Role of Religious Belief in Theories*. Notre Dame, IN: University of Notre Dame Press, 1991.

Cohen, H. Floris. *The Scientific Revolution: A Historiographical Inquiry*. Chicago: University of Chicago Press, 1994.

Galileo Galilei. "Letter to Madame Christina of Lorraine, Grand Duchess of Tuscany." 1615. In *Discoveries and Opinions of Galileo*, edited and translated by Stillman Drake, 173–216. New York: Anchor-Doubleday, 1957. Online: http://inters.org/Galilei-Madame-Christina-Lorraine.

Gingerich, Owen. *God's Universe*. Cambridge, MA: Harvard University Press, 2006.

Harrison, Peter. *The Cambridge Companion to Science and Religion*. Cambridge: Cambridge University Press, 2010.

Hutchinson, Ian R. *Monopolizing Knowledge: A Scientist Refutes Religion-Denying, Reason-Destroying Scientism*. Belmont, MA: Fias, 2011.

Jelsma, Tony, F. G. Oosterhoff, Arnold E. Sikkema, and Jitse M. van der Meer. "Does Evolution Require New Theology?" *Reformed Academic*, June 4, 2013. Online: http://reformedacademic.blogspot.com/2013/06/does-evolution-require-new-theology.html.

Lacey, Hugh. "On Relations between Science and Religion." *Science & Education* 5 (1996) 143–53.

Long, David E. *Evolution and Religion in American Education: An Ethnography*. Cultural Studies of Science Education 4. Dordrecht: Springer 2011.

Mahner, Martin, and Mario Bunge. "Is Religious Education Compatible with Science Education?" *Science & Education* 5 (1996) 101–23.

Meer, Jitse M. van der. "Background Beliefs, Ideology, and Science." *Perspectives on Science and Christian Faith* 65/2 (June 2013) 87–103.

Morris, Tim, and Don Petcher. *Science and Grace: God's Reign in the Natural Sciences*. Wheaton, IL: Crossway, 2004.

Nagel, Thomas. *Mind and Cosmos: Why the Materialist Neo-Darwinian Conception of Nature Is Almost Certainly False*. Oxford: Oxford University Press, 2012.

Nord, Warren A. "Religion and Science Courses." In *Does God Make a Difference?: Taking Religion Seriously in Our Schools and Universities*, 241–62. Oxford: Oxford University Press, 2010.

Pearcey, Nancy R., and Charles B. Thaxton. *The Soul of Science: Christian Faith and Natural Philosophy*. Wheaton, IL: Crossway, 1994.

Plantinga, Alvin. *Where the Conflict Really Lies: Science, Religion, and Naturalism*. Oxford: Oxford University Press, 2011.

Polkinghorne, John. *Belief in God in an Age of Science*. New Haven, CT: Yale University Press, 1998.

Poole, Michael. "'. . . For More and Better Religious Education.'" *Science & Education* 5 (1996) 165–74.

Potvin, Patrice, and Patrick Charland. "The Implications of Two Competing Approaches to Education: The Way to Tackled Science/Religion Issues in Science Classes." In *Science and Religion in Education: How to Respond to Children's Questions*, edited by Michael Schleifer and Victoria Talwar, 227–43. Calgary: Detselig Enterprises, 2009.

Poythress, Vern S. *Redeeming Science: A God-Centered Approach*. Wheaton, IL: Crossway, 2006.

Ratzsch, Del. *Science and Its Limits: The Natural Sciences in Christian Perspective*. 2nd ed. Downers Grove, IL: InterVarsity, 2000.

Riopel, Martin. "Children, Science, and Beyond." In *Science and Religion in Education: How to Respond to Children's Questions*, edited by Michael Schleifer and Victoria Talwar, 111–16. Calgary: Detselig Enterprises, 2009.

Schleifer, Michael, and Victoria Talwar, editors. *Science and Religion in Education: How to Respond to Children's Questions*. Calgary: Detselig Enterprises, 2009.

Settle, Tom. "Applying Scientific Openmindedness to Religion and Science Education." *Science & Education* 5 (1996) 125–41.

Sikkema, Arnold E. "Laws of Nature and God's Word for Creation." *Fideles* 2 (2007) 27–43.

———. "Origin Science and Operation Science." *Reformed Academic*, March 14, 2012. Online: http://reformedacademic.blogspot.com/2012/03/origin-science-and-operation-science.html.

Turner, Tom. "Religion: Impediment or Saviour of Science?" *Science & Education* 5 (1996) 155–64.

Walton, John. *The Lost World of Genesis One: Ancient Cosmology and the Origins Debate*. Downers Grove, IL: InterVarsity, 2010.

Weinberg, Steven. *The First Three Minutes: A Modern View of the Origin of the Universe*. New York: Basic Books, 1977.

Weinberg, Steven. *Facing Up: Science and Its Cultural Adversaries*. Cambridge, MA: Harvard University Press, 2001.

Wolters, Albert M. *Creation Regained: Biblical Basics for a Reformational Worldview*. Grand Rapids: Eerdmans, 1985, 2005.

Wolterstorff, Nicholas. *Educating for Shalom: Essays on Christian Higher Education*. Grand Rapids: Eerdmans, 2004.

Woolnough, Brian E. "On the Fruitful Compatibility of Religious Education and Science." *Science & Education* 5 (1996) 175–83.

Wren-Lewis, John. "On Babies and Bathwater: A Non-Ideological Alternative to the Mahner/Bunge Proposals for Relating Science and Religion in Education." *Science & Education* 5 (1996) 185–88.

6

Educating for Faithful Presence

JUNE HETZEL *and* TIM STRANSKE

Introduction

IN THIS CHAPTER WE will define what James Davidson Hunter means by *faithful presence* and briefly describe four well-intentioned Christian models of engagement ("Relevance To," "Defensive Against," "Purity From," and "Creating Christian Culture") that have factionalized the world from Christianity.[1] Secondly, we will outline theological underpinnings of faithful presence, including God being faithfully present to us, us being faithfully present to God, and us being faithfully present to each other, our tasks, and spheres of influence.[2] And finally, we will propose a model for educating for faithful presence that incorporates calling and foundations in Christ, discipleship and modeling, and ministry through incarnational presence.

1. Hunter, *To Change the World*, 213–19.
2. Ibid., 240–44.

What Is Faithful Presence and Where Has Christianity Failed?

Faithful presence is about 1) God being faithfully present to us, 2) us being faithfully present to God, and 3) us being faithfully present to each other, to our tasks, and to our spheres of influence.[3] Hunter argues for engagement with the world in what he calls *faithful presence*, fashioned after the Israeli diaspora to Babylon.[4] As the multicultural world of postmodernism rejects attempts by any group to impose their views of right and wrong, somewhat like the Babylonians rejected the God of Israel, Hunter argues for a model of engagement with the world called *faithful presence.* As Jeremiah prophesied to Judah before the diaspora, the Israelis were to build and live in houses, plant and eat from gardens, marry and have children, and seek the welfare of the city where they were sent into exile.[5] Israel's faithful presence in seeking the welfare of the city would be a blessing to all. Israel was to experience Yahweh's presence with them and they were to individually and corporately worship Yahweh. Out of this love relationship with the one true God, Israel was to seek the welfare of the city where they were sent into exile, becoming a blessing to the nations.

Decrying the failure of the church's engagement of the world in the late modern period and especially in the recent postmodern, post-Christian era, Hunter suggests that Christians' primary means of engagement with the world, while well-intentioned, fall short of God's mission for the church and the purpose of humankind to glorify God. Hunter identifies these approaches as "Defensive Against," "Relevance To," and "Purity From" models. The "Defensive Against" model launches assaults on secular society, holding up a fist to fight *against* issues (e.g., pornography, abortion) and to fight *for* issues (e.g., creationism, traditional family).[6] This approach tends to build parallel institutions to the secular world, in areas such as education and law, isolating the church from secular society and promoting clashes as the primary means of engagement.[7] The "Relevance To" approach seeks to "make it a priority of being connected to the pressing issues of the day."[8] "Relevance To" approaches are often observed in the seeker-church movement and the

3. Ibid.
4. Ibid., 276–79.
5. Jer 29:5–7.
6. Hunter, *To Change the World*, 214–15.
7. Ibid., 214.
8. Ibid., 217.

emergent church movement.[9] The caution with the "Relevance To" approach is the potential marginalization of orthodox doctrines of the church in an effort to be relevant to the community where Christians have already been vilified due to their irrelevant approaches to being present in the community. Finally, Hunter discusses the "Purity From" approach where Christians "increasingly withdraw into their own communities,"[10] creating a "utopian enclave" that separates Christians from being salt and light in the world. The first two approaches, "Defensive Against" and "Relevance To," argue for political solutions to enforce biblical conceptions of righteousness and justice, respectively, while the third approach, "Purity From," withdraws from the political arena to establish a separate Christian community.

In contrast, Hunter argues for the church to live in community in *faithful presence*, avoiding the disengagement of the "Purity From" model where individuals seek to remain godly through withdrawal from deep engagement with the world and extreme activism from the "left" or "right" that often severs relationships of believers with non-believers, isolating the influence of believers in the community context.[11] Though Hunter included Crouch's conception of "Creating Christian Culture" as part of the "Defensive Against,"[12] we actually conceive of this position as a fourth category that seeks to promote both biblical righteousness and justice through influencing culture and legislation.

Figure 1 illustrates these four models in quadrants defined by two perpendicular axes. The vertical axis represents conceptions of *justice* held personally through those held voluntarily in community to those enforced by government. Similarly, the horizontal axis represents conceptions of *righteousness* held personally through those held voluntarily in community to those enforced by government. In the center of the diagram, in the tension between desiring to do good personally and pursuing that good for others, Hunter suggests that the church community should live in faithful presence, making disciples and avoiding the factionalizing often caused by passionately maximizing differences. For faithful presence with the world, Hunter argues for a "dialectic of affirmation and antithesis"[13] where the Christian church community uses its resources to bring good for others but without forcing moral behavior and judgment upon others as has been the historical case of domination.

9. Ibid., 215.

10. Ibid., 218.

11. Ibid., 218–19.

12. Ibid., 28–29.

13. Ibid., 281–82.

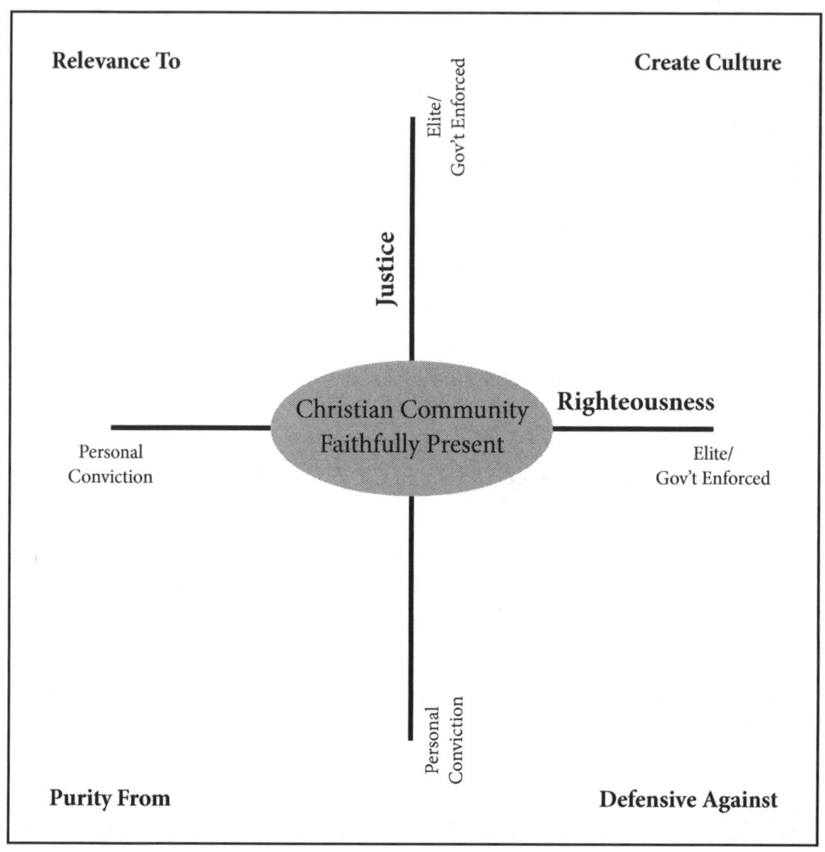

Figure 1: Model for Faithful Presence

Theological Underpinnings of Faithful Presence

As described by Hunter, faithful presence is about 1) God being faithfully present to us, 2) us being faithfully present to him, and 3) us being faithfully present to each other, to our tasks, and to our spheres of influence.[14] First, God is faithfully present to us. He pursues us, he chooses us,[15] he draws us,[16] he calls us,[17] he invites us to come.[18]

14. Ibid., 240–44.
15. Deut 7:6.
16. Jer 31:3.
17. Isa 43:1.
18. Matt 11:20; Hunter, *To Change the World*, 241.

Secondly, God identifies with us. "He remembers that we are dust"[19] and were "born in the likeness of men."[20] He identifies with us because he was God incarnate, and we know he had compassion for those who were in need.[21] Our Savior lived and walked among us.

Third, God is faithfully present to us in the "life that he offers."[22] He is the fountain of life,[23] the source of life,[24] the light of men,[25] the bread of life.[26] Christ said, "I came that they might have life, and might have it abundantly."[27] "The life that God offers is marked by goodness, peace, truth, beauty, joy, fruitfulness . . . the shalom of flourishing."[28]

Finally, this life is only offered because of Christ's atoning sacrificial love.[29] Hence, God's faithful presence to us is marked by his pursuit of us, his identification with us, the life he offers, and his sacrificial love.[30] This active, covenantal, purposeful love of us by the Other is the purpose for which we were created, demanding a response to be faithfully present to him, to our tasks, and to our sphere of influence.[31]

In response to God's faithfulness, we practice being present with God in our daily living. As he is fully present with us, we are to be fully present with him. We worship God individually and corporately. We pray to God individually and corporately. We practice the disciplines of the Christian life, pursuing individual and corporate spiritual disciplines that mark the Spirit-led life, such as prayer, the sacraments, meditating on the Word, study, simplicity.[32]

Secondly, in response to God being faithfully present with us, we practice being fully present to God as we are faithfully present to each other, that is to those within and without the community of faith. This means living

19. Ps 103:14.

20. Phil 2:7.

21. Matt 15:32; 20:29–34; Hunter, *To Change the World*, 242.

22. Hunter, *To Change the World*, 242.

23. Ps 36:9.

24. John 1:4.

25. John 1:4.

26. John 6:35.

27. John 10:10.

28. Hunter, *To Change the World*, 242.

29. 1 John 2:1–2; 4:10.

30. Hunter, *To Change the World*, 242–43.

31. Ibid., 240–48.

32. Calhoun, *Spiritual Disciplines Handbook*; Foster, *Prayer*; Foster, *Spiritual Classics*; Hunter, *To Change the World*.

a holy life within the body of Christ as well as serving and welcoming the stranger.[33] Jesus said, "Whatever you did for the least of these brothers of mine, you did for me."[34]

Third, we are to be faithful to our tasks. God placed us in the garden and gave us dominion over the earth.[35] Work is part of our stewardship of the earth. We are to do our work as unto the Lord, not as unto men.[36] We honor God in our faithfulness to our work, but our allegiance is not to our tasks, but our allegiance is unto God, the one and only, for whom we work as we worship him through our daily work.

Finally, we are to be faithfully present to God in our sphere of influence. The power we have in our spheres of influence is to be exercised "in conformity to the way of Jesus: rooted in intimacy with the Father, rejecting the privileges of status, oriented by a self-giving compassion for the needs of others . . . and committed indiscriminately to the good of all."[37]

How Can We Educate for Faithful Presence?

To educate for faithful presence is to "inculcate just sentiments"[38] for the good in such a way that the hunger and thirst for the one true God is central to one's energy and emotions. The primary good of loving God and being present with God, as he is present with us, takes precedence over secondary goods, whether it be an education, a strong marriage, justice, or other personal interests. For example, to promote justice is to promote a good; however, if your life focus is to promote justice (a secondary good) over the focus of loving God (the primary good), you will eventually move towards a state of spiritual disintegration. However, if your primary good is to love and glorify God above all (e.g., William Wilberforce), God may use you for justice (e.g., abolition of slavery), but it is not a result of your effort. Rather, it is God's work and will *through* you and *in* you as you are faithfully present to him. As St. Augustine stated, "You gathered me together from the state of disintegration in which I had been fruitlessly divided. I turned from unity in you to be lost in multiplicity . . . by pleasing myself and by being ambitious

33. Lev 19:33–34; Matt 25:34–40.

34. Matt 25:34–40.

35. Gen 2:15.

36. Col 3:23–24.

37. Hunter, *To Change the World*, 247.

38. Lewis, *Abolition of Man*, 14.

to win human approval."[39] The temptation away from faithful presence to God is always the distraction of secondary goods and unjust sentiments.

To educate for faithful presence requires a *discipleship model* so that students leave our educational institutions equipped and motivated to be faithfully present to God and others through the power of his Spirit.[40]

When Jesus educated, he first called, then discipled, and finally sent out (see Figure 2). His disciples, however, were not alone in their ministry. They had the Holy Spirit, the Helper, residing in them. As they abided in the Vine,[41] they accomplished their God-given tasks in response to God's ever-present love in them.

Discipleship Model	Gradual Release	Educating for Faithful Presence
Calling	Instructional Input	Calling: Foundations in Christ
↓		↓
Discipleship	Guided Practice	Discipleship: Modeling and Practicing
↓		↓
Ministry	Independent Practice	Ministry: Incarnational Presence

Figure 2: Learning Models

In examining the educational model of *gradual release*, we find similar transitions to Jesus' approach to teaching: instructional input, guided practice, and independent practice. There is a season of learning, a season of doing, and a season of working independently from the teacher.

In considering a model for *educating for faithful presence*, we begin with our calling and foundations in Christ. Then, there must be a season of discipleship that models incarnational living in Christian community, providing tangible practice for being faithfully present with God and others. Finally, the students go out from the school as graduates, and they independently practice being present with God and incarnationally present with others.

39. Augustine, *Confessions*, Book II, i (I).

40. John 15:4–5.

41. John 15.

Calling: Foundations in Christ

First and foremost, our students need to know in their head and in their heart their need for the Savior, "For in him we live and move and exist."[42] Our identity and life are all about him. As St. Augustine prayed, "You are the one true and good lord of your land, which is my heart."[43]

Not only from Jesus's example, but from other biblical figures like Joseph, Daniel, and Esther, students discover how important it is to know who they are and whose they are. The Apostle Paul said, "For me to live is Christ."[44] The old self that seeks its own must die. The new self that is raised is not the same me, it is "Christ in me."[45] That new self avoids the rivalry and conceit that seeks its own, but rather regards "one another as more important than himself,"[46] laying down the pursuit of shadows and "ambition to win human approval,"[47] focusing upon one's identity in Christ and forsaking all other loves.

Spirit-dependency is cultivated in the prayer life. No matter how much cognitive knowledge students gain, hearts must change. Students can in daily prayer present themselves as a living sacrifice,[48] recollect who they are in Christ,[49] lay open their hearts in honesty before the Lord,[50] pray for discernment to see what God is doing and how their hearts are responding,[51] and hear the Word of the Lord and abide in him.[52] Prayers of intention assist in opening students' hearts to receptivity to the Spirit.[53]

Discipleship: Modeling and Practicing

As students watch their teachers live in community with Christians and non-Christians, they must see that we, as teachers, also need to be reconciled with God, even as the blasphemer and persecutor of the church Saul

42. Acts 17:28.
43. Augustine, *Confessions*, Book II, iii (5).
44. Phil 1:20.
45. Gal 2:20.
46. Phil 2:3.
47. Augustine, *Confessions*, Book II, i (I).
48. Rom 12:1–2.
49. Phil 3:7–9.
50. Ps 15:1–2; 139:23–24.
51. Eccl 7:13–14.
52. Heb 4:12; John 15:5.
53. Coe, "Prayers of Intention," 1–2.

was reconciled to him.[54] Students need to see and hear our testimonies. As we model reconciliation to God and others, he allows us to be his ambassadors to encourage reconciliation of others to himself.[55]

Students observe how we respond to what is going on around us. As Paul modeled his faith in God when he was shipwrecked,[56] bit by a viper,[57] and put into a difficult situation by others' methods of witnessing,[58] men and women were drawn to Christ. While teaching his disciples, Jesus indicated that, "When (a student) is fully trained, he will be like his teacher.[59] Our faithful presence allows us to be the "salt of the earth"[60] and "the light of the world"[61] to our students.

Once students understand their need for their Savior and receive the Holy Spirit as their teacher, a starting place for sanctification and the practice of living out faithful presence begins. However, even if students have not yet received Christ as their Savior, their exposure to God's faithful presence can come through the teacher modeling faithful presence in the classroom, as well as through the curriculum. Hence, planned and spontaneous opportunities to practice and experience faithful presence are present every day in the classroom.

To practice faithful presence, one can incorporate internships, practicums, mentoring, tutoring, and serve days into the curriculum. In science, one can incorporate ecology projects so as to better steward the earth. In social studies, one can facilitate community service, work in soup kitchens, start SOS clubs for community projects, and encourage involvement in student council and campus clubs. In language arts, students can develop classroom newspapers, writing skills, conversational skills, listening skills, and public speaking so as to be winsomely present and serve their community. For math application, students can practice tithing, giving to the poor, and helping with micro-businesses across the globe. There is no end to how one might model and provide opportunity for practicing faithful presence in the curriculum.

Part of faithful presence also includes building a community that encourages and supports each other. Solomon taught that community brought

54. 1 Tim 1:12–17.

55. 1 Cor 5:17–21.

56. Acts 27.

57. Acts 28:3.

58. Phil 1:15–17.

59. Luke 6:40.

60. Matt 5:13.

61. Matt 5:14.

strength when he wrote, ". . . though a man might prevail against one who is alone, two will withstand him—a threefold cord is not quickly broken.[62] The writer of Hebrews indicates this principle holds for the church.[63] When our colleague Dennis Eastman, PhD, served at a charter school, focusing on meeting the needs of at-risk and foster children, he noted that every means to inspire students to behave and perform academically was relationally based. If a teacher did not establish a strong relationship with the students, the high schoolers almost never worked to their potential. He gathered around him faithful teachers that built strong relationships with the students. Dr. Eastman himself was surprised when his school showed the greatest Academic Performance Index improvement of any school in the state of California in 2008.[64]

Ministry: Incarnational Presence

As teachers we duplicate who we are. As Jesus lived in community with his disciples, so we have lived incarnationally with our students—eating, drinking, walking, studying, crying, and doing ministry together. Our students have seen us go through the challenges of life—trial, affliction, and even persecution.[65] They know that when we are weak[66] and when we experience loss[67] our faith in God—his presence with us and our presence with him—remains firm. Our incarnational presence with our students and with the community has reflected Spirit dependency[68] and now our students are leaving us to practice the same.

Incarnational presence, however, does not come merely from our students practicing. In other words, our students, when they leave us, cannot be faithfully present to God and others in their own strength alone. Rather, God produces the fruit of his Spirit by our students abiding in Christ and his Word abiding in them.[69] As students have experienced our incarnational love, experienced a life of prayer or being prayed for, studied God's Word, and experienced a loving community, they have become more attuned to living in accordance with his Word, growing with the solid food for the

62. Eccl 4:12.

63. Heb 10:24–25.

64. California Department of Education.

65. 2 Cor 4:7–9.

66. 2 Cor 12:9.

67. John 11:32–36.

68. John 15:4–5.

69. John 15:7.

mature.[70] Experiencing the joy of God's work in their lives, gratefulness and worship freely flow from their lives; they have developed holy habits in our classrooms under the tutelage of the Spirit[71] and now go out practicing faithful presence in their daily work.

One of our university graduates, Michael Long, is an example of a student going out and practicing faithful presence through incarnational living. After graduating from Biola University, Michael taught faithfully in the South Whittier school district. As students, parents, and fellow teachers noticed his deep care for his students and consistent academic results, he was nominated as Teacher of the Year, eventually becoming Teacher of the Year for the state of California in 2008.[72] At each juncture, he faithfully gave honor to God for what God had allowed him to accomplish. Inwardly, he said, "Well, God, this is probably the end of the competition for me, but I want to speak transparently about what has allowed me to be successful with my students, and it is your work in my life."[73] Michael did not try to pressure others to do what he did, nor hide what he believed was the source of his ability. Rather, he was faithfully present with God and others, serving in his sphere of influence, and God blessed with changed lives.

Summary

In essence, the goal of the educator is first to respond to God's faithful presence in his or her own life, to model it, to practice it, and to encourage its development in his or her students' lives—through relationship and through the curriculum—and then watch the Spirit of God produce the fruit and woo youth to himself. When we educate for faithful presence, a gradual release discipleship model assists in preparing students to live the Christian life by being faithfully present to God and others. Educating for faithful presence encourages dependence upon the Spirit of God.[74] The Spirit-led life is not about accomplishing more. Rather, the Spirit-led life is a life of increasing dependency upon the Spirit, that is, practicing faithful presence. From this wellspring flows the good, as God is faithfully present with us

70. Heb 5:13–14.

71. Eph 3:14–21.

72. Los Angeles County Office of Education, "Teachers of the Year."

73. Michael Long, personal communication.

74. John 15:4–5.

and we are faithfully present with him, to others, to our tasks, and to our community.[75]

Reflection Questions

1. What are some biblically based mandates and who are some biblical role models that compel us to educate for faithful presence?
2. How do we see biblical characters, such as Daniel, Esther, or Mordecai, demonstrate faithful presence within their contexts?
3. How do we help our students to understand and relate to the world without being morally or intellectually derailed? How do we help our students remain faithfully present in the world, yet set apart?
4. What temptations do you experience in your own life as it relates to love of secondary goods that inhibit your being fully present to God and loving him first (the primary good)?

Recommended Reading

Book of Daniel, chapters 1–6, on the life of Daniel.
Book of Esther, chapters 1–10, on the lives of Esther and Mordecai.
Book of Genesis, chapters 37–50, on the life of Joseph.
Hunter, James Davidson. *To Change the World: The Irony, Tragedy, and Possibility of Christianity in the Late Modern World.* Oxford: Oxford University Press, 2010.
Lewis, C. S. *The Abolition of Man.* New York: Harper Collins, 2001.

Bibliography

Augustine, Saint. *Confessions: A New Translation by Henry Chadwick.* Oxford: Oxford University Press, 2008.

Calhoun, Adele Ahlberg. *Spiritual Disciplines Handbook: Practices That Transform Us.* Downers Grove, IL: InterVarsity, 2005.

California Department of Education. "2008 Growth Academic Performance Index (API) Report." For Nova Academy Early College High. Online: http://api.cde.ca.gov/AcntRpt2008/2008GrowthSch.aspx?allcds=30666700106567.

Coe, John. "Prayers of Intention." La Mirada, CA: Talbot School of Theology, Institute for Spiritual Formation, 2010. Online: http://www.solidarityrising.org/documents/Prayers_of_Intention.doc.

Crouch, Andy. *Culture Making: Recovering Our Creative Calling.* Downers Grove, IL: InterVarsity, 2008.

75. Hunter, *To Change the World*, 240–44.

Foster, Richard J. *Prayer: Finding the Heart's True Home*. New York: Harper Collins, 1992.

Foster, Richard J., and Emilie Griffin. *Spiritual Classics: Selected Readings for Individuals and Groups on the Twelve Spiritual Disciplines*. San Francisco: HarperSanFrancisco, 2000.

Hunter, James Davidson. *To Change the World: The Irony, Tragedy, and Possibility of Christianity in the Late Modern World*. Oxford: Oxford University Press, 2010.

Lewis, C. S. *The Abolition of Man*. New York: Harper Collins, 1974.

Long, Michael. Personal communication. Biola University, 2008.

Los Angeles County Office of Education. "Teachers of the Year: Michael Long." Teacher2Teacher. Online: http://teacher2teacher.lacoe.edu/michael-long.aspx.

PART TWO

Philosophical Foundations

7

Educating for the Good Life[1]

Perry L. Glanzer

I enjoy reading my students' obituaries. They provide moments of moral clarity in my life as an educator. Perhaps I should note that the obituaries I read are those from living students in my moral development class. I relish this assignment, because the time for flip-flopping about different approaches to various ethical dilemmas passes and the call to a commitment is made. The students must show their hands and reveal who they want to be—their highest life aspirations and ideals.

When this occurs, I find students often favor the use of virtue language. They want to be loving, kind, caring, etc., but what I find important is that they do so within the context particular identity roles. They write about being loving wives, caring husbands, and encouraging moms and dads. They share their hopes about raising kind and loving children. They want to be remembered for loving their sisters and brothers deeply, being faithful to God and their spouses, and caring for their neighbors. They envision tremendous sacrifices, such as adopting five children, feeding and caring for the homeless in the local town or in foreign lands, and educating untouchables and showing them love. Their language of moral imagination demonstrates that the practice of virtue and our concepts of the good life

1. Portions of this article first appeared in Perry L. Glanzer, "Building the Good Life: Using Identities to Frame Moral Education in Higher Education," *Journal of College and Character* 14/2, 177–84 (DOI: 10.1515/jcc-2013-0023). I am grateful to the publisher, De Gruyter, for permission to use portions of it.

are caught up with their present and future identities. In this chapter, I argue that educating for the good life must involve helping students understand who they are and the moral elements of their various identities.

The Morally Foundational and Integrative Role of Identity

You cannot know what you should do unless you know who you are. In other words, to know what it means to be a good person, you have to know what a person is. Much of contemporary education avoids this issue. One recent scholarly attempt to address this fundamental question can be found in Christian Smith's *What Is a Person?* Smith identifies the highest human capacity as "interpersonal communion and love."[2] If we are to delve more deeply into human personhood and why love should be considered our highest capacity, Christians believe we must do so in light of the overall biblical narrative regarding our identity.

The Bible starts by reminding us that God created us, male and female, in his own image (Gen 1:27). It is upon this identity that Christian teachers must build any effort to engage in moral education. The reason is that this identity provides a key to understanding our divine and human purpose. What does it mean to be made in God's image? Scholars have identified a number of different elements, with one understanding being that we image God by being God's representatives on earth.[3] The Apostle Paul draws upon this perspective, but he also adds an additional element based on what we know about God through Christ, when he states: "Therefore be imitators of God, as beloved children. And walk in love, as Christ loved us and gave himself up for us, a fragrant offering and sacrifice to God" (Eph 5:1–2, ESV). In particular, he calls Christians to imitate God's virtues (e.g., love) and these virtues are usually understood and expressed within the context of identities (e.g., we are loved by God in a similar way that a parent loves his or her child).

Just as God is revealed to us in the Bible through a variety of what can be called social identities (e.g., king/lord, father/mother, friend, shepherd, teacher, potter, master, manager, and more) while never capturing God's full divinity, so also we can understand ourselves through the various identities we take upon ourselves (all the while realizing these identities cannot ever capture our full humanity). We are individuals, family members, friends,

2. Smith, *What Is a Person?*, 54.

3. See for example, Middleton, *Liberating Image*; and Grenz, *Social God and the Relational Self*.

neighbors, professionals or workers, men and women, citizens, and members of various groups.

Developing these identities involves moral elements, as can be seen from simply asking students what it means to be a good student, neighbor, citizen, friend, woman, husband, mother, or son. Just as we understand God and Christ by understanding what it means to be a good parent or a good shepherd (Ps 23; Matt 18:12–14; Luke 15:4–7), we gain insight into the good life by understanding and practicing what it means to be good in our various identities. The first step of moral education then involves helping students identify these elements.

Identifying the Moral Elements of a Good Identity Role

What does it take to be good or great in a particular identity role? Anyone can discover this basic moral knowledge and related categories. To help students engage in this discovery, I usually ask them to answer this question using a common identity role, such as being a good basketball player or being a good husband or wife. They can identify a number of elements, but they rarely identify all ten moral elements that I believe they need to consider.

The first element is setting and characters. In basketball, we need a basket, balls, a court, and teammates. What do you need for a good marriage? Do you need anything beyond two (or more) people? What role do the state, religion, families, civil society (i.e., nongovernmental communities), or nature play? What natural gifts and abilities do the principal characters need to engage in this role? It is hard to play basketball without the use of one's hands and feet. Can a physically and mentally handicapped person engage in the practice of marriage? Pat Robertson caused a stir recently when he mentioned that he thought divorce could be an option when facing a spouse with Alzheimer's—a striking contrast to the practice we found in the popular movie *The Notebook*, where a husband cares for a wife with dementia. Is an individual still married if she or he suffers from dementia? We must clarify the essential as well as the divine and fallen elements of the setting that make the practice of an identity possible.

Second, students must consider ends or purposes when examining these practices. What is the difference between the Harlem Globetrotters and the San Antonio Spurs? One plays for entertainment and the other primarily plays to win a NBA championship. What is the purpose or purposes of marriage? Is it merely pleasure and happiness or are there deeper reasons such as oneness, sanctification, or even theological witness?

Third, what are the rules? A person cannot play a game without knowing the rules. In basketball, the player cannot double dribble. Who writes the rules and enforces them? God, nature, state, or a group in civil society (e.g., church, mosque, or synagogue)? Most students never think of God's created order or nature as playing any refereeing role and largely think of the state as the primary arbiter of moral rules. Is "Thou shalt not commit adultery" still one of the rules of marriage or should the rules committee rewrite that one?

Fourth, what are the most important virtues or character qualities for the identity role's successful practice? As Aristotle noted, virtue acquisition requires continual practice. Similarly, in basketball, dribbling, passing, and shooting require the same. In marriage, do love, humility, patience, love, faithfulness require a similar form of habituated practice? Furthermore, the acquisition of virtues varies according to the purpose of the practice. Spinning a basketball on both hands is a virtue acquired by practice for a Harlem Globetrotter, but it is not a virtue for NBA players. This is the reason why a famous moral educator Lawrence Kohlberg criticized what he called the "bag of virtues" approach to moral education.[4] He thought the bags were often arbitrary. In actually, we must agree upon the purpose of a particular role or the end of life as a whole in order to agree upon the virtues necessary for the flourishing of that particular role or of life as a whole.[5]

The fifth and sixth elements are wisdom and the coaches who have it. Wisdom is neither rules nor behavioral virtues, but the knowledge that comes from excellent practice. This kind of expert knowledge is the kind acquired by someone who has observed and practiced in the field (e.g., think of Solomon's wisdom literature about life). Someone who has played and observed basketball for years can often predict whether a player will make a three-point shot or a free throw by looking at the mechanics of a shot, or whether the shot was taken after receiving a pass from a certain place on the floor and in a certain rhythm of the game. In marriage, this type of wisdom involves figuring out how to love your spouse in unique ways. Does loving one's spouse mean buying flowers, showing more physical affection, taking out the trash, changing diapers, or changing the car's oil (or perhaps all of the above)?

Similarly, we expect coaches or mentors to possess this type of wisdom. If one examines the autobiographies of great athletes, such as the tennis players Andre Agassi and Pete Sampras, one finds that even at the pinnacle of success in their sport they still had coaches. The greatest athletes in the

4. Kohlberg, *Philosophy of Moral Development*.

5. MacIntyre, *After Virtue*.

world still need coaches who can provide them with the wisdom to perfect their practice. The same proves true with any other human practice such as marriage, friendship, being a good citizen, or practicing life as a whole.

Seventh, you have to practice under a coach to develop the virtues and gain wisdom. The benefits of what are called "deliberate practice" in sports such as basketball with a wise coach or mentor are well known.[6] Do we need students to practice before they enter the game of marriage? What does practice look like? We can actually look at social science research to realize that cohabitation is really not an effective form of practice for marriage.[7]

Eighth, through practice we can gain increased moral imagination. When a point guard such as Jeremy Lin, Steve Nash, or Chris Paul drives into the lane, he can see and imagine things others cannot. He is creating ways to enhance his team. In marriage, we often call this romance. In making sense of and practicing life, we also need this kind of creative imagination.[8]

Ninth, there are those who have achieved excellence in the practice, what we might call *models* (or *heroes* or *saints*): those who incarnate the best of all of these elements. My son has posters on his wall of those models in basketball. In marriage, one might think of the example of Greg Manning and his wife Lauren. She was engulfed by flames in the World Trade Center attack. She said that she initially prayed to die, but her love for her son and husband helped her fight for life. After being placed in a drug-induced coma, "Greg ignored Lauren's unconscious state, reading poetry to her and playing her favorite CDs, all the while reassuring her that she was loved, that he would take care of her, that everything would be okay. During his home shifts, he took Tyler to birthday parties and play dates, read and sang to him, and documented his development on videotape for Lauren's future viewing."[9] In the end, doctors had to replace more than 80 percent of Laura's skin. The chroniclers of their ordeal recount:

> Exactly 3 months after admission to the hospital, Lauren saw her new, scarred face for the first time. The predictable shock and sadness were tempered by the fact that her husband had prepared her through repeated reminders that she always had been and always would be his soul mate, and in his eyes was as beautiful as ever.[10]

6. Colvin, *Talent Is Overrated.*
7. Wilcox, *Why Marriage Matters*, 304.
8. Smith, *Desiring the Kingdom.*
9. Peterson and Seligman, *Character Strengths and Virtues.*
10. Ibid., 304.

It is important to recognize that all the above elements work together in a modeling situation. Love would look differently if one were showing love as a teacher, citizen, neighbor, or parent. Furthermore, Greg exemplified wisdom in the midst of love. Also, if he committed adultery during this time to fulfill a sexual need that was not being met, the story would not be so powerful since he violated a rule of the practice of marriage and demonstrated certain vices. Models also prove vitally important because they capture the emotional aspect of the good life in ways that instruction using commands, general virtues, mentoring, or practices can never do. They inspire.

Finally, it is important to realize these models are often inspired by something else—a story that holds all of these things together. What narrative guides this practice and what is its story? When my son engages in the practice of basketball, he asks, "Dad, what team are you going to be?" He wants to place the practice in an already existing story to give it meaning, life, excitement, and drama. He pretends it is the NBA championship. Is there a metanarrative of a love story that gives marriage excitement, drama, and purpose? Christians claim that God's love story with the world provides us with the most profound one.

Why All the Elements Are Important

God has created a morally complex world. By introducing students to all of these elements, we can avoid truncated forms of moral education that focus only on one or two of these components and avoid other essential parts. Harvard administrators' recent attempt to require its freshmen class to sign a "freshman pledge" provides a good example. It sought to create good academic citizens. The core of the pledge stated:

> In the classroom, in extracurricular endeavors, and in the Yard and Houses, students are expected to act with integrity, respect and industry, and to sustain a community characterized by inclusiveness and civility. As we begin at Harvard, we commit to upholding the values of the College and to making the entryway and Yard a place where all can thrive and where the exercise of kindness holds a place on par with intellectual attainment.[11]

Why should students uphold the virtues of integrity, respect, industry, civility, inclusiveness, and kindness? The pledge does not really say. What about the definitions and different understandings? Will one person's

11. As cited in Lewis, "Freshman Pledge."

honesty be another person's incivility? The pledge offers students little guidance with this critical issue. The Harvard pledge only provides virtues, without any of the other elements necessary for thinking about what it means to be a good student and a good neighbor at Harvard. Students do not receive an explanation of the moral origins of these virtues, definitions, or readings that might explain the rich reasons for them.

This last omission is the most serious. Rules or definitions of virtue can only be effectively established by moral traditions or communities that conceptualize a specific human end derived from particular narratives. Based on this conception of human flourishing, communities then seek to establish certain rules and embody, prioritize, and exemplify particular virtues. Yet, many higher education programs appear to seek an intellectual community devoid of a guiding tradition or narrative, because such trappings prove restrictive. The mission of Harvard College (which is the undergraduate program at Harvard University) even boasts,

> Harvard seeks to identify and to remove restraints on students' full participation, so that individuals may explore their capabilities and interests and may develop their full intellectual and human potential. Education at Harvard should liberate students to explore, to create, to challenge, and to lead.[12]

This pledge is like asking someone to learn to dribble a ball without providing him or her any context of the game for which such a virtue might be helpful. The Harvard College pledge has no story and no saints.

Granted, Harvard College probably does not hope to form moral saints. One might argue that it merely wants kind and civil students. A pledge written by a committee supplies a basic community ritual, so perhaps it remains a small beginning to forming a slightly more vigorous moral community. Yet, bags of virtues designed to focus on community citizenship will likely be less compelling than advancing a robust moral vision of how students can develop their full human potential. Our moral knowledge and practice needs to recognize this complexity. After all, the moral instruction found in the Bible contains all of these elements. Moral educators must consider this complexity and help students in all ten of these areas.

Identity Conflicts and the Good Life

Once educators understand the moral elements of an identity role, they can better understand the complex moral implications of what Christians

12. Harvard College, "About Harvard College."

understand as the fall. Moral conflict continually occurs in our lives in multiple forms. First, we face the challenge of pursuing excellence within a particular practice and with particular moral elements of the practice (e.g., Will I show self-control and study for the test? Will I violate a moral rule by cheating on the test? Do I study only for my own self-esteem and glory?). This type of moral conflict occurs between our two most fundamental identities as humans made in God's image and sinners. As Paul outlines in Romans 7, we fight among our identities about what to do, "For I do not do the good I want, but the evil I do not want is what I keep on doing" (Rom 7:19, ESV). Paul Bloom from Yale argues, "an evolving approach to the science of pleasure suggests that each of us contains multiple selves—all with different desires, and all fighting for control."[13] The new science is merely old theology. As Paul writes, "Now if I do what I do not want, it is no longer I who do it, but sin that dwells within me" (Rom 7:20, ESV). At the end of this verse, Paul recognizes that an alien identity has entered humanity, and it is killing us.

Second, we must realize that merely because we think we have controlled this alien identity in one area, it does not mean those moral elements will transfer to another identity area. We may be honest at church but dishonest at school. We may be courageous at work, but cowards when interacting with our neighbors. We must consider what psychologists have "discovered" and most people recognize. Behavior does not exhibit "cross-situational stability."[14] Christians simply confess, as Paul does, that we are sinners and hypocrites. According to the conception presented above, this should be no surprise since there are reasons linked both to creation and the fall. With regard to creation, we always learn and acquire virtues in particular identity role contexts, and it is not easy to transfer the virtues between roles. Jumping in basketball and ice skating are both jumping, but they are quite different. Similarly, I may be quite creative in my professional job, but I may lack creativity when thinking about how to celebrate my spouse's birthday. Such moral development requires Spirit-filled inspiration and practice and our sinfulness often prevents us from receiving such inspiration or engaging in such practice.

Finally, we need to realize that we may also face conflicts between competing identity goods (e.g., Should I be a good student and study for the exam, or be a good friend and listen to my best friend's relationship struggles?). We face this issue every day. Should I be a good professional and work more on this lecture for work or spend time with my wife and kids?

13. Bloom, "First Person Plural," 90.

14. Appiah, *Experiments in Ethics*.

We are constantly faced with the question of how we integrate all of these competing selves, desires, and loves. We must order our loves and figure out how to prioritize our identities. What Jesus identified as the greatest commands of loving God and one's neighbor are the obvious way that Christians start to order their loves. The problem, of course, is we cannot do it alone.

Redemption

Identity shapes our whole understanding of the moral life. If one reads through the New Testament with a focus upon identity, one finds that it emerges as a major theme to virtually every book. The Gospels center on the question of Jesus' identity as the Christ who can save us from our sins. After Paul discusses his frustration with the alien identity that leads him to sin he asks, "Who will deliver me from this body of death?" The answer: "Thanks be to God through Jesus Christ our Lord!" (Rom 7:25, ESV).

The importance of Christ's identity has profound implications for our identity and our moral lives. This is why the writers of the epistles usually spend the first half or more of their letters, as in Romans, Galatians, Ephesians, and others, helping us understanding our own identity in light of God's story and particularly what Christ has done for us. Only then, do they start to give ethical commands. Unlike the civility code at Harvard, the biblical writers recognize that we need to understand our larger story, our identity, and the rationale for rules, virtues, and wisdom before we can be persuaded by it. Moreover, we need the triune God's help to empower and mentor us as we seek to practice living the good life. Finally, Christ's loving sacrifice provides for us the ultimate model of God's love and therefore the ultimate model (recall Eph 5:1) and God's spirit empowers us to acquire the virtues we need to follow that model.[15]

Conclusion: Becoming Morally Excellent

If Christian educators wish to be excellent coaches or mentors in the good life, they themselves must be experienced identifiers with and imitators of Christ. There is a reason most great sports coaches or music teachers have themselves engaged extensively in the practice. Yet, as any good coach

15. See also Matt 20:25–28; Mark 10:42–45; Luke 14:27–33; John 15:12, 20–21; Rom 6:6–11; 1 Cor 10:33—11:1; 2 Cor 1:5; 4:10; Gal 2:20; 5:24; Eph 5:1–2; Phil 1:29; 3:10–11; Col 1:24; 2:20—3:1; 2 Tim 3:12; Heb 11:1—12:5; 1 Pet 2:20–21; 3:14–18; 4:12–16; 1 John 2:6; 3:11–16; Rev 12:10–11. For additional writing about this issue see Hays, *Moral Vision of the New Testament*.

knows, one must begin at different developmental stages depending upon the moral stage of the practitioner. In this area, some scholarship about various stages of reasoning or different practices for acquiring particular virtues can provide helpful guidance and wisdom.[16] Nonetheless, such scholarship will always remain only partial help in the holistic development of human beings made in God's image to love and be loved.

Reflection Questions

1. Why is identity foundational to ethics?
2. What are the different elements of a good identity role?
3. Pick a practice and see if you can identify the elements of that practice (e.g., being a neighbor, creating a business, parenting, etc.)
4. Can you find examples from the Bible where the different moral elements are addressed?
5. Why is it important to consider all of the elements?
6. What are the moral reasons for identity conflicts?

Recommended Reading

Hays, Richard. *The Moral Vision of the New Testament*. San Francisco: Harper Collins, 1996.

MacIntyre, Alastair. *After Virtue: A Study in Moral Theory*. 3rd ed. Notre Dame, IN: Notre Dame University Press, 2007.

Peterson, Christopher, and Martin Seligman. *Character Strengths and Virtues: A Handbook and Classification*. New York: Oxford University Press, 2004.

Smith, Christian. *What Is a Person?: Rethinking Humanity, Social Life and the Moral Good from the Person Up*. Chicago: University of Chicago Press, 2009.

Bibliography

Appiah, K. A. *Experiments in Ethics*. Cambridge, MA: Harvard University Press, 2008.

Bloom, Paul. "First Person Plural." *The Atlantic* 302/4 (November 2008). Online: http://www.theatlantic.com/magazine/archive/2008/11/first-person-plural/307055/.

Colvin, Geoff. *Talent Is Overrated: What Really Separates World-Class Performers from Everybody Else*. New York: Penguin, 2010.

16. Kohlberg, *Philosophy of Moral Development*; Peterson and Seligman, *Character Strengths and Virtues*.

Grenz, Stanley. *The Social God and the Relational Self: A Trinitarian Theology of the Imago Dei*. Louisville: Westminster John Knox, 2001.

Harvard College. "About Harvard College." Online: http://www.college.harvard.edu/icb/icb.do?keyword=k61161&tabgroupid=icb.tabgroup84748.

Hays, Richard. *The Moral Vision of the New Testament*. San Francisco: Harper Collins, 1996.

Kohlberg, Lawrence. *The Philosophy of Moral Development: Moral Stages and the Idea of Justice*. Essays on Moral Development 1. San Francisco: Harper & Row, 1981.

Lewis, Harry. "The Freshman Pledge." Bits and Pieces blog. Online: http://harry-lewis.blogspot.com/2011/08/freshman-pledge.html.

MacIntyre, Alasdair. *After Virtue: A Study in Moral Theory*. 3rd ed. Notre Dame, IN: Notre Dame University Press, 2007.

Middleton, J. Richard. *The Liberating Image: The Imago Dei in Genesis 1*. Grand Rapids: Brazos, 2005.

Peterson, Christopher, and Martin Selgiman. *Character Strengths and Virtues: A Handbook and Classification*. New York: Oxford University Press, 2004.

Smith, Christian. *What Is a Person?: Rethinking Humanity, Social Life and the Moral Good from the Person Up*. Chicago: University of Chicago Press, 2009.

Smith, James K. A. *Desiring the Kingdom: Worship, Worldview, and Cultural Formation*. Grand Rapids: Baker, 2009.

Wilcox, Brad. *Why Marriage Matters: Thirty Conclusions from the Social Science*. 3rd ed. New York: Institute for American Values, 2011.

8

Evangelism in the Classroom

Elmer John Thiessen

It is frequently said that evangelism or proselytizing has no place in the classroom.[1] Teaching *about* religion is deemed to be acceptable, but not the teaching *of* religion, which is generally associated with indoctrination. Neutrality is still seen by many as the ideal for teachers in the classroom. Another expression of opposition to evangelism in the classroom is found in the recent debate surrounding the question of how to treat controversial issues in schools. Some scholars maintain that if an issue is controversial, then teachers must be careful "to teach the question nondirectively."[2] Others distinguish between public and private values and then go on to suggest that teachers should avoid trying "to promote their own personal opinions in school."[3] Typically, religion is considered to be a controversial or private matter, and so it follows that evangelism is thought to be out of place in the classroom.

The fundamental problem with the above expressions of opposition to evangelism is that teachers cannot help but influence their students to

1. Jeff Astley reviews some expressions of this opposition to evangelism in general schooling and non-confessional religious education in "Evangelism in Education," 184.

2. This is the position taken by Michael Hand in an essay mainly concerned with defining the notion of controversial, "What Should We Teach," 220.

3. See for example the advice given to teachers by the British Citizenship Foundation, "Teaching About Controversial Issues."

some degree, whatever their religious or non-religious position happens to be, and however hard they try to remain neutral. Most of us, I am sure, can point to teachers in our lives who inspired and influenced us in significant ways. More generally, we are always influencing others, and that influence often includes explicit persuasion, evangelism, or proselytizing. It is in the nature of a human being to proselytize. As John Haughey has said, "it seems to be endemic to the way we are as human beings to promote with others what we ourselves have come to understand as true and good."[4] We are in fact proselytizing animals. We are also by nature, proselytized animals.[5] The classroom is one very important context in which proselytizing and being proselytized occurs.

More specific problems with the above expressions of opposition to evangelism in the classroom should also be noted. It is not easy to separate teaching about religion from the teaching of religion. Indoctrination is notoriously difficult to define, and it can be argued that it is possible to teach for commitment in a way that is not educationally suspect.[6] The ideal of neutrality has been shown to be problematic, especially in light of the insights of a postmodern epistemology.[7] The notion of "controversial" is itself controversial.[8] The public/private distinction is similarly problematic.[9] The above problems would suggest that instead of categorical condemnations of evangelism in the classroom, we need a careful articulation of what is and what is not acceptable in terms of a teacher exerting religious persuasive influence in the classroom.

Sometimes it is Christians themselves who object to evangelism or proselytizing in the classroom. Trevor Cooling, for example, in his recent book, *Doing God in Education*, maintains, "Proselytizing is not appropriate in an inclusive and fair classroom."[10] And yet, the central thrust of Cool-

4. Haughey, "Complex Accusation of Sheep-Stealing," 266.

5. For an expansion of these points, see Thiessen, *Ethics of Evangelism*, 142–45.

6. For an extended defense of teaching for commitment with regard to religion, see Thiessen, *Teaching for Commitment*.

7. I develop this argument in Thiessen, *Defence of Religious Schools*, 196.

8. For a treatment of various notions of "controversial," see Cooling, "What is a Controversial Issue?"

9. See Thiessen, *Defence of Religious Schools*, 105–7.

10. Cooling, *Doing God in Education*, 61. Cooling has argued that he was here using the term "proselytizing" in its pejorative sense, as referring to unethical evangelism ("Evangelism in the Classroom: A Response to Elmer Thiessen," 261). However, in this same article it is clear that Cooling is also opposed to persuasive evangelism in the classroom, although he does accept non-persuasive influence on the part of a Christian teacher in the classroom. Cooling has also expressed opposition to evangelism in the classroom in an earlier work, and here he talks specifically about "evangelism"

ing's work is to argue against the ideal of neutrality as espoused, for example, by the British Humanist Association. But if neutrality is impossible, it would seem difficult to avoid evangelism or proselytizing in the classroom. Indeed, Cooling goes on to suggest that the teacher's faith can be seen as an educational resource, though the expression of that faith needs "to be carefully managed in light of the sensitive and complex context of the modern school."[11] Here Cooling seems to be opening the door for evangelism in the classroom—at least a little. There is a tension in Cooling's position suggesting that his earlier statement needs more careful nuancing.

The purpose of this essay is to provide a more careful exploration as to what is and what is not acceptable by way of evangelism or proselytizing in the classroom, drawing on my recent work, *The Ethics of Evangelism: A Philosophical Defense of Ethical Proselytizing and Persuasion*.[12]

I use the words "evangelism" and "proselytizing" interchangeably, and take them to mean any efforts at religious influence or persuasion.[13] While the main focus of my book and this article is on religious persuasion, it should be noted that the terms "evangelism" and "proselytizing" are not limited to this domain. These terms can be and often are applied to nonreligious domains like commercial advertising.[14] Within the educational context, we can also apply these terms to the broader notion of worldviews, and teachers' efforts to persuade students about their own worldview. We must also be careful not to think only of deliberate efforts to evangelize. Influence and persuasion can occur in many forms. Thus evangelism or proselytizing can be intentional or unintentional, direct or indirect, overt or covert. In this paper I will focus mainly on intentional and verbal persuasion in the area of religion. While my primary focus will be on the teacher, I will also touch on how all this relates to students and the aims of education.

(*Christian Vision*, 112). Brian Hill also argues that "it would be both illegal and immoral, under conditions of compulsory schooling and assessment, to use the classroom for explicit evangelism" ("Values in Free Fall?," 50).

11. Cooling, *Doing God in Education*, 61.

12. Thiessen, *Ethics of Evangelism*.

13. The term "proselytizing" is often used to refer to unethical evangelism, but I find this usage arbitrary and confusing. For my rationale for this assessment and for a more careful definition of evangelism or proselytizing, see Thiessen, *Ethics of Evangelism*, 8–17.

14. Thiessen, *Ethics of Evangelism*, 15–16.

Some Personal Reflections

I begin with some reflections on my own teaching career, hoping this will serve as a useful touchstone for further analysis. I have spent most of my career teaching philosophy in secular post-secondary educational institutions. Since I like to practice what I preach—I have written a book entitled *Teaching for Commitment*—I have been very open about my own Christian commitment in the classroom.[15] I have experimented with different ways to declare my commitment. Whatever the approach, at some point in time I warn my students (with a smile) that they are stuck with a Christian philosopher, and that my Christian commitment will color everything that I say in the classroom.

An introductory ethics course has always been my favorite. In this course I challenge the rampant relativism in student attitudes towards ethics, and explore various foundations for objective universal ethical norms, including a religious foundation. I am open about my own convictions about ethical foundations and even try to persuade my students concerning the same. But there are some self-imposed constraints as to what I do by way of evangelism in the classroom. In a secular classroom my defense of the Christian faith necessarily takes place in the context of pluralism. A Christian foundation to ethics is therefore presented alongside Kantian and utilitarian approaches to ethics. I make it a point to subject a Christian foundation to ethics to critique, just as I critique Kantian and utilitarianism theories of ethics. I tell my students repeatedly that they can disagree with me in class discussions. Indeed, I welcome disagreement and argument. I try very hard to create an atmosphere in the classroom where students are free to challenge my own position.

All of this, I believe, is quite in keeping with the goals of a liberal education. It is simply a mistake to assume that evangelism and education are necessarily incompatible. Indeed, I concur with Jeff Astley, "Education and evangelism may be closer neighbors than many suspect."[16] The sharing of a teacher's religious convictions, if done in the right way, can lead to further learning on the part of students. It can help students to become rational and critical thinkers as they examine their own convictions about religion. It can also help students understand the nature of healthy commitment, especially with regard to beliefs that are controversial. With proper modeling, students also learn how to influence others in an ethical manner concerning the beliefs they hold dear.

15. Thiessen, *Teaching for Commitment*.

16. Astley, "Evangelism in Education," 190.

I also believe that my approach to teaching from and for commitment is in keeping with ethical principles that should govern evangelism in the classroom. In my most recent book I devote two chapters to articulating and defending fifteen criteria to distinguish between ethical and unethical proselytizing.[17] These criteria are developed in relation to a broader social context. What I want to do now is to apply the relevant criteria to the classroom setting.

Ethics and the Limits of Ethical Principles

Ethics is itself a controversial topic. So where does one begin when treating the ethics of evangelism, especially when one is trying to bridge the divide that often exists between skeptics and religious adherents? I start by affirming the dignity and worth of the human being, which I believe is a necessary prerequisite of any adequate ethical theory. It was Immanuel Kant, in the eighteenth century, who gave us the modern and secular version of an ethical theory based on the dignity of persons. For Jews and Christians, this dignity is of course grounded in the fact that each person is created in the image of God. So my treatment of the ethics of evangelism begins with this foundational principle, which I believe is shared by most reasonable and morally sensitive people.

Before I move on to work out the implications of this foundation, a few cautionary notes might be in order. While I consider ethics and ethical principles to be ultimately objective and universal, their application is to some degree relative to context. Ethical principles tend to be abstract. In the end they need to be contextualized. We should also expect that differing contexts might just result in differing applications of the same ethical theory and principles. The ethics of evangelism in different educational settings might look somewhat different. Unless otherwise noted, I will from now on focus on the context of elementary and secondary, state-maintained, secular schools.

It is also important to realize that ethics cannot be exhaustively defined in terms of principles or specific criteria. Despite the limitations of rule-oriented ethics, I believe attempting to define ethical criteria still has some merit.

17. Thiessen, *Ethics of Evangelism*, chs. 7–8. I provide a summary of these criteria in Appendix 1 of the same book. All the criteria listed in the rest of this chapter are taken from this Appendix, pp. 234–37.

Dignity and Care

I begin with two broad criteria that I consider to be foundational to all the rest. The first gives expression to the principle of dignity I have already referred to as the foundation of ethics being assumed in this paper. The principle of dignity is a broad principle and as such might be thought to be unhelpful in distinguishing between ethical and unethical evangelism. However, I believe the principle of dignity has some concrete practical implications for evangelism. But a stress on the dignity of persons is not enough. Kantian ethics has been criticized for leading to an overemphasis on human rights. So I believe this principle needs to be coupled with a principle of care for persons.

> Dignity criterion: Ethical proselytizing is always done in such a way as to protect the dignity and worth of the person or persons being proselytized. Proselytizing becomes unethical when it reduces the proselytizee to the status of an object or a pawn in the proselytizing program of any religious institution or religious organization.
>
> Care criterion: Ethical proselytizing must always be an expression of concern for the whole person and all of his or her needs—physical, social, economic, intellectual, emotional, and spiritual.

It is surely self-evident that professional and ethical teachers need to uphold the dignity of each and every student, and that this needs to be coupled with a genuine care for students. This also has implications for teachers exerting religious (or non-religious) influence in the classroom. Students must never be seen as mere objects of a teacher's proselytizing program. Ethical teachers care for their students, and insofar as is appropriate and possible, care for them as whole persons. However, given the educational context of the classroom, ethical teachers are committed to ensuring that the educational needs of their students remain uppermost. Teachers also need to protect the dignity and worth of each student regardless of their religious or non-religious beliefs. Indeed, as will be shown later, protecting the dignity of students is tied to respecting the religious or non-religious identity students inherit from their family background.

Coercion

The freedom to make choices is central to the dignity of persons. Ethical proselytizing will therefore respect the freedom of persons. Coercive evangelism is immoral. It is rather easy to articulate the essence of the coercion criterion as a basis for distinguishing between ethical and unethical evangelism. Difficulties quickly emerge when it comes to describing exactly what coercive evangelism means. The concept of coercion is rather slippery. There are also different kinds of coercion—physical, psychological, and social.

Physical coercion is easier to deal with. The physical coercion criterion can be stated quite simply: "Proselytizing involving the use of physical force or threats is immoral."[18] It would obviously be wrong to try to convert a student by threatening him or her with a beating.

The more difficult kinds of coercion are psychological and social. Vagueness seems to be inescapable in trying to define what is involved in psychological or social coercion. Each of these notions is also multifaceted, and it is impossible to do justice to all the dimensions of psychological or social coercion.

The basic idea behind the psychological coercion criterion can again be stated quite simply: Ethical proselytizing avoids psychological coercion. But what is psychologically coercive? The problem here is that normal human interactions involve some degree of psychological manipulation of one person in relation to another. Here it should be noted that I am using the term "manipulation" in a morally neutral sense. There is a certain degree of psychological manipulation that we need to accept as inescapable and even healthy, and hence not morally blameworthy. I maintain that it is only *excessive* psychological manipulation that raises moral concerns.

Let me apply this to the teacher in the classroom. A good teacher will use a variety of psychological techniques in order to keep order and discipline in the classroom. But should the use of such techniques be considered manipulative in a pejorative sense? Not necessarily. But at some point, psychological manipulation can become excessive and then moral concerns begin to surface. The same problem of vagueness arises with regard to social coercion. Parents and teachers obviously wield a certain degree of authority, power, and control over their children or students. This is not the place to explore the complexity of such power-imbalances. But at some point, power and control over others can become excessive and then moral concerns arise.

18. Thiessen, *Ethics of Evangelism*, 234, cf. 167–69.

Here then are two additional criteria of ethical proselytizing that relate to the above discussion.

> Psychological coercion criterion: Ethical proselytizing avoids excessive psychological manipulation. There are various ways in which proselytizing can be (excessively) psychologically manipulative. (a) Proselytizers should avoid intense, repeated and extremely programmatic approaches to bringing about conversions. (b) Care must be taken to avoid exploiting vulnerability. This becomes especially important when dealing with children, young people, vulnerable adults, and individuals facing personal crises. (c) Excessive appeals to emotion and fear must also be avoided.

> Social coercion criterion: While acknowledging that some degree of power and control is inescapable in proselytizing, excessive expressions of power, or the exploiting of power imbalances when proselytizing, is unethical.

These criteria raise a key question. When does psychological manipulation or the exercise of power and control become excessive? It is simply not possible to define precisely when one has crossed the line. As I argue in my book, it is therefore best to deal with the psychological and social criteria on a case-by-case basis.

A controversial case of proselytizing in a Bronx, New York, public school classroom raises some key questions related to the psychological and social coercion criteria under consideration.[19] A student in a fifth-grade classroom died in a drowning. Mildred Rosario, the fifth-grade teacher in this school, had to make some choices as to how to respond to students who were asking her where the accident victim now was. She responded by saying he's "in heaven." The children then began asking a series of related questions such as "What is heaven like?"

> According to reports, Rosario invited students who did not want to participate in her religious discussion to leave the classroom, but none did. She then asked "if anyone would like to accept Jesus as their personal savior." Rosario explained in a written report submitted to the New York Board of Education that all of the students raised their hands in response.[20]

As might be expected, not all of the students felt comfortable with what their teacher did. One of the students called home immediately after

19. I draw on a description of this case by Steve Benen, "Wrong Answer."

20. Benen, "Wrong Answer," 7.

class. This led to several telephone calls from parents asking the principal for an explanation. This in turn prompted the school administrators to call Rosario in for a disciplinary hearing. After presenting her with the concerns of the parents, Rosario admitted that she had engaged in proselytizing, but also argued that there was nothing wrong with what she had done. She refused to promise to abstain from such activities in the future. She was fired from her position on June 12, 1998, four days after the incident.

Clearly Rosario was trying to respond to students who were deeply distraught over the death of a classmate. Surely trying to provide some comfort to distraught students is a good thing, as was Rosario's responding to her students' feelings and questions in a personal and caring way. She therefore satisfied the care criterion of evangelism discussed above.

However, I believe Rosario acted immorally by using this occasion, when her young students were very distraught, to do some evangelism. She was exploiting the vulnerability of young children in emotional turmoil. As a general rule, I would suggest that the greater the emotional turmoil of children, the more inappropriate it is to engage in evangelism. Rosario was also exploiting her position as a teacher, as someone in authority over her students, and this is no doubt the bigger issue here. It is no surprise that all of the students raised their hands in response to her question as to whether anyone wanted to accept Jesus as their personal savior. That is what young students will typically do in response to an appeal by a caring teacher. But what Rosario did here was clearly ethically wrong. She was exploiting a power imbalance in order to evangelize.

Generalizing, teachers are in a position of authority in the classroom. Hence, caution is in order when a teacher is open about his/her religious or non-religious beliefs. Students must never feel pressured to agree with the religious or non-religious beliefs of their teacher. When writing essays that might touch on religious themes, students should feel perfectly free to disagree with the beliefs expressed by the teacher. That is why I repeatedly tell my students that they can disagree with me and still get an "A" grade on a paper. Such reassurance would be even more important with younger students, who are more prone to pleasing the teacher.

Epistemological/Ethical Concerns

Another set of criteria to distinguish between ethical and unethical evangelism has to do with the intersection of epistemology and ethics.

Rationality Criterion: Proselytizing involves persuasion to convert. Ethical persuasion includes the providing of information in order to make such a decision. It also includes giving reasons for the proposed change of heart and mind. Proselytizing that attempts to sidestep human reason entirely is unethical.

> Truthfulness criterion: Ethical proselytizing is truthful. It seeks to tell the truth about the religion being advocated. It is truthful also with regard to what it says about other religions. Integrity characterizes the ethical proselytizer. Proselytizing accompanied by hidden agendas, hidden identities, lying, deception, and failure to speak the truth should be condemned as immoral.
>
> Humility criterion: Ethical proselytizing is characterized by humility. Proselytizing becomes unethical when it becomes arrogant, condescending, and dogmatic in the claims being made.

What might surprise the reader is the extent to which these criteria reflect some of the typical aims of education. Education is about searching for truth and the cultivation of reason. Ethical evangelism too must satisfy the criteria of rationality and truth. Thus, within an educational context, ethical evangelism must include the giving of reasons for the religious convictions held by teachers as well as students. Here it might be objected that it is simply inappropriate to apply the notions of rationality and truth to the area of religion, and hence the criteria of rationality and truth cannot be used to define ethical evangelism. This argument however rests on a narrow Enlightenment understanding of the notion of rationality and a relativist understanding of truth. Given what one writer has called "soft rationalism," a humbler rationalism that is aware of its limitations, religion too becomes a "reasonable" enterprise, and one to which the notion of truth can still be applied.[21]

Ethical proselytizing is also truthful. The teacher will therefore encourage truthfulness in all claims being made about or against religion. This means that the teacher should be willing to admit unpleasant truths about the religion he/she holds. Care also needs to be taken to be truthful when talking about other religions. Students will also be looking for integrity in the teacher. A teacher who does not practice what he preaches will not be very effective in doing evangelism, but more important, such a lack of integrity is unethical. Another key requirement is the avoidance of hidden agendas in the classroom. That is why it is so important for teachers to be

21. Thiessen, *Ethics of Evangelism*, 62–76.

open about their religious or non-religious commitments, which invariably shape the content of their teaching.

Religious persuasion, when occurring in the classroom, must also be practiced with humility. Arrogance, a condescending attitude, and dogmatism have no place in the classroom, either on the part of the teacher or students. Here it might be objected that evangelism is inherently arrogant. Clearly, a person who has certain convictions believes that he or she has the truth, whether these convictions are religious or non-religious. Such a person will also believe that those disagreeing with her do not have the truth. This should not in itself be viewed as arrogant. Indeed, if claims to truth are viewed as arrogant, then claims to the effect that there is no truth are equally arrogant. As Alvin Plantinga has noted, "These charges of arrogance are a philosophical tar baby: Get close enough to them to use them against the exclusivist and you are likely to find them stuck fast to yourself."[22] We all disagree with others about a lot of things. And we all persuade others in terms of our present limited understanding of the truth. Such persuasion can be done humbly, even admitting that one is open to being proven wrong.[23] Such an attitude is an essential characteristic of ethical religious persuasion in the classroom.

Tolerance and Identity

The above criteria, insofar as they make reference to other religions, also point to another very important criterion of ethical evangelism, involving tolerance. Unfortunately, misconceptions about the nature of tolerance abound. The traditional concept of tolerance meant only to endure, to put up with (from the Latin *tolerare*)—nothing more than that. It did not mean one had to like something. Indeed, the need for tolerance arises precisely because one doesn't like the other person's ideas, for example. We tolerate an item always in relation to some other priority that we consider higher. We believe respect for persons is more important than fighting over a disagreement about ideas. This does not mean that truth is not important. It has been well said that error has no rights, but people do. That is why we endure or put up with ideas and practices and institutions that we do not like.[24]

Today, however, this is frequently spoken of condescendingly as "mere tolerance," and it is seen as not good enough. Today a further demand is made of the tolerant person, namely, the requirement of fully accepting and

22. Plantinga, "Defense of Religious Exclusivism," 177.

23. Thiessen *Ethics of Evangelism*, 59–62.

24. For a more detailed treatment of these points, see ibid., 106–8.

even agreeing with what is different. Indeed, to disagree with someone is to be intolerant. The preferred substitute for tolerance today is mutual acceptance of each other's ideas as equally valid. I believe this contemporary understanding of tolerance is fundamentally mistaken. It rests on a relativistic understanding of truth which is itself problematic.[25] It is also fails to do justice to the higher priority that lies behind the need for tolerance—respect for persons is more important than fighting over a disagreement about ideas. Thus we need to shift the focus from beliefs held to persons holding the beliefs. We may disagree with another's beliefs but we still respect them as persons.

> Tolerance criterion: Ethical proselytizing treats *persons* holding beliefs differing from that of the proselytizer with love and respect. While it does not preclude fair criticism of other religious or irreligious beliefs, it treats the same with respect, and avoids hostile attitudes or the use of insulting and abusive language against other religions and worldviews.

What does this mean in the classroom? As has already been argued, within the context of a pluralist classroom, teachers and students will need to acknowledge that there are competing claims to truth. Students making differing claims to religious or non-religious truth need to be treated with respect. But this does not entail that there can be no criticism of religious positions held by others in the classroom. And engaging in such criticism should not in itself be equated with intolerance. It is only if such criticisms are made using insulting or abusive language, or if the teacher or a student display hostile attitudes to the religion being criticized, that the teacher or the student should be accused of being intolerant and unethical.

The tolerance criterion is closely related to the final criterion of ethical proselytizing I want to consider, the identity criterion.

> Identity criterion: Ethical proselytizing will take into account and show some respect for the communal identity of the proselytizee. Proselytizing which completely disregards the dignity of the individual as rooted in his or her social attachments is immoral.

Especially at the elementary levels of schooling, teachers need to take into account the communal identity of their students, the homes they come from, and their families' religious (or non-religious) affiliation. Education needs to build on the primary culture within which children have been raised. Evangelism too needs to treat this primary culture of students with

25. I expand on this point in ibid., 62–71.

sensitivity. Again, this does not mean that there cannot be criticism of the primary cultures of students, especially as they mature. But such criticism must always be done in such a way that the dignity of the student is upheld. And so we are brought back to the principle of the dignity of persons, the principle with which we began and which underlies all the criteria that we have considered.

Cooling, Thiessen, and the British Humanist Association

I conclude with a brief comparison of my position with that of the British Humanist Association, and Cooling's critique of the BHA referred to earlier in this essay. I agree with Cooling's critique of the BHA, which wants to rule out all religion in the classroom in the name of neutrality. Neutrality is impossible, and finally just a cover for the imposition of a secular or humanistic curriculum in our schools.[26] What is needed is more integrity. Teachers need to be honest about their convictions in the classroom, including their religious (or non-religious) convictions.

What Cooling fails to see is that his critique of neutrality in teaching entails that proselytizing is in fact inescapable. Teachers cannot help but exert persuasive influence over their students with regard to the convictions they hold. Such persuasion, however, must be done in a professional and ethical manner. It is here where Cooling and I are largely in agreement. Cooling adopts a pragmatic approach to "doing God in education" and calls for "courageous restraint" in giving expression to one's faith within a secular pluralistic context.[27] Restraints include a willingness "to accept that the truth you personally hold dear is contestable in wider society," and "to let fairness temper one's advocacy of truth as you understand it." Also, follow the Golden Rule.[28] For the teacher in the classroom, "this means welcoming the expression of points of view by pupils and in the syllabus that you personally think are flawed, sometimes fundamentally so." I agree with all of this, except for Cooling's earlier prohibition of proselytizing in the classroom. What Cooling needs is more courage in admitting that proselytizing is appropriate in the classroom, if practiced with ethical integrity.

I return to the personal narrative with which I began my exploration of the ethics of evangelism in the classroom. My own experience involves teaching philosophy in a post-secondary educational context, with relatively

26. Cooling, *Doing God in Education*, 56.

27. Ibid., 61–63.

28. I also include the Golden Rule as one of the criteria to distinguish between ethical and unethical evangelism; see Thiessen, *Ethics of Evangelism*, 237, 208–10.

mature students. In describing my experience, I outlined some constraints as to what is allowed by way of evangelism in this educational context. In this essay I have for the most part focused on a quite different educational context—elementary and secondary schooling—and this is Cooling's focus as well. Here we are dealing a captive audience of young and very impressionable children who by law are forced to be in school. I believe the ethical restraints in doing evangelism within this context are more stringent. Indeed, it might be argued that the restraints involved in this particular context are so stringent that the resulting approach to evangelism or religious influence in the classroom is nearly indistinguishable from the neutral approach being advocated by the BHA.

So perhaps the differences between Cooling, the British Humanist Association, and myself are not that significant after all, at least from a *practical* point of view. I believe there are still some differences, not the least of which has to do with honesty in describing what is really going on in the classroom with respect to evangelism.[29]

Reflection Questions

1. Is neutrality in the classroom possible? Desirable?
2. What makes an issue "controversial" for a classroom? What implications follow for teaching?
3. Are human beings by nature proselytizing and proselytized animals?
4. Jeff Astley maintains, "Education and evangelism may be closer neighbors than many suspect." Critically evaluate.
5. Critically evaluate the ethical constraints on religious persuasion on the part of the teacher in the classroom as given by Cooling and Thiessen. Can you think of some additional constraints?

Recommended Reading

Astley, Jeff. "Evangelism in Education: Impossibility, Travesty or Necessity?" *International Journal of Education and Religion* 3/2 (2002) 179–94.

Cooling, Trevor. *Doing God in Education*. London: Theos, 2010.

29. This chapter is a condensed and revised version of an essay that first appeared in the *Journal of Education and Christian Belief* 17/2 (Fall 2013). I want to thank David Smith, Trevor Cooling, and several anonymous readers for their helpful comments on earlier drafts of this paper.

Snook, I. A. *Indoctrination and Education.* London: Routledge, Kegan Paul, 1972.

Thiessen, Elmer J. *The Ethics of Evangelism: A Philosophical Defence of Ethical Proselytizing and Persuasion.* Crownhill, Milton Keynes: Paternoster; Downers Grove, IL: IVP Academic, 2011.

Bibliography

Astley, Jeff. "Evangelism in Education: Impossibility, Travesty or Necessity?" *International Journal of Education and Religion* 3/2 (2002) 179–94.

Benen, Steve. "Wrong Answer (Religion in Schools)." *Church & State* 51/8 (1998) 7–8.

British Citizenship Foundation. "Teaching About Controversial Issues: Guidance for Schools." Online: http://www.citizenshipfoundation.org.uk/lib_res_pdf/0118.pdf.

Cooling, Trevor. *A Christian Vision for State Education.* London: SPCK, 1994.

———. *Doing God in Education.* London: Theos. 2010.

———. "Evangelism in the Classroom: A Response to Elmer Thiessen." *Journal of Education and Christian Belief* 17/2 (2013) 33–53.

———. "What Is a Controversial Issue?: Implications for the Treatment of Religious Beliefs in Education." *Journal of Beliefs and Values* 33/2 (2012) 169–81.

Hand, Michael. "What Should We Teach as Controversial?: A Defense of the Epistemic Criterion." *Educational Theory* 58/ 2 (2008) 213–28.

Haughey, J. C. "The Complex Accusation of Sheep-Stealing: Proselytism and Ethics." *Journal of Ecumenical Studies* 35/2 (1998) 257–68.

Hill, Brian V. "Values in Free Fall?: Religious Education and Values in Public Schools." *Journal of Christian Education* 51/3 (2008) 43–55.

Plantinga, Alvin. "A Defense of Religious Exclusivism." In *Philosophical Challenge of Religious Diversity*, edited by and 172–92. New York: Oxford University Press, 2000.

Thiessen, Elmer J. *The Ethics of Evangelism: A Philosophical Defense of Ethical Proselytizing and Persuasion.* Crownhill, Milton Keynes: Paternoster; Downers Grove, IL: IVP Academic, 2011.

———. *In Defence of Religious Schools and Colleges.* Montreal: McGill-Queen's University Press, 2001.

———. *Teaching for Commitment: Liberal Education, Indoctrination, and Christian Nurture.* Montreal: McGill-Queen's University Press; Leominster, UK: Gracewing, 1993.

9

The Peculiar Hope of the Educator[1]

Nicholas Wolterstorff

In a recent communication to me by a professor of education, he observed that though teaching is a "profession of hope"—his words—there has been surprisingly little explicit reflection by educators about hope. He noted that in the profession there is a curious combination of professional optimism with a general sense of educational crisis, the result being that teachers get a confusing message about hope. On the one hand, hope is held to be intrinsic to the concept of teaching; on the other hand, hope is often not present in the reality of teaching. He quoted one teacher as saying, "If I could leave teaching, I would go tomorrow. . . . I'm not sure I have much hope left." He concludes by saying, "We need a theory of hope."

I have never thought in any sustained way about hope in general, nor have I thought in any sustained way about the hope of the educator. So I was about to set these comments aside as an interesting observation about the present state of teaching when a voice inside me stopped me in my tracks and said that it would be cowardly not to accept them as a challenge. So that's how it happened that my topic is "The Peculiar Hope of the Educator."

1. This essay was originally presented as a lecture by Nicholas Wolterstorff to the School of Education at Trinity Western University, Langley, BC, in conjunction with The Re-Envisioning Christian Humanism and Higher Education Lecture Series, March 4–18, 2013. The lecture series was sponsored by the Canada Research Chair in Interpretation, Religion and Culture.

What I have to say will fall far short of the theory of hope that my correspondent says is needed; it will not advance much beyond preliminary reflections on hope and on its role in teaching.

The Nature of Hope

I am a philosopher. So let me begin as philosophers ever since Socrates have been in the habit of beginning, namely, with the relevant "What is it?" question. What is hope? I judge that a good way to begin our address to this question is with the characteristically lucid analysis of hope that Thomas Aquinas gives in his *Summa theologiae*.[2] Hope, says Aquinas, is a special form of desire. It is unlike *fear* in that its object is a good of some sort—or at least something that the agent regards as a good. It is unlike *joy* in that its object is a future good, whereas the object of joy is a present good. It is unlike the desire for small things in that, in Aquinas' words, its "object is something arduous and difficult to obtain." We do not "speak of anyone hoping for trifles which are in one's power to have at any time." And it is unlike *despair* in that "this difficult thing is something possible to obtain: for one does not hope for that which one cannot get at all."

Let me recap and amplify Aquinas' analysis. Hope is unlike fear in that whereas the object of fear is some evil that threatens to befall someone, the good for which one hopes is a good in someone's life, perhaps in one's own life, perhaps in the life of someone else. Looking ahead, intrinsic to teaching is the hope for some good in the lives of one's students. The good for which one hopes may or may not be a good that human beings have some hand in bringing about; one might hope that the asteroid hurtling toward earth misses us.

Hope is a form of desire, says Aquinas, specifically, desire for some future good. This seems clearly right. Aquinas notes that joy also bears a relation to the good, but that the relation of hope to the good is different from the relation of joy to the good. Whereas hope is desire for some future good, we experience joy or delight in some present good.

Aquinas also distinguishes hope from despair, and rightly so, obviously. In drawing the distinction Aquinas does not actually say that despair resembles hope in that despair is also a form of desire for some future good; I interpret him as assuming that, however. Whether or not he is assuming that, it seems to me true. What then distinguishes hope from despair is that when one hopes for some future good, one believes that there is at least a

2. Thomas Aquinas, Summa theologiae, Q. 40, art. 1, resp.

chance that the good one desires will come about, whereas when one despairs of some future good, one believes that there is no chance of the good that one desires coming about.

The other point Aquinas makes about hope is that we speak of hoping for something only when the future good that we desire is "something arduous and difficult to obtain." We don't speak of "hoping for trifles which are in one's power to have at any time." This too seems to me to be correct. It would be quite silly for me to say, for example, that one of the things I hope for is that I will be able to spell the word "the" the next time I want to.

Let me now go beyond Aquinas and suggest two additional contrasts. Hope is also related to, but distinct from, *expectation*. To expect something to happen is to believe that it probably will happen, whereas to hope that something will happen is to believe that there's a chance it will happen—maybe a good chance, maybe only a slim chance. Further, what one *expects* to happen may or may not be something that one desires, whereas hope is always for a desired good. What one expects to happen may be some evil that one dreads.

Someone might wonder at this point whether expectation excludes hope; if I expect something to happen, do I then not hope for it to happen? I think expectation does not exclude hope. It seems to me to make perfectly good sense to say, "I hope that Obama wins; in fact, I expect that he will." What hope adds to expectation in such a case is desire. That expectation does not exclude hope will become important when we discuss the role of hope in teaching.

Second, it appears to me that hoping is also to be distinguished from *longing*. I remember talking to a Russian, a decade or so before the breakup of the Soviet Union, about the absence of religious freedom in his country. I would characterize the attitude he expressed as longing for a time when he, as an Orthodox Christian, could worship freely but holding out no hope of that happening in his lifetime. He saw no chance of its happening. Longing, as I will understand it, is desiring some future good when one sees no chance of its coming about.

But if that's what longing is, how is longing different from despair, which I also characterized as longing for some future good that one sees no chance of coming about? I think the difference is one of focus. When we speak of *longing* for something we focus on the future good that is desired, whereas when we speak of *despairing* of something we focus on there being no chance of the desired good coming about. The attitude of the Russian that I talked to could be characterized as longing for freedom of religion but despairing of that happening.

Let me summarize my analysis of the difference between expectation, hope, and longing. To expect some future good is to believe that that good will probably come about; one may or may not desire it. To hope for some future good is to desire that good and to believe that there is at least a chance that it will come about; one may believe that there is more than a chance, that it will probably come about. To long for some future good is to desire that good but to believe that there is no chance of it coming about.

That's my analysis of hope. It's well short of a theory, but for our purposes here it will be sufficient. Let me now move on to some comments about the structure of the activity that we call "teaching."

The Structure of Teaching

Teaching is shaped by desire, the desire to effect some change in the student—a change for the better, of course. Having judged that it would be a good thing in the life of the student if he knows some things that presently he does not know, if he knows how to do some things that presently he does not know how to do, or if he is disposed to do some things that presently he is not disposed to do, the teacher aims at bringing about those changes.

But as we all know, one can aim at teaching and not be successful. Then one hasn't actually taught; or to view it from the converse side, the student wasn't actually taught. Teaching didn't happen. Our verb "to teach" is what is sometimes called a "success" term. It's like the verb "to kick" in that regard. Aiming to kick someone is not sufficient for kicking to occur; someone has to be kicked.

We use our English word "love" to refer to a number of quite different phenomena. One thing we call "love" is what one might call *love as attraction*; love as attraction consists of being drawn to something on account of its worth, as when one says, "I love the late Beethoven string quartets." Another thing we call "love" is *love as benevolence*; love as benevolence consists of aiming to advance the good in someone's life. Aiming to teach someone is inherently an act of love, specifically, an act of love as benevolence. We who are teachers don't always think of trying to teach someone as inherently an exercise of love; perhaps we do so only infrequently. But that's what is—inherently, not incidentally. To aim at teaching someone is to aim at enhancing the good in the student's life; and that is love as benevolence.

It may be that some people who are employed as teachers aim at nothing more than "presenting the material," as we say. "Take it or leave it" is their attitude. These are not teachers; they are not trying to teach. Aiming simply to present the material is not to be identified with trying to teach. The person presenting the material may be in love with the material, but love for the material is not to be identified with love as benevolence for the student. If one's sole aim is to present the material, one will be disappointed only if, for some reason, one does not succeed in doing that—perhaps a disturbance breaks out in the hallway before one has finished presenting the material. By contrast, the person who genuinely tries to teach is disappointed if the change for the better that she desires in the students does not come about. The person who just presents the material has no such desire.

In trying to teach, especially in trying to teach young children, the good that one desires to bring about is a highly distinctive good. One aims at contributing to inducting the student into the human community and into some part of its cultural heritage—or more precisely, at inducting the student into *some particular segment* of the human community. More precisely yet, one aims at contributing to bringing it about that the student will *flourish* in some particular segment of the human community and that she herself will *contribute to the flourishing* of the community. When I speak here of flourishing, I have in mind the biblical concept of *shalom*.[3] Shalom is flourishing.

The teacher thus aims at formation, unavoidably so. And that makes teaching a deeply responsible activity; to intentionally aim at the formation of someone, especially at the formation of a young child, is an activity that carries with it deep responsibility.

The reason I speak of the teacher as aiming at *contributing* to inducting the student into some particular segment of the human community and into some part of its cultural heritage, rather than straightforwardly saying that the teacher *aims* at that, is that teachers are far from alone in aiming at such induction. Parents do so as well, and friends. They all contribute. The words, "aims at contributing to inducting the student into the human community and into some part of its cultural heritage" are a mouthful. So let me henceforth save words by saying that teachers aim at *contributing to socializing and enculturating the student.*

It is up to oneself whether one *tries* to teach something to some student. It is not up to oneself whether one *does in fact* teach that thing to that student—that is to say, whether one is successful in one's aim. As I noted earlier, "to teach" is a success term. In order actually to teach a student one has to adapt one's ends and means to the student's present capabilities—which presupposes, of course, that one has a pretty good idea of what those

3. See Wolterstorff, *Educating for Shalom.*

present capabilities are. One does not try to teach calculus to a first-grader who has not yet learned arithmetic. Teaching is inherently adaptive to its recipients.

Some of a student's present capabilities depend on native talent, but many, if not most, of them also depend on the nature and extent of the socialization and enculturation that the student has already undergone. The kindergartner whose parents have often read to her has capabilities that the kindergartner to whom no one has ever read lacks—even if the native talent of the two students is the same. It's important to keep in mind this distinction between a student's present capabilities and a student's potential. The student's potential goes well beyond her present capabilities. The teacher aims, among other things, at enhancing the student's capabilities so that they come closer to the student's potential.

The point just made is that whether one does in fact teach something to some student depends on whether that student is presently capable of learning that thing. To this it must be added that it also depends on the active cooperation of the student. Whether teaching occurs depends not just on what the agent of the teaching does, namely, the teacher, but also on what the recipient of the teaching does, namely, the student. Both must be active. Teaching does not consist of pouring something called "subject matter" into the minds of students. In all sorts of ways the student must actively contribute to the process, or the aimed-at socialization and enculturation will not occur. She has to listen attentively, look attentively, read carefully, speak up, write, think, perform exercises. Whether something is actually taught depends as much on the activity of the student as it does on the activity of the teacher.

Earlier I noted that "to teach" and "to kick" are both success terms. In respect to what I have just now noted, teaching is very different from kicking. I can kick someone without any active contribution on that person's part. I cannot teach someone something without active contribution on that person's part.

Whether or not the teacher actually teaches something to the student—whether she succeeds in her aim of contributing to the induction of the student into some segment of the human community and into some part of its cultural inheritance—is thus in good measure out of her hands and in the hands of that immature young student who needs to be inducted. Seen from this angle, teaching is a very paradoxical activity. Someone who is, say, an office manager also works with human material. But an office manager is not trying to induct into the human community people who have to cooperate in that induction or it won't happen. They have already been inducted.

Parenthetically, it's worth noting that teaching is very different, in the respect noted, from scholarship. Whether or not one is successful in one's scholarly activities is by and large in one's own hands. Scholarship, in general, is not vulnerable to the cooperation of recipients in the way that teaching is. Put it like this: whether or not teaching occurs is both agent-dependent and recipient-dependent. Whether scholarship occurs is, for the most part, just agent-dependent.

The Place of Hope in Teaching

From these all-too-brief reflections on the nature of hope and on the structure of teaching, let us now move on to the topic we wanted to get to, namely, the place of hope in teaching. In doing so, it will be important to keep in mind the distinctions I drew among expectation, hope, and longing. Let me repeat them. To *expect* some future good is to believe that that good will probably come about; one may or may not desire it. To *hope* for some future good is to desire that good and to believe that there is at least a chance that it will come about—perhaps a good chance, perhaps a slim chance. To *long* for some future good is to desire that good but to believe that there is no chance of it coming about.

When I was teaching graduate seminars at Yale the students were invariably bright, industrious, well trained in the habits of the scholar, and well prepared. I had a good idea of what I could expect from them, and those expectations were high. Looking back, I don't think that I hoped for more; I don't think I hoped for more than I expected. Hope was not absent. I did hope, I did desire some change for the good in the students; I was by no means indifferent. I did not simply aim at presenting the material. But by and large, what I hoped for is also what I expected.

Now and then it happened that a student's work did not live up to my expectations. I had expected, say, that he could write better than, as it turned out, he could. Since I hoped for what I expected, I was in that case disappointed. And sometimes students surprised me by going beyond my expectations. But as I recall, I did not hope to be surprised in this way, so I wasn't disappointed when I wasn't. Maybe I should have hoped for more than I expected; maybe some professors in my situation do. But I don't recall that I did. I think I felt that, for the most part, the students were living up to their potential, so what more was there to hope for?

If I did leave the classroom disappointed, it was usually not because my hopes for the students were disappointed but because my hopes for myself were disappointed: I felt that I had done a poor job of explaining something, or a student had pointed out something that, once noted, was so blindingly obvious that I kicked myself for not having noticed it myself. I'm sure there are classrooms in elementary and secondary schools that are exceptional in the same way that my graduate school seminars were exceptional. But they are, indeed, just that: exceptional. The teachers in such classrooms experience no more than occasional disappointment. Teaching is, for them, very nearly an unalloyed delight, as it was for me.

If all classrooms were exceptional in this way it would probably never occur to anyone to think about the place of hope in teaching; in my own case, nothing in my Yale seminars provoked me into thinking about it. It's the other classrooms that provoke us into thinking about hope, especially those that are exceptional in the other direction—exceptionally bad.

Let us suppose that what we are dealing with is a stereotypical American inner-city classroom in, let's say, the first grade. The teacher is freshly minted; she has just graduated from college or university where she majored in elementary education. There she acquired some idea of the level of achievement to be expected from first-graders. So that's what she aims at, that's what she desires, that's what she hopes for.

But the students in front of her are poorly prepared for formal schooling; their socialization and enculturation are, in this respect, seriously deficient. They lack the present capability of doing what their young teacher expects of them. Most of them, maybe all of them, have the *potential* for living up to her expectations; they are not lacking in innate ability. That's not the problem. The problem is that their socialization and enculturation have been such that they don't presently have the capability. Their socialization and enculturation have also been such they have not acquired the dispositions that would enable them to contribute to the educational process in the way that's required for their teacher actually to teach what she aims to teach, actually to succeed in what she hopes for. They can't sit still; their minds wander off; they don't listen.

The young teacher becomes profoundly disappointed. Her hopes are dashed. She regards herself as a failure. She finds no joy in her teaching. She is depressed. The idealism with which she entered the profession, inspired in her by her college or university professors, is now completely gone. She wonders whether she should look for some other line of work. But she decides to stick it out for a few more years.

So what should she do next year? She now knows fairly well what she can expect of her students, far less than what she expected when she began teaching the previous year. Should she now lower her aims so that they match her expectations? Should she now hope to achieve no more than she can reasonably expect to achieve?

Let us suppose that she is not without hope. She has not fallen into indifference; she is not resigned to simply presenting the material and maintaining some semblance of order in the classroom. She still hopes to effect some change for the good in her students. So far as I can see, it is never right for the teacher to give up hope, never right for her to give up the desire for bringing about some good in the lives of her students, never right to become indifferent. In a word, it is never right for her to give up on love for her students—that is, love as benevolence, love aimed at bringing about some good in the lives of her students.

The question is not whether she should give up hope; she should never do that—though I understand why teachers sometimes do. The question is whether she should reduce her hopes so that they reach no higher than her expectations. That way she will only occasionally be disappointed—only when a student fails to live up even to her low expectations. I judge that this is the main question to be addressed when we ask about the place of hope in teaching.

Let's be sure that we understand the question. It is rather often said that when teachers lower expectations, they lower achievement; I have no doubt that this is true. But the term "expectations" is here being used in a different sense from that in which I am using it. Expectations in this sense are requirements, demands, challenges—as when the teacher says, "I expect all of you to have read pages 103 to 129 by next class period."

What I mean by "expectation" is not that. To expect something, in the sense in which I am using the term, is to believe that it is likely to happen. The teacher has come to certain conclusions about what she is likely to achieve. The question is not whether she should lower her expectations, that is, her beliefs as to what her students can achieve; that would be appropriate only if her expectations as to what her students can achieve are still unreasonably high. The question is whether she should lower her hopes so that she no longer desires to achieve more than what she expects to achieve.

Ambulance attendants often try to get a patient's heart beating again even though they don't think it's likely that they will succeed; they do so as long as they think there is some chance of succeeding. Hope in their case exceeds expectation. Should teaching be like that? Or should teaching be like trying to get the patient's heart beating again only if one thinks that one is likely to be successful?

I don't think the right answer to this question is just obvious. But my view is that the teacher should be like the ambulance attendant. Teachers in difficult situations of the sort I have described should hope for more than they expect. They should hope to spark some awakening in their students, some change of attitude, some curiosity, some delight, some wonder, some awe, on occasion some horror, even when they don't really expect it. Of course this hope must now and then be gratified; if what one hopes for never happens, one's hope dies. It's because ambulance attendants sometimes succeed in getting someone's heart beating again, when there's only a chance and not a likelihood of being successful, that they keep on trying.

I shall never forget what a Dutch monk once said to me when we were discussing the state of the Dutch Catholic Church. He found the state of the church depressing. But then he said this: "Even when the grass looks entirely brown, always, when you get down on your knees and look closely, you will see some blades of green."

That leads me to add that, in good measure, we teachers don't know when we are successful; that makes teaching quite different from most other professions. Let me offer a true anecdote that, at the same time, can serve as a metaphor. Some years ago a former student happened to be back on campus and looked me up in my office. She told me that for quite some time she had wanted to tell me the following: she remembered almost nothing of what I had taught in class (I cringed), but her life was changed by a casual remark I had made in the hallway; she repeated the remark. I had no memory of saying that; I had to take her word for it.

Much of teaching is like that. We work hard at trying to bring about some change for the good in the student; in the course of doing so, we may bring about some truly significant change that is quite different from what we aimed it, and we may never know that we did. It is for this reason also that hope should not be reduced to expectation. Another point to be taken from the anecdote is that teaching is not limited to classroom lesson plans.

If I am right in saying that, even in difficult situations, hope should not be tamped down so that it does not exceed expectation, if no matter how difficult one's classroom situation may be one should hope for more than one expects, then it follows that, in all but the most exceptional situations, teachers live with disappointment—not guilt, let's be clear, but disappointment. What one hoped for did not happen. Perhaps what one expected happened, but not what one hoped for.

Conclusion

In concluding, let me bring longing back into the picture. I have suggested that the teacher in the American inner-city classroom should not tamp down her hopes so that they do not exceed her expectations. She should hope for more than she expects. Let me now add that she should long for even more than she hopes. She should long for the day when the students who show up in her inner-city classroom are not socially and culturally deprived. She, along with all of us, should be like the Russian I mentioned who saw no chance of ever being allowed to worship freely but who nonetheless longed deeply for such freedom. We should never cease to say, "This should not be." We should hope for more than we expect and long for more than we hope.

What saddens the committed inner-city teacher is not just that her hopes are so often dashed. What saddens her about the present situation is that there is no hope of the potential of her students being realized. The waste of human potential, the fact that for many of her students there is no hope of their ever truly flourishing in human community and of their contributing to the flourishing of community, no hope of their enjoying the shalom of the community and of contributing to its shalom—that is truly sad.

We long for signs of the coming of the kingdom.

Reflection Questions

1. How might the Christian educator demonstrate a uniquely Christian practice of hope in the K–12 classroom? Think of specific examples.
2. Among all the ideas and reflections about hope and the teacher-educator that Wolterstorff mentions, which do you believe would be the most effective? Which do you believe would be most practical?
3. What are some possible ways that God could use your specific interests, educational or otherwise, to make a positive impact in the life of a student?
4. How is hope understood by teachers, parents, and students in the public and private education system? Is there a difference? Think of both explicit and implicit examples.

Recommended Reading

Egea, Denise. *Levinas and Education: At the Intersection of Faith and Reason*. New York: Routledge, 2008.

Loomis, Steven, and Paul Spears. *Education for Human Flourishing: A Christian Perspective*. Downers Grove, IL: InterVarsity, 2009.

Pelikan, Jaroslav. *The Idea of the University: A Reexamination*. New York: Yale University Press, 1992.

Van Brummelen, Harro. *Walking with God in the Classroom: Christian Approaches to Teaching and Learning*. Colorado Springs, CO: Purposeful Design, 2009.

Bibliography

Wolterstorff, Nicholas. *Educating for Shalom: Essays on Christian Higher Education*. Grand Rapids: Eerdmans, 2004.

10

Truth, Traditional Teaching, and Constructivism

Rev. Keith Mitchell

In this fast paced world of ideas, postmodern concepts, and deconstructionist thought Christian teachers are sometimes left to wonder what an appropriate pedagogy in educating individuals is. The influence of the likes of John Dewey, Paulo Freire, Jean Piaget, and others has tended to catapult traditional means into somewhat of a spiral downwards. The rise of constructivist thought with its postmodern influence can be quickly seen as "evil" because of its secular roots. The constructivist approach is then relegated to the side by well-meaning Christian educators who then tenaciously hold on to past traditional means of education. This chapter espouses God's truth as the basis of all methodologies and then applies this concept to traditional and constructivist epistemologies. This dissertation then suggests amalgamating both forms of educational approach based on the educational needs of the individual.

The Truth

Jeremiah 10:12 expresses that all of God's creation was founded on his wisdom and made through his power and understanding. We know that God is truth and so, therefore, it must be deduced that God's truth pervades all of his creation alongside his wisdom, power, and understanding. However, the effects of the fall we see contended in Genesis 3 indicate that humanity rebelled against God himself and this truth was distorted. In that we now acknowledge that humanity has attempted to hinder God's truth as Romans 1:18 informs us. However, the truth referred to in Romans 1:18 is a general truth that all can access rather than the truth of Christ and the gospel.[1] It is this general truth that is engaged in this dissertation on traditional versus constructivist teaching.

At the heart of thought is that it is agreed that all truth is God's truth. Knowlton and Shaffer outline a construction of God's truth in their work that distinguishes between personal truth and God's truth.[2] Therein, they argue that "Construction is not creating something new; it is putting together ideas in a personally meaningful and honest (and thus "truthful") way."[3] In this we are enabled by a sense of confidence that exploring varying and non-traditional concepts, approaches, and methods in education is a relatively pliable venture alongside the use of an interpretative biblical framework. However, if we disagree with the conceptualization that truth is embedded in this world then we can tend to develop a more suspicious, anxious, and fearful outlook to new pedagogical principles, particularly birthed from a more so-called secular market.

George Knight expressed that "All other sources of knowledge must be tested and verified in light of scripture."[4] Knight enunciated assumptions surrounding the fallen human state as:

1. Humans exist in a supernatural universe in which the infinite Creator God has revealed himself to finite minds on a level they can comprehend in at least a limited fashion.
2. Humans beings are created in the image of God and, even though fallen, are capable of rational thought.
3. Communication with other intelligent beings (people and God) is possible in spite of humanity's inherent limitations and the imperfections and imprecision of human language.
4. The God who cared enough to reveal himself to people also cared enough to protect the essence of that revelation as it was transmitted through succeeding generations.

1. Morris, *Epistle to the Romans*, 78.
2. Knowlton and Shaffer, "Shifting Toward A Constructivist Philosophy," 116.
3. Ibid., 21.
4. Knight, *Philosophy & Education*, 168.

5. Human beings are able to make sufficiently correct interpretations of the Bible, through the guidance of the Holy Spirit, to arrive at Truth.

Now this does not deduce that all societal concepts are accepted without critique. In fact Paul the apostle tells Christians in Romans 12:2 to be transformed by the renewing of their minds, and in 2 Corinthians 10:5 instructs to "take captive every thought to make it obedient to Christ." Through these verses we are presented with a need to learn the ability and skill of critiquing concepts and ideologies. Where conceptualizations directly stand against the knowledge of God then we can discern inerrancies and demolish these arguments through debate, or contextualize them within a workable Christian framework. Paul at the Areopagus in Acts 17:16–34 debated with the Stoic philosophers by utilizing their local religion (v. 22–23) and secular authors (v. 28). Therefore, engaging with worldly ideas should not be feared. In 1 John 4:18 it is stated that perfect love casts out all fear. "We should understand our culture by discovering those elements in it that are highly esteemed and recognizing its primary stories."[5] It is about meaning making in the process of student learning. So, therefore, the debate about utilizing a constructivist methodology in teaching need not be feared if gleaned through a biblical framework.

Talking on epistemology affects one's conception of education regarding basis, view of persons, and proposed goals and purposes. Pazmino said that the "stance on values, in conjunction with a corresponding view of reality and truth, will determine the choice of purposes and goals in the education process."[6] Therefore, educators need to ensure that their choice of methodology correlates with their political, social, economic, and relational circumstances.

The New Testament maintains that knowledge or truth must be related to love (2 John 1) and that all truth is God's truth, for he alone is the source of all knowledge, wisdom, and understanding (Col 2:2–3). "The problems facing the Christian educator is how to maintain in creative tension those truths discerned through study in various disciplines with the truths revealed in Scripture while at the same time being guided by love for God, others, and creation."[7]

Christian developmentalists in their epistemology would most likely align to a belief "that there are unchanging and reliable absolutes in the universe (absolute metaphysics) and yet at the same time they acknowledge

5. Clifford and Johnson, *The Cross Is Not Enough*, Kindle loc. 5492–93.

6. Pazmiño, *Foundational Issues in Christian Education*, 96.

7. Ibid., 98.

that one's perception of God and the world are conditioned by one's own mental structures and experiences (relative epistemology)."[8] There is a need for the Christian to claim that Scripture is the source of knowledge and epistemological authority for God's truth to be ensured.[9]

Pazmiño suggests six epistemological observations in this regard:

1. The biblical perspective is that all truth is God's truth, so there is therefore no secular/sacred truth distinction.
2. The truth of Christian revelation is true to what actually exists in the universe so Christians can pursue truth without fear of ultimate contradiction.
3. Forces of evil seek to undermine the Bible, distort human reasoning, and lead persons to rely on their own inadequate and fallen selves in pursuit of truth.
4. The Bible is concerned not with abstract truth but with the truth as related to life, therefore, knowing in the biblical sense is applying the perceived knowledge to daily life.
5. The various sources of knowledge available to Christians (the special revelation of Scripture, the general revelation of the natural world, and reason) are complementary and should be used in light of the biblical pattern.
6. Given the unity of truth, the acceptance of a Christian epistemology cannot be separated from the acceptance of a Christian metaphysics.[10]

Therefore, the intention in the development of a critiquing mind in student learning is for individuals to ultimately be able to discern truth for themselves. This means avoiding an approach that indoctrinates the student such that they become dependent upon the teacher or educator. Indoctrination "is to teach even supposedly sound beliefs and values in such a manner that students are incapable of reconsidering them, whether at school or in later life."[11] Inappropriate teaching content can be taught in a soft-sell gentle and tentative teaching manner such that it becomes a form of indoctrination where students are not enabled to think for themselves. Some forms of pedagogy can fit into a hard-sell schema and so may need challenging but so too should bad content be challenged. So the form of teaching is important in adopting an appropriate pedagogical methodology. "Teach-

8. Wilhoit, *Christian Education and the Search for Meaning*, 94.

9. Knight, *Philosophy & Education*, 168.

10. Pazmiño, *Foundational Issues in Christian Education*, 98–99.

11. Beck and Kosnik, *Innovations in Teacher Education*, 74.

ing which neglects appeal to experience and reason and induces excessively strong psychological attachment to ideas inhibits the later dropping of beliefs which further learning suggests are mistaken."[12] Reliance and trust that the Holy Spirit is at work is an essential assumption in enabling individuals' development of the discernment of truth (John 15:26).

Traditional Teaching

"Students educated in a setting that stresses performance learn that technique, rules, and memory matter more than context, authenticity, and wholeness."[13] Brooks previews the presuppositions of traditional teaching as:

1. Teachers disseminate information and expect students to replicate this information.
2. Limited truth is explored by provision of textbooks provided by teachers.
3. A lot of alone time in learning rather than cooperation. Minimal higher order thinking encouraged.
4. Students are discouraged in learning through the teacher determining the correct answer and students showing that knowledge.
5. There is an assumption of a fixed world rather than the construction of new knowledge; work towards attaining conventional understandings.[14]

Wilhoit adds to these the assumptions that students are essentially apathetic towards learning, that they are blank slates in need of being written upon, and that knowledge in itself is what transforms an individual.[15]

Many of the teachers who subscribe to the more traditional view of teaching would agree that knowledge inevitably leads to transformation and its application via the transmission process through a more didactic form.[16] This pedagogical concept has tended to be recognized as the "banking" concept of education where the student is seen as a container to deposit

12. Ibid., 76.
13. Brooks and Brooks, *In Search of Understanding*, 8–9.
14. Ibid., 6–7.
15. Wilhoit, *Christian Education*, 98–99.
16. Ibid.

information and knowledge into so as to ensure that learning takes place.[17] It is generally agreed that the philosophical basis of a teacher's precept towards education effects the outworking of that ideology. So it is accepted that an educator's beliefs surrounding personhood leads to the organization, sequence, and structure of instruction in the classroom. The traditional form of teaching practice, such as that prescribed by Brooks (1999), can be based on a fear or misdemeanor that students are not capable of sufficient rational thought and the development of the necessary skills in the critique of the world. Therefore, students require someone else more competent to do that for them through a traditional approach. However, many a teacher has seen the effect of passivity and lessened domain of learning from their students through the more traditional means of education.

Constructivism

Constructivism is an expanding approach to education in many teaching settings and environments since its inception over the last few decades. Westwood's research on constructivism displayed that constructivism is a theory about human learning rather than a method of teaching.[18] He considers John Dewey (1933), Jean Piaget (1983), and Jerome Bruner (1961) as the forerunners of constructivist principles as they focused on a child-centered approach to learning rather than a teacher-directed one. Westwood explained that Lev Vygotsky (1962, 1978) expanded this basis of constructivism and developed what is now coined as "social constructivism" or "structuralism." Vygotsky aimed to differentiate his work from Piaget's claim on the need for collaborative social interaction and communication in the process of learning. A pervading assumption of constructivism is "that children are self-motivated and self-regulating beings who will acquire the fundamental skills of reading, writing, spelling, calculating and problem solving as by-products of engaging in, and communicating about age-appropriate, meaningful activities every day."[19]

The pedagogical developments in teaching have moved from behaviorism to cognitivism and now to constructivism approaches surrounding education. This proliferation has moved constructivism into diverse areas of thought and concept in this early part of the twenty-first century.[20] In

17. Crotty, *Foundations of Social Research*, 153.

18. Westwood, *Teaching Methods*, 4.

19. Ibid.

20. Applefield, Huber, and Moallem, "Constructivism in Theory and Practice," 37.

fact Hattie explains and evidences research showing that deeper thinking is elicited from a more constructivist approach rather than direct questions that illicit factual recall.[21]

Essentially constructivism has become more of a descriptor of learning rather than a model of pedagogical precept because of its diverse expression and divergence in its development and evolution.[22]

> Constructivism is an epistemological view of knowledge acquisition emphasizing knowledge construction rather than knowledge transmission and the recording of information conveyed by others.[23]

A challenge to move towards a more constructivist form of learning has been proposed by the likes of Knowlton and Shaffer, who outline that in more traditional forms of education,

1. memorization does not indicate understanding;
2. it places the teacher as a judge or legislator;
3. it involves individual student effort void of the social interactions of learning; and
4. it tends toward an understanding to develop in the student that ideas and concepts are compartmentalized and separate from content areas.[24]

A constructivist approach to learning, despite being aligned to postmodernism and epistemological relativism, does not in itself mean that absolute truth is dispensed with. Rather a constructivist approach, if moderated appropriately, can be constructed with thought and critique such that God's truth is still foundational and educators can focus on the social, cognitive, and pragmatic areas of child education.

But in fairness it must be noted that constructivist teaching has its critics. Bowers claims that the constructivism formulated by Dewey, Piaget, and Freire is anthropocentric in its understanding of human nature and relationships and is dismissive of varying cultural ways of knowing.[25] He espouses that the imperialism of Western thought as imposed within the theory is dissenting against other non-Western cultures and is, therefore,

21. Hattie, *Visible Learning*, 26–29.
22. Windschitl, "Framing Constructivism," 131.
23. Applefield, Huber, and Moallem, "Constructivism in Theory and Practice," 37.
24. Knowlton, and Shaffer, "Shifting Toward a Constructivist Philosophy," 118–19.
25. Bowers, *False Promises of Constructivist Theories of Learning*, x–xii.

against the globalization of constructivist theory. His point is valid and so adoption of a constructivist approach without critique of context should be heeded.

Constructivism and the Scriptures

Adopting interruption and creating a safe space to engage in teaching practice becomes the norm in constructivist teaching. This interruptive approach can be seen in multiple examples of Jesus' approach to teaching. He was interjected at various times by the likes of Jairus surrounding his daughter's illness (Matt 9:18–19). He was then interrupted by a woman bleeding for twelve years and in need of healing (9:20). On many occasions Jesus was moved with compassion for the people and their needs and responded thereon rather than pursuing his own teaching agenda (Matt 9:36; 14:14; 23:37). With the woman of Samaria Jesus demonstrated openness and acceptance despite the cultural issues of a Jewish man avoiding talk with a non-Jewish woman (John 4:1–26). His bridging of the gap in working from her interest led to her learning about the Messiah and eventual following of Jesus himself. All these demonstrate a student-centered approach rather than a teacher-directed approach towards learning.

In that, education takes place as there is consideration of the person being impacted rather than the person delivering the information. Jesus himself claimed that he came to serve and give his life as a ransom (Matt 20:28; Phil 2:11–13). Obviously, this means that teachers need to be better positioned with knowledge than their students to be able to adapt to changing thoughts and issues. It does mean an interrupted curriculum instead of fulfilling a desire to complete certain requirements. However, the gains in learning of the student seem to outweigh this minor diversion.

Adding to the biblical picture of constructivist ideology, William Yount discusses the concept that learners need learn to think for themselves.[26] He sources his argument by comparing biblical examples of people presented with freedom to make their own decisions in life against the controlling approach of the Pharisees. He presents examples of choices made by various people—albeit bad decisions—like: the rich young ruler, Judas' betrayal, Thomas's doubt, and Peter's denial of the Lord. We see here that Jesus did not intervene or pressure a change in decision in these people. Rather, in grace he worked with where they were at in their stage of learning. Yount then contrasts these examples against the denial of freedom presented by

26. Yount, *Created to Learn*, 357–58.

the Pharisees, who desired to create fear and engaged control in achieving their purposes in learning. Development of self-thought and self-processing is an important component in the education process of the individual that a constructivist approach can enable.

Synthesizing Constructivism and Traditional Teaching

It must be said that varying the teaching method has its place in child learning and development and so discerning the most appropriate setting, whether a traditional or more constructivist approach to teaching, is a skill to be developed in itself. It is generally accepted that an appropriate balance is realized when selecting the methods of instruction. This selection should be determined by the type of learning required in a lesson, considering such matters as age, ability, and capability of individual students. Louise Ellis suggests

1. More directive strategies have greater impact on students with learning difficulties than other methodologies.
2. A balanced approach to methodologies delivers better student outcomes with more positive results.
3. Educators require knowledge and understanding of both approaches so that they can amalgamate the best of both approaches effectively.
4. Teachers require a belief that all students are able to learn, even those-with special needs or learning difficulties.[27]

Research is showing that "direct" methods are more worthwhile in earlier stages of learning, where more foundational skills surrounding literacy and numeracy are required so that students are better prepared for the less structured activities.[28] In this it can be deduced that more traditional forms of teaching can be amalgamated alongside more constructivist forms when the students' needs and abilities are considered with the particular aspect of learning that is required.

Peter Westwood's exploration of pedagogical methods suggests a three-stage model of knowledge acquisition that can complement both traditional and constructivist learning concepts.[29] He first indicated a Stage 1 where initial knowledge acquisition is more didactic in approach. This

27. Ellis, *Balancing Approaches*, 53.

28. Westwood, *Teaching Methods*, 17.

29. Ibid., 6–7.

then develops into Stage 2 where advanced knowledge is constructed by the student. Finally, the process of learning advances into Stage 3 where proficiency is developed through a totally constructivist methodology. The discerning educator will be the one who is able to determine where the transition between stages takes place for the individual student. This approach respects the individual's ability to learn at the center, enables the skill of *how* to learn to take place, and encompasses interdependence for an individual reflective of the freedom that is found in the gospel of Jesus Christ. Therefore, in light of all truth being God's truth, alignment to a biblical framework can be espoused when amalgamating constructivist thought against traditional methodologies.

Conclusion

So, as we conclude we can see that an appropriate interplay of ideas and concepts on the issue of truth, traditional teaching, and constructivism can be attained within a Christian framework. In this a teacher needs to learn the skill and technique of amalgamation of thought between these varying ideologies whilst acknowledging the usefulness of each concept at varying levels and stages of the education process of students. The practicalities so as to transition from a traditional teaching model to a more constructivist approach have been not the purpose of this chapter. However, if in fact a teacher desires to alter their approach to adopt a more constructivist expression this will depend on the educational context in which they operate and the level of authority in which they have to be able to implement change. I may suggest that challenging presuppositions and formulating a biblical basis of truth is a great place to commence in reforming a teaching environment and altering the educational system. Traditional teaching methods and constructivism have their place in the schema of pedagogical methodology and can be amalgamated appropriately. The discerning teacher led by Christ's Holy Spirit, enabled with a firm Christian framework, and who is willing to engage with societal ideologies will be the educator to make educational environment changes effectively.

Reflection Questions

1. What are your presuppositions surrounding students and their learning abilities and processes?

2. In what areas of education could a traditional and/or constructivist approach function effectively such that the students are engaged and dynamic in their learning?
3. What practical aspects surrounding a more constructivist form of teaching are impeding its implementation in your learning environment?

Recommended Reading

Beck, Clive, and Clare Madott Kosnik. *Innovations in Teacher Education: A Social Constructivist Approach*. Suny Series, Teacher Preparation and Development. Albany: State University of New York Press, 2006.

Educational Broadcasting Corporation. "What Does Constructivism Have to Do with My Classroom?" Workshop: Constructivism as a Paradigm for Teaching and Learning. Concept to Classroom. 2004. Online: http://www.thirteen.org/edonline/concept2class/constructivism/index_sub2.html.

Knight, George R. *Philosophy & Education: An Introduction in Christian Perspective*. 4th ed. Berrien Springs, MI: Andrews University Press, 2006.

Pazmiño, Robert W. *Foundational Issues in Christian Education: An Introduction in Evangelical Perspective*. 3rd ed. Grand Rapids: Baker, 2008.

Westwood, Peter S. *Teaching Methods: What Teachers Need to Know About*. Camberwell, Vic.: ACER, 2008.

Bibliography

Applefield, James M., Richard Huber, and Mahnaz Moallem. "Constructivism in Theory and Practice: Toward a Better Understanding." *High School Journal* 84/2 (December 2000–January 2001) 35–53.

Beck, Clive. *Better Schools: A Values Perspective*. New York: Falmer, 1990.

Beck, Clive, and Clare Madott Kosnik. *Innovations in Teacher Education: A Social Constructivist Approach*. Suny Series, Teacher Preparation and Development. Albany: State University of New York Press, 2006.

Bowers, C. A. *The False Promises of Constructivist Theories of Learning: A Global and Ecological Critique*. New York: P. Lang, 2005.

Brooks, Jacqueline Grennon, and Martin G. Brooks. *In Search of Understanding: The Case for Constructivist Classrooms*. Alexandria, VA: Association for Supervision and Curriculum Development, 1999.

Clifford, Ross, and Philip Johnson. *The Cross Is Not Enough: Living as Witnesses to the Resurrection*. Grand Rapids: Baker, 2012. Kindle ed.

Crotty, Michael. *The Foundations of Social Research: Meaning and Perspective in the Research Process*. Thousand Oaks, CA: Sage, 1998.

Ellis, Louise A. "Balanced Approach Needed for Students with Learning Difficulties." *Research Developments* 14 (2005). Online: http://research.acer.edu.au/cgi/viewcontent.cgi?article=1019&context=resdev.

———. *Balancing Approaches: Revisiting the Educational Psychology Research on Teaching Students with Learning Difficulties*. Camberwell, Victoria: Australian Council for Educational Research, 2005.

Hattie, John. *Visible Learning : A Synthesis of over 800 Meta-Analyses Relating to Achievement*. New York: Routledge, 2009.

Kalantzis, Mary, and Bill Cope. *New Learning : Elements of a Science of Education*. New York: Cambridge University Press, 2008.

Knight, George R. *Philosophy & Education : An Introduction in Christian Perspective*. 3rd ed. Berrien Springs, MI: Andrews University Press, 1998.

———. *Philosophy & Education : An Introduction in Christian Perspective*. 4th ed. Berrien Springs, MI: Andrews University Press, 2006.

Knowlton, Dave S., and Suzanne C. Shaffer. "Shifting Toward a Constructivist Philosophy for Teaching Biblical Principles in K–12 Christian Schools." *Christian Education Journal* 1 (Fall 2004) 116–29.

Morris, Leon. *The Epistle to the Romans*. Pillar New Testament Commentary. Grand Rapids: Eerdmans, 1992.

Pazmiño, Robert W. *Foundational Issues in Christian Education: An Introduction in Evangelical Perspective*. 3rd ed. Grand Rapids: Baker, 2008.

Westwood, Peter S. *Teaching Methods: What Teachers Need to Know About*. Camberwell, Vic.: ACER, 2008.

Wilhoit, Jim. *Christian Education and the Search for Meaning*. 2nd ed. Grand Rapids: Baker, 1991.

Windschitl, Mark. "Framing Constructivism in Practice as the Negotiation of Dilemmas: An Analysis of the Conceptual, Pedagogical, Cultural and Political Challenges Facing Teachers." *Review of Educational Research* 72/2 (Summer 2002) 131–75.

Yount, William R. *Created to Learn: A Christian Teacher's Introduction to Educational Psychology*. Nashville: Broadman & Holman, 1996.

11

Education for What Matters

Aims for Christian Schooling

TED NEWELL

THIS CHAPTER REVIEWS HISTORICAL and current thinking about schooling's aims, and proposes a clear aim for Christian schooling in North America in the twenty-first century. The occasional thinker asks whether education needs aims, any more than the existence of a town needs aims, or knowing ultimate reality would be "aimed." However, the view of most is that education is an intentional, "aimed" activity.[1] Kieran Egan says, "To know what the curriculum should contain requires a sense of what the contents are for. If one lacks a clear sense of the purpose of education, then one is deprived of an essential means of specifying what the curriculum should contain."[2]

Up to modernity, around 1500, the content of education was the library of great books, and the aim of education was a person with mind sharpened and character formed by them.[3] A rich body of content is still prescribed by perennialists and essentialists, as in the Great Books program of R. M. Hutchins or Mortimer Adler's Paideia Project. To Hutchins or Adler, de-

1. Standish, "Education without Aims?," 41.
2. Egan, "What Is Curriculum?," 14.
3. Ibid., 9.

mocracy depends on an electorate equally equipped to consider society's issues, so all voters should have a quality education. All citizens will serve as the elite. No less an aim than strong reasoning ability was moral character. For example, the film *The Emperor's Club* (2002) portrays a candidate for political office who underlines the need for character by showing that he is far below the standard of his Great Books schooling. The aim of classical education is to fit humanity to the orderly character of the cosmos.

Note from classical education that it is as clear to talk about the *attributes* of an educated person as about *aims*. The philosopher R. S. Peters urges that education is always an activity with an intention; therefore, education is always aimed. Saying "aims of education" is only repeating oneself. Peters would abolish talk of aims, though most philosophers continue to see value in it.[4] Significantly, the insight implies that any definition of education already includes its aims, and sidelines others—a reason why this chapter focuses on "schooling."[5]

Classical education also leads us to see how aims sift a school's offerings and weight them. D. C. Phillips, a philosopher of education, asks, "Why is evolution included, or excluded . . . within the standard high school subject Biology? Why is Driver Education part of the high school curriculum, and methods of birth control usually not. . . . Is the justification that is given for teaching Economics in some schools coherent and convincing?"[6]

Aims point to more than weighted content. They point educators toward methods that develop desired aptitudes in graduates. Topic areas are a long-understood *what*—that is, content. By contrast, Egan calls educational methods the *how* of curriculum. In classical schooling the *how* is not often an issue because the *what* takes up the horizon. However, later forms of schooling see that chosen methods can also work toward aims. "[O]ne uses progressivist methods because they are a part of what you are trying to achieve educationally, not simply because they are the most efficient method of ensuring memorization of some knowledge."[7]

Nel Noddings summarizes:

> [G]reat aims are meant to guide our instructional decisions. They are meant to broaden our thinking—to remind us to ask why we have chosen certain curriculums, pedagogical methods, classroom arrangements, and learning objectives.[8]

4. Peters, "Education as Initiation."

5. White, *Aims of Education Restated*, 4; Noddings, *Philosophy of Education*, 27; Peters, Woods, and Dray, "Aims of Education," 29–49.

6. Phillips, "Philosophy of Education."

7. Egan, "Students' Development in Theory and Practice," 25–41.

8. Noddings, "What Does It Mean to Educate the Whole Child?," 9–10.

Aims and Human Potential

Any society's education has unique aims. Noddings notes that there cannot be one final aim of education because "the aims of education are tied to the nature and ideals of a particular society."[9] Elsewhere she acknowledges, "aims differ across cultures and times and among individuals . . . people contest . . . the very methods and procedures by which we might establish and assess our goals . . ."[10]

For example, the fulfillment of learning at which Plato aimed was the ability to see through the delusive, ever-changing world to perceive the abstract—literally, out-of-this-world—ideals of Truth, Goodness, and Beauty. Use of human reason in discussion and contemplation was the way to fulfillment. By contrast, Jean-Jacques Rousseau's ideal was a perfect citizenry developed by one-on-one natural education. Rousseau could imagine such an education because he believed human nature to be good until corrupted by society. Herbert Spencer, again, desired a utilitarian education of the most (practical) worth. John Dewey put forward a problem-solving adaptation for a future of evolutionary growth. These examples indicate that education is always imagined within some conception of reality. Each example translates beliefs about human nature into education. Each example aims for a unique human "good." Thus, there is Islamic education, Waldorf education, modern education—and hundreds more. Education is the initiation process of a culture and worldview. Education is not a "one size fits all" activity, but a culturing process.[11] Recognizing that education varies by worldview prepares one to recognize how Christian faith speaks not only to apparently "spiritual" matters, such as character development or a chapel policy, but to the whole of schooling.

Modern Aims

This section looks at three prominent suggestions for aims in the modern era. Paul Standish gives a rough-and-ready approach by noting three possible foci: "first, to serve the needs of society; second, to pass on and develop those ways of knowing and understanding which are the common heritage; third, to help individual learners to develop, either through a process of unfolding from within or through an authentic creation of themselves."[12]

9. Ibid.
10. Noddings, "Response to Suppes."
11. Peters, Woods, and Dray, "Aims of Education," 27.
12. Standish, "Education without Aims?," 35.

I comment on the three foci as a way to work towards a confessional Christian aim that is alert to mainstream concerns.

Emile Durkheim, a professor of education as well as a founder of the modern discipline of sociology, made *social adjustment* the aim in *Education and Sociology.* On first reading, this aim sounds not radically different from the classical ideal of conformity to the orderly cosmos:

> Education is the influence exercised by adult generations on those that are not yet ready for social life. Its object is to arouse and to develop in the child a certain number of physical, intellectual and moral states which are demanded of him by both the political society as a whole and the special milieu for which he is specifically destined.[13]

For Durkheim, society's needs indicate the aim of schooling. The "certain number" of attributes useful in "political society" or a line of work will divide the aim into components. John Franklin Bobbitt, founder of the modern field of curriculum studies, followed the same pattern. Bobbitt listed no fewer than 160 major educational objectives by nine areas, from the ability to use language in all ways required for proper and effective participation in community life to the "ability to entertain one's friends, and to respond to entertainment by one's friends."[14] Bloom et al.'s *Taxonomy of Educational Objectives: Handbook 1, the Cognitive Domain* (1956) listed thousands of objectives. It was followed by a similar taxonomy in *Handbook 2, the Affective Domain* (1956). The pattern is that education aiming for social adjustment divides present-day social life into specific, testable objectives.[15]

What assessment might Christians make of social adjustment as aim of schooling? First, the objectives are connected only as phenomena of cultural life. Pupils who persistently ask about the need for schooling will never get a better answer than, "You must complete your education in order to find a place in society." Education grounded in present-day society cannot point beyond the status quo. Critique of society would not be possible since the authority for schooling is existing society. However, any contemporary prophet must rely on some source of truth outside the system. While classical education desired pupils to be adjusted to ultimate reality, a social adjustment aim makes reality to be no greater than society. For genuine motivation, schooling's rationale must go deeper than economics. From

13. Durkheim, *Education and Sociology*, 71.

14. Bobbitt, *How to Make a Curriculum*, 11–29; cited in Eisner, "Educational Objectives," 86.

15. More on narrow objectives is in Van Dyk, "Goals and Objectives."

a Christian perspective and many secular perspectives, social adjustment cannot be a complete rationale for schooling.[16]

A second suggested aim in modernity has been *individual autonomy*. Autonomy seems like an opposite aim to social adjustment, meaning in the original sense, "self-governed."[17] Dearden's classic article pointed to the philosopher Immanuel Kant as originator of the autonomy aim.[18] Kant's pursuit of autonomy comes from optimism about humanity; he located moral truth not in religion but in the individual conscience. Self-direction comes from an innate sense of duty that is found in all human beings. Conscience is therefore a sufficient guide to behavior. When a person obeyed the imperatives within, she was acting responsibly.[19] Rational autonomy is an aim of education for a liberal society.

Is autonomy a valid aim for Christian schooling? Yes and no. In driver education, the instructor wants graduates to drive a car without supervision—not to write their own traffic rules. One should be autonomous in a restricted sense, of personally appropriating beliefs. For example, the psalmist prays to have the true God implant the truth within him (Ps 119). A divine promise for the New Covenant is that the Law would be written on the hearts of God's people (Ezek 37). The sure way to remain in covenant with God was to love him and serve him from the heart. In the sense of personal appropriation, autonomy is desirable. Yet Hebrew and Jewish thinking never failed to observe human twistedness, from our first parents' seduction, to Cain's successors' faithless behavior, through even the chosen people. Patriarchs, mostly good kings who fail, as well as false prophets are all examples. Romans 1–5 and Ephesians 2 teach that humans are alienated from God from conception, resulting in sinful acts. Thus, a worldview centered on the crucifixion of the Son of God must balance optimism with historical realism. Autonomy is the weak sense is almost the same as maturity and thus a definite aim. Strong autonomy, in the sense of leading all pupils to write their own rules or decide a life course independent of their formation, is problematic from a Christian and from some secular points of view.[20]

The third suggested aim of modern education comes from American philosopher John Dewey (1859–1952). Dewey proposed that education

16. Dewey, *Democracy and Education*, 139–41.

17. Dearden, "Autonomy and Education," 58.

18. Ibid., 58–59.

19. Ibid., 59, cited in Standish, "Education without Aims?" 37.

20. Winch, "Autonomy as an Educational Aim."

should aim for "growth" as open as evolution.[21] Humans have come far; who knows where further adaptation might take the human race?

Dewey's open-ended aim has something right about it. In the optimistic Victorian era, the poet A. E. Housman justified the study of classics as part of an elaborate treasure-finding game:

> It is to some such game of hide-and-seek that we are invited by that power which planted in us the desire to find out what is concealed, and stored the universe with hidden things that we might delight ourselves in discovering them.[22]

Housman's aim of knowledge for knowledge's sake might remind Christians that the first generations of modern scientists sought to understand the book of creation to know its Creator. Science had the extrinsic aim of gaining knowledge of the true God through his works, and thus aimed toward deeper worship.[23] Wonder should be fostered by a Christian education worthy of the name. God is inexhaustible, so knowledge about God is inexhaustible.

Dewey's open-ended aim of knowledge for knowledge's sake can also be assessed in Christian perspective. On the positive side, being human is never fixed. We are always in time, active even in sleep. To live the present life is to participate in the divine workweek leading toward the cosmic Sabbath (Gen 1, Heb 4, Rev 21). On the other hand, again, the downside potential of human nature is deep.[24] Dewey famously had to make clear that growth in burglary is not the growth he wants.[25] Neither would he aim for cancerous growth, nor unlimited population growth, nor growth in ignorance. Dewey's non-negotiables emerge as values that underpin liberal democratic society, which would seem to be his genuine aims. In Christian perspective, open-ended growth cannot be an adequate aim.

Each of the three selected aims—social adjustment, autonomy, and growth—have merits that need to be reconsidered in a Christian framework.

21. Dewey, *Democracy and Education*, 62; White, *Aims of Education Restated*, 18; Noddings, *Philosophy of Education*, 20–27.

22. Housman and Housman, *My Brother, A. E. Housman*, 65.

23. Harrison, "Bible and the Emergence of Modern Science."

24. Bernfeld, *Sisyphus*; cited in Suppes, "Aims of Education"; Felman, *Jacques Lacan and the Adventure of Insight*; Britzman, *After-Education*.

25. Noddings, *Philosophy of Education*, 26; Dewey, *Experience and Education*, 36.

Christian Schooling Hands On a Tradition

In Christian perspective, human potentials are understood from revelation. The potentials indicate aims for education. Basically, created humans exist to maximize the glory of God. Believers will not cease in eternity a continuing education of wonder, love, and praise. Human capacities (also "talents" or "gifts") are for worship of God by serving others. Christian education thus extends well beyond moral or religious aspects of life.

Education, though, is always carried out in a particular historical and social context. How to translate a high-level aim into curricular principles? How could "God fully honored" be translated into schooling? Which aims should Christian schools be seeking to fulfill?

Several ways of developing aims are open to us. We could draw principles for learning or evaluation from specific verses.[26] We could develop a comprehensive biblical theology of education. Either of these approaches imagines that it is possible to start from scratch. Yet another approach is to borrow the aim of prominent Christian philosopher Nicholas Wolterstorff, who desires education for "shalom." This Hebrew word indicates rightly ordered, just relationships throughout society. For Wolterstorff, shalom means a politically left-of-center society practicing social justice. As David Gushee observes, Wolterstorff's aim would not suit the board or administration of many—perhaps most—conservative Christian colleges. It appears that "shalom" is an aim like "God fully honored." These aims are general statements that can be made specific by a variety of Christian traditions.[27]

An aim that I wish to explore is education from and for a tradition. The schooling of a religious minority such as Catholic, Reformed, evangelical, or fundamentalist Christians for vocation, family life, and civic life in Western societies now presents significant challenges. How can minority subcultures and the lives of graduates be enhanced by better schooling? Can Christian schools rise to become centers of cultural vitality?

A fresh way of thinking about aims is suggested by Harry Fernhout. Fernhout seeks to understand schooling in a way that will sponsor lived discipleship, not inert head knowledge. From theologian N. T. Wright's insight that worldview is a lived-out Story, Fernhout identifies four elements in a worldview: Memory, Vision, Symbols, and Ethos. Briefly, Memory is the history of a society or subculture as currently understood. The Story also implies a more or less compelling Vision of the preferred future of a people.

26. Waterink raises cogent objections: *Basic Concepts in Christian Pedagogy*, 37–40.

27. Gushee, "Future of Baptist Higher Education," 47.

A society lives out its Story through Symbols, including rituals. The fourth element is an Ethos or way of living that fits the worldview. Fernhout's lived worldview concept is freeing for an education trying to escape a persistent bias toward the cognitive. If worldviews are lived out by symbols, rituals, and a way of living, formation efforts can never be only rational efforts.[28]

Memory is an especially fertile notion. A new generation does not passively absorb a tradition as if they were being indoctrinated. Memory is formed in a dialogue between the Story and the experiences of events. Students do not absorb a worldview by a one-way flow of communication from teachers. The upcoming generation must continually renew the society's Memory, just as individual memory is continually reshaped by life's events. Students rework the meaning of the Story in their own historical experiences. As teachers adapt material for students they effectively conduct a dialogue with students with the aim of conscious cultural buy-in.[29] The alternative to renewing Memory is that a distinct society will not continue. Thus teachers learn from the rising generation—and, of course, vice versa. Traditions can be abandoned, twisted, or strengthened. Traditions can be revived too, as in recent Basque, Gaelic, Islamic, and Hindu revivals. These traditions are resisting a modernity that subordinates local Stories to the technological rumble of progress. Revived traditions are evidence that these societies continue to negotiate and resist modernity through their own means.[30] Christian renewal is also a real possibility in Western societies.

Notice four implications of a tradition-building or cultivational approach to education. First, the approach is narrative. Its aim is not structures built up from facts but both means and desires to live the Story. It is a non-empiricist approach. It is always aiming to build up an integrated picture.

A second implication of a cultivational approach is that it is oriented to whole persons. All aspects of schooling including humanistic and scientific studies, music, drama, school societies, sports, and more are part of a deliberate process of cultivation. Humans beings are not reducible to brains in a petri dish, nor ghosts in a machine. We are creatures of many dimensions—imaginative, artistic, musical, political, critical, historical, narrative, and more. Therefore, a school should be a vital laboratory of cultural participation in all dimensions.[31]

Thirdly, the cultivational model is culturally attuned by nature. Schooling is formal enculturation. The cultivational approach adapts to the

28. Fernhout, "Christian Schooling."

29. Joldersma, "Introduction," xv, xviii–xix.

30. Taylor, *Modern Social Imaginaries*, 1, 195.

31. Gushee, "Future of Baptist Higher Education," makes a similar proposal.

current time and place by its nature. Explorations of culture should affirm the good as well as expose contemporary anti-biblical assumptions. Christ must transform culture, including schooling.

A fourth implication of the cultivational approach is that it seeks right dispositions. It wants not only knowledgeable disciples but responsive ones.[32] The character of teachers who encourage initiation is thus vital to success.[33]

The aim of narrative wisdom places the three aims of mainstream philosophers in perspective. The first aim, social fit, is reshaped by the cultivational approach's interactivity. The tradition must be renewed generation by generation using the Story resource. Fit is a legitimate aim. The body analogy of 1 Corinthians 12–14 affirms it. But there the fit of the members is not in the body of the church but in Christ. The potential of critique is built-in. The second aim, autonomy, is better understood as willing participation in Christ's freedom way: "in your light we see light" (Ps 36:9). The third aim, knowledge for knowledge's sake, is reshaped to avoid an idolatry of book learning. Like the early European scientists, the cultivational approach seeks knowledge towards better worship. Wonder is an expected byproduct.

Learning for Wisdom

Statements of aims do not always translate into local school change, of course. In Reformed schools, for example, John Hull sees many more Christians educating than genuinely Christian education being done.[34] Four observations may give shape to a cultivational curriculum.

First, a cultivational approach explicitly aims toward godly wisdom. Story awareness will identify challenges to the faith in modern living. The aim is able interpreters who know their Story well enough to approve what is good and turn from what is harmful (Phil 4:8). Wisdom is not a passive trait. The biblical wisdom literature and the New Testament show that it is both the ability to discern good and evil and to act wisely (Heb 5:14). Unafraid of the world, a graduate accepts the good gifts of God and sorts out negations. For discernment to grow, the Bible should be taught with an eye to both ancient and Western cultural contexts. Pupils should gain the ability to test knowledge claims against Christian belief. The cultivational approach is not defensive: extra-biblical knowledge claims can challenge and expand knowledge. Whitehead affirms as much when he avows, "There is only one

32. Stronks and Blomberg, *Vision with a Task*.

33. Wolterstorff, *Educating for Shalom*, 141–52.

34. Hull, "Aiming for Christian Education."

subject-matter for education, and that is Life in all its manifestations. . . . What we should aim at producing is men [*sic*] who possess both culture and expert knowledge in some special direction. Their expert knowledge will give them the ground to start from, and their culture will lead them as deep as philosophy and as high as art.[35]" Wisdom is to be able to see through the particulars to gain a picture of the whole, to sift knowledge claims.

To state the aim clearly: Cultivational education succeeds when Kingdom agents exercise wisdom to image God and refuse idols. Kingdom agents will resist all stunting "isms" and act responsibly for family, church, and civil life.

Second, the aim of narrative wisdom reorganizes and weights the curriculum. Whitehead advised not to teach any area which cannot be related to life or practice. Since inert knowledge is literally useless, do not teach it. This startling insight means that it is better to teach less but more deeply. Whitehead says:

> The result of teaching small parts of a large number of subjects is the passive reception of disconnected ideas, not illumined with any spark of vitality. Let the main ideas which are introduced into a child's education be few and important, and let them be thrown into every combination possible.[36]

If connected wisdom is the aim, curriculum designers should choose subjects to achieve it. For example, mathematics has an honored place in the traditional school curriculum. The high regard has its origin in the Platonic and Pythagorean belief that mathematics exercises the mind and develops ability toward abstractions. For Pythagoras, mathematics was the hidden key to the universe. The significance of mathematics should be underlined for students: its order genuinely reflects a reliable, predictable, wonderful Creator. Noddings suggests that mathematical techniques can be set in the human context of their discovery. More broadly, the wisdom aim can ask how much mathematics is required. Students can be bored or confused by the subject in their later school years. Many know the subject at advanced levels will never be picked up again. Kieran Egan urges the alternative: "We need, for the educational benefit of children, to reconstruct our curricula and teaching methods in light of a richer image of the child as an imaginative as well as a logico-mathematical thinker."[37]

35. Whitehead, *Aims of Education*, 14.

36. Ibid.

37. Egan, *Teaching as Story Telling*, 17.

Third, the wisdom aim is not soft on content. Whitehead urged, "The problem of education is to make the pupil see the (forest) by means of the trees." Again, "All practical teachers know that education is a patient process of the mastery of details, minute by minute, hour by hour, day by day."[38] To connect knowledge with life requires that pupils know the stuff. The Bible does not envisage education as agreeable effort or as play. Learning requires a discipline that bears fruit.

Fourth, a cultivational approach can embrace social reparation such as reconciliation efforts. Since the tradition must be reappropriated by a new generation, a school should be an agent of social justice or environmental efforts. Racial reconciliation, for example, is appropriate in any school in a community with two or more races.

The cultivational approach underwrites clear-sighted administration. Faculty hires and curriculum development efforts for example can be tailored to the educational mission. Faith-consistent teaching can be encouraged. Discipline can avoid utilitarian or manipulative traps that diminish personal dignity.[39]

Summary

It seems as if nothing in schooling is as important as aiming aright. Because aims and definitions of education are closely related, the search for aims is also a question about the ideal graduate. Modern aims have included socialization, autonomy, and growth. In Christian perspective, each of the modern aims has good aspects but is only partial. A cultivational approach that avoids one-sided emphasis on reasoning and aims for a wisdom fully expressed in the divine-human Christ is an appropriate goal for Christian schooling.

Response Questions

1. What are some aims for a Christian high school? What is the highest level or ultimate aim?
2. Should one rely only on teaching and testing information in an academic way to achieve the aims of Christian education? Why or why not?

38. Whitehead, *Aims of Education*, 14.
39. For an alternative example, see Inlay, "Values."

3. Is schooling a more extensive process than implied by objectives set out in state or provincial curriculum documents?
4. How important is the "hidden" curriculum (structural curriculum, the learning from procedure and practices) in schooling? Can aims cover the hidden curriculum also?

Recommend Reading

Dewey, John. *Democracy and Education: An Introduction to the Philosophy of Education.* New York: Macmillan, 1921. See chapter 8, "Aims in Education."

Egan, Kieran. "What Is Curriculum?" *Journal of the Canadian Association for Curriculum Studies* 1/1 (2003) 9–16.

Suppes, Patrick. "The Aims of Education." In *Philosophy of Education 1995: A Publication of the Philosophy of Education Society*, edited by Alvin Neiman. Online: http://web.archive.org/web/20060614153742/http://www.ed.uiuc.edu/EPS/PES-Yearbook/95_docs/suppes.html.

White, John. *The Aims of Education Restated.* International Library of the Philosophy of Education 22. London: Routledge; Boston: Kegan Paul, 1982.

Whitehead, Alfred North. *The Aims of Education & Other Essays.* New York: New American Library, 1949.

Bibliography

Bernfeld, Siegfried. *Sisyphus: Or, The Limits of Education.* Translated by Frederic Lilge. Berkeley: University of California Press, 1973.

Bobbitt, John Franklin. *How to Make a Curriculum.* Boston: Houghton Mifflin, 1924.

Britzman, Deborah P. *After-Education: Anna Freud, Melanie Klein, and Psychoanalytic Histories of Learning.* Albany: SUNY Press, 2003.

Dearden, Robert F. "Autonomy and Education." In *Education and the Development of Reason*, vol. 3: *Education and Reason*, edited by Robert F. Dearden, Paul H. Hirst, and R. S. Peters, 58–75. International Library of the Philosophy of Education 8. London: Routledge, 1975.

Dewey, John. *Democracy and Education.* New York: Macmillan, 1921.

———. *Experience and Education.* New York: Simon and Schuster, 2007.

Durkheim, Emile. *Education and Sociology.* Translated by S. Fox. Glencoe, IL: Free Press, 1956.

Egan, Kieran. "Students' Development in Theory and Practice: The Doubtful Role of Research." *Harvard Educational Review* 75/1 (2005) 25–41.

———. *Teaching as Story Telling: An Alternative Approach for Teaching and Curriculum in the Elementary School.* Chicago: University of Chicago Press, 1989.

———. "What Is Curriculum?" *Journal of the Canadian Association for Curriculum Studies* 1/1 (2003) 9–16.

Eisner, Elliot W. "Educational Objectives—Help or Hindrance?" In *The Curriculum Studies Reader*, edited by David J. Flinders and Stephen J. Thornton, 85–91. 3rd ed. New York: Routledge, 2009.

Felman, Shoshana. *Jacques Lacan and the Adventure of Insight: Psychoanalysis in Contemporary Culture*. Cambridge, MA: Harvard University Press, 1987.

Fernhout, H. "Christian Schooling: Telling a World View Story." In *The Crumbling Walls of Certainty: Towards a Christian Critique of Postmodernity and Education*, edited by I. Lambert and S. Mitchell, 75–96. Sydney: Centre for the Study of Australian Christianity, 1997.

Gushee, D. P. "The Future of Baptist Higher Education." In *Integrating Faith and Learning in an Ecumenical Context*, edited by Donald D. Schmeltekopf and Dianna M. Vitanza, 25–51. Waco, TX: Baylor University Press, 2006.

Harrison, Peter. "The Bible and the Emergence of Modern Science." *Science and Christian Belief* 18/2 (2006) 115–32.

Housman, Laurence, and A. E. Housman. *My Brother, A. E. Housman: Personal Recollections Together with Thirty Hitherto Unpublished Poems*. Port Washington, NY: Kennikat, 1969.

Hull, J. E. "Aiming for Christian Education, Settling for Christians Educating: The Christian School's Replication of a Public School Paradigm." *Christian Scholar's Review* 32/2 (2003) 203–24.

Inlay, L. "Values: The Implicit Curriculum." *Educational Leadership* 60/6 (2003) 69–71.

Joldersma, Clarence. "Introduction." In *Educating for Shalom: Essays on Christian Higher Education*, by Nicholas Wolterstorff, edited by Gloria Stronks and Clarence Joldersma. Grand Rapids: Eerdmans, 2004.

Noddings, Nel. *Philosophy of Education*. 2nd ed. Boulder, CO: Westview, 1995.

———. "Response to Suppes." In *Philosophy of Education 1995: A Publication of the Philosophy of Education Society*, edited by Alvin Neiman. Online: http://web.archive.org/web/20060203115059/http://www.ed.uiuc.edu/EPS/PES-Yearbook/95_docs/noddings.html.

———. "What Does It Mean to Educate the Whole Child?" *Educational Leadership* 63/1 (2005) 8–13.

Peters, R. S. "Education as Initiation." In *Philosophy of Education: An Anthology*, edited by Randall Curren, 55–67. Malden, MA: Blackwell, 2007.

Peters, R. S., J. Woods, and W. Dray. "Aims of Education: A Conceptual Inquiry." In *The Philosophy of Education*, edited by R. S. Peters, 11–57. Oxford: Oxford University Press, 1973.

Phillips, D. C. "Philosophy of Education." *The Stanford Encyclopedia of Philosophy*, edited by E. N. Zalta. Spring 2009 ed. Online: http://plato.stanford.edu/archives/spr2009/entries/education-philosophy.

Standish, Paul. "Education without Aims?" In *The Aims of Education*, edited by Roger Marples, 35–49. Routledge International Studies in the Philosophy of Education 7. New York: Routledge, 1999.

Stronks, Gloria Goris, and Doug Blomberg, editors. *A Vision with a Task: Christian Schooling for Responsive Discipleship*. Grand Rapids: Baker, 1993.

Suppes, Patrick. "The Aims of Education." In *Philosophy of Education 1995: A Publication of the Philosophy of Education Society*, edited by Alvin Neiman. Online: http://web.archive.org/web/20060614153742/http://www.ed.uiuc.edu/EPS/PES-Yearbook/95_docs/suppes.html.

Taylor, Charles. *Modern Social Imaginaries*. Durham, NC: Duke University Press, 2004.

Van Dyk, John. "Goals and Objectives: Pathways to Educational Myopia?" *Pro Rege* 23/3 (1995) 19–24.

Waterink, Jan. *Basic Concepts in Christian Pedagogy*. Grand Rapids: Eerdmans; St. Catherines, ON: Paideia, 1954.

White, John. *The Aims of Education Restated*. International Library of the Philosophy of Education 22. London: Routledge; Boston: Kegan Paul, 1982.

Whitehead, Alfred North. *The Aims of Education & Other Essays*. New York: New American Library, 1949.

Winch, Christopher. "Autonomy as an Educational Aim." In *The Aims of Education*, edited by Roger Marples, 74–84. Routledge International Studies in the Philosophy of Education 7. New York: Routledge, 1999.

Wolterstorff, Nicholas. *Educating for Shalom: Essays on Christian Higher Education*. Edited by Clarence Joldersma and Gloria Stronks. Grand Rapids: Eerdmans, 2004.

12

Faith in the Humanities

KAREN SWALLOW PRIOR

A Rough Time for the Humanities

SINCE HIGHER EDUCATION'S MID-TWENTIETH-CENTURY shift away from the liberal arts (in liberal arts institutions, no less)[1] toward a more utilitarian, career-oriented educational paradigm, the humanities have had it rough. Within the context of conservative Christianity and its institutions of higher learning, which have not been immune to pragmatism's reign,[2] the humanities have it even rougher. Add to this decades-long trend the more immediate concerns about the pursuit of four-year degrees in a climate marked by a bad economy, a surplus of workers with four-year college degrees, and a persistent lack of jobs,[3] and one wonders if the humanities education can—or should—survive.

Of course, the uncertain bond between church and culture, more generally, and between church and the humanities, more specifically, that has endured for millennia can't be blamed on the bad economy of the moment: the tie between church and culture has been knotted messily since

1. For a detailed report on the decline of liberal arts curricula in the latter half of the twentieth century, see National Association of Scholars, "Dissolution of General Education."

2. See, for example, Murray, *Evangelicalism Divided.*

3. Zagier, "College for All?"

the inception of the church. Nevertheless, both Scripture and evidence show that when the relationship between church and culture is correctly balanced, the beneficiaries of that proper balance are individual believers, the church body, and the culture at large.

"What Has Athens to Do with Jerusalem?"

As early as the third century, Tertullian, a Roman lawyer and convert to Christianity, was one of the first to pinpoint this problem when he posed the question that has echoed within the church, in one form or another, ever since: "What indeed has Athens to do with Jerusalem? What concord is there between the Academy and the Church?"[4] In other words, of what possible use or value could the pagan learning of the Greeks be to the followers of the Messiah who came from the Hebrews? Dallas Willard fleshes out the question even further in explaining what is connoted by the opposing terms *Athens* and *Jerusalem*. "Athens refers to the capacity of unaided human thought to grasp reality," Willard explains, "the human mind's ability to grasp (some) reality by thinking, and Athens symbolizes that world-shaping discovery." He continues:

"Jerusalem, by contrast, refers to the declaration of reality and gift of knowledge from a supreme, personal divinity who cares about what happens in human life and intervenes to give direction to the human enterprise."[5]

This view of the uneasy relationship between the life of the intellect and the life of the spirit as being at odds with one another is an example of what H. Richard Niebuhr, in his classic text *Christ and Culture*, identifies as the view of Christ "against culture."

The issue of the relationship between God's people and their culture predates Tertullian, of course, and the Christian church too. Many of the Old Testament codes God commanded the Israelites to follow accomplished, among other things, the separation of his people from the surrounding pagan cultures. Yet, total separation from the culture is neither demanded nor possible. Indeed it was in excelling in the knowledge and skill in all learning and wisdom of his captors that Daniel and his fellow captives brought glory to God. When brought before King Nebuchadnezzar, Daniel, Hananiah, Mishael, and Azariah were found by the king to be "ten times better than all the magicians and astrologers that were in all his realm."[6] In mastering the surrounding culture in order to magnify God, Daniel exemplifies a very

4. Tertullian, *Prescription Against Heretics* 7, in *Ante-Nicene Fathers*, 3:246.

5. Willard, Foreword, in Poe, *Christianity in the Academy*, 9.

6. Dan 1:17–20.

different view of culture than that of Tertullian. While it would be difficult to argue that it approaches the other end of Niebuhr's scale ("transformer of culture"), it may in fact exemplify what James Davison Hunter describes, in his important book *To Change the World: The Irony, Tragedy, and Possibility of Christianity in the Late Modern World*, as a "faithful presence" in the culture.

One can find Daniel's engaging approach to culture in the early church even after Tertullian's haunting question. About a century after Tertullian, St. Augustine drew upon Old Testament examples to develop his own view of the church transforming the culture. To understate the case, Augustine's stance on culture is complicated and not entirely consistent across the body of his work. Coming from a pagan background and schooled in rhetoric and philosophy outside of the Christian faith, Augustine understandably expressed opposition to many of the ideas and values that shaped his life before conversion. Nevertheless, Augustine seems to have been unable to help himself, despite his best efforts, to claim for the kingdom's purposes all wisdom and eloquence, regardless of where it might be found. Augustine is, of course, recognized for the undisputed claim that all truth is God's truth: "For all truth comes from the one who says, 'I am the truth.'" Later, in the same text, Augustine restates it this way: "A person who is a good and a true Christian should realize that truth belongs to his Lord, wherever it is found."[7] In the same work, Augustine asserts that Christians can put the "Egyptian gold" of pagan philosophy and learning into the Lord's service as long as that "gold" is tested by Scripture to determine whether or not it truly is gold. For example, rhetorical skills such as those Augustine learned before his conversion could be employed, he argues, in the service of advancing truth: "It is not the aim of the eloquence or the intention of the speaker that the truths or the eloquence should in themselves produce delight; but the truths themselves, as they are revealed, do produce delight by virtue of being true."[8] Augustine distinguishes here between eloquence for its own sake and eloquence in the service of truth. Thus, in appropriating the values and knowledge of his culture for the advancement of God's kingdom, Augustine clearly fits Niebuhr's description of a "transformer of culture" in that "he redirects, reinvigorates, and regenerates that life of man, expressed in all human work . . ."[9]

In the eighth century, Alcuin of York, a scholar, poet, and abbot who served Charlemagne as master of the Palace School in France, echoed the

7. Augustine, *On Christian Teaching*, 6, 47.

8. Ibid., 64–65.

9. Niebuhr, *Christ and Culture*, 209.

question of Tertullian from centuries earlier, but this time focusing more narrowly on literature. In 797, concerned about a growing fascination among the monks of Lindisfarne with the legendary Norse warrior Ingeld, Alcuin wrote a letter to their bishop in Lindisfarne. In it he asked, "*Quid enim Hinieldus cum Christo*?" or "What has Ingeld to do with Christ?"[10] Apparently, Alcuin thought the monks' time would be more profitably spent on things other than the heroes of story and legend.

This line of thinking about literature has continued to thread its way through the fabric of church history. One of the most notable purveyors of such antagonism—a view of literature that exemplifies what Niebuhr describes as "Christ against culture"—is the seventeenth-century British Puritan and theologian Richard Baxter. In a sermon titled "The Sinfulness of Flesh-Pleasing," Baxter cautioned Christians to "take heed of a delight in romances, playbooks, feigned stories, useless news, which corrupt the mind, and waste your time."[11] Baxter is most famous for this additional advice on reading:

> Make careful choice of the books which you read: let the holy scriptures ever have the pre-eminence, and, next to them, those solid, lively, heavenly treatises which best expound and apply the scriptures, and next, credible histories, especially of the Church . . . but take heed of false teachers who would corrupt your understandings.[12]

Presumably, in following Baxter's prescription, after reading the Bible, followed by commentaries, church history, and then other history, there wouldn't be much, if any, time left for plays and poetry.

In the eighteenth and nineteenth centuries, British evangelicals, following in the footsteps of their Puritan forebears, offered objections that were slightly less severe than Baxter's but otherwise similar. By this time, the literary form making the most gains in popularity and availability was the newly developing genre of the novel. Even in cases when objections to the novel's content (more often than not, tales of illicit and/or romantic love) didn't apply, evangelicals of the period expressed a number of anxieties over the activity of novel reading generally. Numerous sources voiced concern over the novel's tendency to weaken the mind's ability to read more serious material, produce too much familiarity with the secular world, and simply to waste time. Furthermore, echoing earlier concerns of Puritans,

10. Mitchell and Robinson. *Beowulf*, 35.

11. Baxter, "Sinfulness of Flesh-Pleasing."

12. Ibid.,

evangelicals were leery of all fictional tales because, being untrue, they were therefore lies.[13]

A Brighter Cord in the Tapestry of Church History

Yet, despite the hand wringing by believers across the ages toward literature, another brighter cord is woven into the tapestry of church history by those who view human culture—even pagan literature—as part of the fullness of God's world.

The first such thread perhaps comes from the Apostle Paul, who, in the famous passage of Acts 17, quoted the pagan Greek poet Aratus—a student of stoicism of the late fourth century BC—in order to point the philosophers debating on the Areopagus toward the one true God.[14] As a result, the passage relates, some were saved. Like Daniel in the Old Testament, as described above, Paul saw the relationship of the church and culture as one in which the church is empowered to engage the culture. In order to quote Aratus as he did, Paul clearly had not only exposed himself to the ideas and works of the pagan culture around him (and perhaps this took place before his conversion to Christianity), but he was conversant enough with them even after his conversion to quote a passage from memory which—although not connected in any way to the God of Scripture—he could use to draw connections between it and the one true God.

Some centuries later, a masterpiece of Old English literature, *Beowulf*, exemplifies, perhaps, what Niebuhr describes as a synthesis of Christ and culture. While insufficient records exist to delineate the exact progression of this pagan heroic tale into a Christianized text, the evidence suggests that at some point a poem that emerged out of the Anglo-Saxon oral tradition was later transcribed by a monk (very few outside the church were literate at the time) and embellished with enough Christian elements to turn what was once a pagan folk epic into one of the earliest written expressions of Christianity in English. While the Christian embellishment is not enough entirely to overwhelm its deeply pagan worldview, *Beowulf* stands as one of the earliest examples in English of the power of the gospel to transform a culture.

13. For more on this subject, see my dissertation, "Hannah More and the Evangelical Influence on the English Novel," 85–121.

14. Yet, apparently even this passage has been used to argue against engagement with the culture. Harry Lee Poe reports that some theologians have argued that the relatively low number of converts recorded in Acts 17 is evidence that Paul's approach was wrong. Poe, *Christianity in the Academy*, 25.

In the sixteenth century, Sir Philip Sidney formulated one of the earliest expressions of a poetics—that branch of literary criticism that addresses the nature, forms, and underlying laws of all literature (not just poetry)—that is distinctly Christian. Sidney argued in his *Defence of Poetry* (published posthumously in 1595) that the "end of all earthly learning [is] virtuous action" and that of all the sources of learning, the poet is "monarch" of all "sciences"[15] (*science* here is meant in the etymological sense of its Latin root, *knowledge*). In other words, what Sidney boldly asserts is that poetry, as the highest and greatest means of knowledge, is the best spur to virtue. In further describing the poet as, in making poetry, giving honor to "the heavenly Maker of that maker,"[16] Sidney's defense of poetry (and, effectively, all literary art) is rooted not in pragmatic or utilitarian terms, but in the very doctrine of creation. The goodness of poetry includes its practical effects ("virtuous action"), but is not limited to pragmatic value: simply reflecting the Maker through making makes the act of creating literary art good.

In the century following Sidney, the Puritan poet and pamphleteer John Milton offered a defense of literature grounded in Christian liberty.[17] In his 1644 *Areopagitica*, a passionate argument against the Licensing Act of the Puritan-led Parliament (and one of the precursors to the prohibition in American jurisprudence of prior restraint), Milton defends a free press on a specifically Christian basis. In so doing, Milton distinguishes between innocence (which does not know evil), and virtue (which is the intentional choosing of good over evil), and he suggests that the best way to be acquainted with evil (which in the context of *Areopagitica* is particularly heretical doctrine) is vicarious exposure through liberal ("promiscuous") reading. He writes:

> As therefore the state of man now is; what wisdome can there be to choose, what continence to forbeare without the knowledge of evill? He that can apprehend and consider vice with all her baits and seeming pleasures, and yet abstain, and yet distinguish, and yet prefer that which is truly better, he is the true warfaring Christian. I cannot praise a fugitive and cloister'd vertue, unexercis'd & unbreath'd, that never sallies out and sees

15. Sidney, *Defence of Poetry*, 29, 39.

16. Ibid., 24.

17. As a Puritan living during the period of bloody civil war that followed the English Reformation, Milton's staunch anti-Catholicism is at the root of his strenuous advocacy for liberty of conscience, Catholicism being linked by Milton and most English Puritans with political and religious tyranny.

> her adversary but slinks out of the race, where that immortall garland is to be run for, not without dust and heat.[18]

In the treatise, Milton focuses mainly on the publication of political and theological writings. Although a great poet himself, he was concerned in this work primarily with the free expression of ideas and not a defense of literature as a form of art and expression of culture. Nevertheless, his standing—having written that great Christian epic poem *Paradise Lost*—as one of the greatest English poets of all time speaks even more pointedly to his view about the relationship between church and culture.

Both Sidney and Milton build upon the foundation established by Daniel, Paul, and Augustine—a foundation for a bold Christian confidence in engaging with the culture outside the church. In combination, the principles articulated by Sidney and Milton create a strong case for the value of literature in particular, not only to human culture but to Christian culture and Christian individuals as well. Sidney's defense focuses primarily on the value of literature as a *form* of art. In *Defence of Poetry*, Sidney argues that poetry is superior to both history and philosophy. While history describes what was, poetry is more philosophical than history because it is not limited only to what has happened but expresses what could and should happen. While philosophy describes what ought to be (rather than what was), poetry can add to that concrete examples of what should be. Thus, according to Sidney, poetry combines the virtues of history and philosophy in being able to depict concretely what ought to be.[19] While Sidney concerns his argument with poetry (and, by extension, all literary forms), Milton's argument for a free press focuses not on the form of a text, but its *content*—even when that content contains the most dangerous ideas in the world: heresy. Milton argued:

> Truth is compar'd in Scripture to a streaming fountain. If her waters flow not in a perpetuall progression, they sick'n into a muddy pool of conformity and tradition. A man may be a heretick in the truth; and if he believe things only because his Pastor sayes so, or the Assembly so determines, without knowing other reason, though his belief be true, yet the very truth he holds, becomes his heresie.[20]

Here Milton claims that if one holds to true ideas simply because nothing else has come along to challenge those ideas, those true ideas are, in fact,

18. Milton, *Areopagitica*, 1006.
19. Sidney, *Defence of Poetry*, 29–32.
20. Milton, *Areopagitica*, 1015.

heresy. The implication is that exposure to oppositional ideas is necessary to a vigorous Christian faith.

The Humanities and Christian Learning Today

Yet, oppositional ideas are exactly what some Christians—parents, pastors, and educators among them—are most nervous about exposing themselves to, let alone those under their care. Even in Christian institutions of higher learning, this tension between church and culture can shift—in either direction—toward an unhealthy balance. Common assumptions, in fact, hold that faith tends to weaken as a result of a college education. But some recent studies show that the situation is a bit more complicated. It seems that some college environments foster an increase in faith while others are linked to a weakening of belief. But which colleges do which is a bit surprising. Research is showing that among college students it is in the secular institutions where faith is more likely to grow and strengthen. The sociological (as well as the biblical) evidence seems to suggest that a holistic approach to faith—one that engages all of life—cultivates a more robust faith.

In a study published in 2005, "How Corrosive Is College to Religious Faith and Practice?," Mark D. Regnerus and Jeremy E. Uecker take on earlier findings that students typically experience a decline in faith during their college years. The authors do concede that the "assumption that the religious involvement of young people diminishes when they attend college is of course true: 64 percent of those currently enrolled in a traditional four-year institution have curbed their attendance habits." But the study goes beyond the typical findings to compare this statistic with that of these students' peers that did not go to college. Among their peers who did not go to college, 76 percent reported a decrease in attendance at their places of worship. Apparently, the majority of people in the college age bracket experience a decline in faith, but those who attend college are less likely to experience the decline than those who don't go to college. The study further found:

> Whereas 20 percent of those that did not pursue college renounced any and all religious affiliation, only 13 percent of four-year college students had done the same. Thus, the assumption that a college education is the *reason* for such a decline gathers little support. . . . Simply put: Higher education is *not* the enemy

> of religiosity. Instead, young people who avoid college altogether display a more precipitous drop in their religious participation.

Yet, as this and other studies show, some college students are clearly experiencing a weakening of faith. And surprisingly, it may be the students at the Bible colleges and Christian schools more so than their counterparts at secular institutions.

A 2010 essay by Edward Dutton in *The Chronicle of Higher Education*, "Finding Jesus at College," argues that, in fact, "there is a correlation between the kind of college [students] attend and their likelihood of developing a radical-conservative religious worldview." However, it turns out that the type of college most likely to produce such a faith, the author's research found, is not the Christian institution, but rather the elite Ivy League and Oxford variety.[21] Dutton's findings confirm earlier research showing that

> Christian students who attend Christian colleges tend to become more liberal during the process of their education. They enroll as fervent evangelicals and leave, in many cases, far less ardent in their faith. The reason is that Bible colleges, unlike many more-prestigious universities, lack a central quality that encourages the formation of fundamentalist student groups and religious experiences.

What is this central quality? According to Dutton, that central quality is the sort of "identity-challenging rite of passage" that occurs in a heterogeneous environment and serves to strengthen one's faith commitment. In contrast to their counterparts at faith-based institutions who, surrounded almost uniformly by like-minded peers, exhibit within such "homogeneity" "a more lenient attitude" toward unbiblical ideas and lifestyles, Dutton found that "Christian students who attend Ivy League and other respected institutions tend to leave more fervently evangelical than when they began college. Such universities tend to challenge students' faith, prompting them to create a 'fortress of identity' to preserve their sense of who they are."

A flaccid faith does not or cannot fulfill the exhortation of 1 Thessalonians 5:21–22: "test everything; hold fast what is good. Abstain from every form of evil" (ESV). The verbs in these verses are muscular verbs, not passive or weak. Through literature, art, and other cultural artifacts, Christians can be exposed to worldviews that oppose the biblical worldview and see pagan philosophies fleshed out and enacted in the lives of those who have followed them, both in history and in literature, and thus put these ideas to the test.

21. Dutton, "Finding Jesus at College."

Even more importantly, if, as James Davison Hunter claims, "Culture is far more profound at the level of *imagination* than at the level of argument,"[22] then Christians can do no better than to acquaint themselves with works of the imagination in order to engage the culture. Christians who are conversant with the prevailing cultural influences and ideologies are not only better equipped to exert their own influence on the culture, but, through the constant exercise of their faith in confronting these ideas, to develop a more muscular faith.

Reflection Questions

1. What are the benefits of a humanities education to a society overwhelmingly preoccupied with pragmatism?
2. Who/what constitute the beneficiaries of the properly balanced relationship between the church and the culture?
3. The respective views of Daniel and Tertullian toward culture differ greatly. In what ways do they differ? Where would their views fall on Richard Niehbuhr's scale of cultural engagement?
4. What answer does Augustine provide as the distinction between eloquence for its own sake and eloquence in service of the truth?
5. What is the value of studying secular literature, art, and other cultural artifacts? How does this correlate to 1 Thessalonians 5:21–22?

Recommended Reading

Cowan, Louise, and Os Guinness. *Invitation to the Classics: A Guide to Books You've Always Wanted to Read.* Grand Rapids: Baker, 1998.

Niebuhr, H. Richard. *Christ and Culture.* San Francisco: Harper, 1951.

Prior, Karen Swallow. *Booked: Literature in the Soul of Me.* Ossining, NY: T. S. Poetry Press, 2012.

Schaeffer, Francis. *How Should We Then Live?: The Rise and Decline of Western Thought and Culture.* Old Tappan, NJ: Revell, 1976.

Veith, Gene Edward. *Reading Between the Lines: A Christian Guide to Literature.* Wheaton, IL: Crossway, 1990.

22. Hunter, "Faithful Presence."

Bibliography

Augustine. *On Christian Teaching.* Translated by R. P. H. Green. Oxford: Oxford University Press, 1997.

Baxter, Richard. "The Sinfulness of Flesh-Pleasing." Online: http://www.puritansermons.com/baxter/baxter4.htm.

Dutton, Edward. "Finding Jesus at College." The *Chronicle Review*, March 7, 2010. Online: http://chronicle.com/article/Finding-Jesus-at-College/64459/.

Hunter, James Davison. "Faithful Presence." Interview by Christopher Benson. *Christianity Today*, May 14, 2010. Online: https://www.christianitytoday.com/ct/2010/may/16.33.html.

———. *To Change the World: The Irony, Tragedy, and Possibility of Christianity in the Late Modern World.* Oxford: Oxford University Press, 2010.

Milton, John. *Areopagitica.* In *The Riverside Milton*, edited by Roy Flannagan. Boston: Houghton Mifflin, 1998.

Mitchell, Bruce, and Fred C. Robinson. *Beowulf: An Edition with Relevant Shorter Texts.* Oxford: Blackwell, 1998.

Murray, Iain. *Evangelicalism Divided: A Record of Crucial Change in the Years 1950–2000.* Edinburgh: Banner of Truth, 2000.

National Association of Scholars. "The Dissolution of General Education: 1914–1993." Princeton, NJ: NAS, 1996. Online: http://www.nas.org/articles/the_dissolution_of_general_education_1914_1993.

Niebuhr, H. Richard. *Christ and Culture.* San Francisco: Harper, 1951.

Poe, Harry Lee. *Christianity in the Academy: Teaching at the Intersection of Faith and Learning.* Grand Rapids: Baker Academic, 2004.

Prior, Karen Swallow. "Hannah More and the Evangelical Influence on the English Novel." PhD diss., State University of New York at Buffalo, 1999.

Sidney, Philip. *A Defence of Poetry.* Edited by J. A. Van Dorsten. Oxford: Oxford University Press, 1966.

Tertullian. *The Prescription Against Heretics.* Translated by Peter Holmes. In *Ante-Nicene Fathers* vol. 3, *Latin Christianity: Its Founder, Tertullian*, edited by Allan Menzies. Grand Rapids: Eerdmans, n.d.

Willard, Dallas. Foreword in Harry Lee Poe, *Christianity in the Academy: Teaching at the Intersection of Faith and Learning.* Grand Rapids: Baker Academic, 2004.

Zagier, Alan Scher. "College for All? Experts Say Not Necessarily." Associated Press, May 13, 2010.

PART THREE

Sociological Foundations

13

School Choice and Church School Education in the United Kingdom

Elizabeth Green

Introduction

Until the last few decades the view that parents have the right to choose an education for their children in line with their religious beliefs was relatively uncontested in the United Kingdom. Christian parents may not always have had access to a state-funded Christian school but the principle of church involvement as a provider of publicly funded education was well embedded in the system. The secularization of society in the UK, the increase of militant atheism, and an orchestrated campaign against state funding for church schools has led to fierce and sometimes hostile debate.

This chapter will outline the way that these debates about school choice and church school education play out in the UK. The UK has devolved government. In Wales and Scotland the public school system is predominantly comprehensive. Comprehensive schools are non-selective and school places are allocated via a geographical catchment. Northern Ireland is a particularly unique setting because of the long history of sectarian divide and in such a brief chapter it is not possible to do justice do the nuances of the debate;

consequently much of the analysis that follows relates to the system in England, where 83.9 percent of the population of the UK lives.[1] The chapter is structured in three main parts followed by some discussion questions. The first section comprises a history of the Dual System in England. The Dual System refers to the provision of state-funded church schools alongside secular state-funded schools. The second section comprises an overview of school choice and the third section will draw these two strands together in an analysis of contemporary themes.

The Dual System

In sharp contrast to the public education system in the United States of America and parts of Canada, approximately a third of all state schools in England and Wales have a religious character.[2] The largest provider by far is the Church of England, with 4,849 schools in England and Wales.[3] Roman Catholic schools make up 10 percent of the national total of schools in England and Wales with 2,257.[4] There are some non-denominational Christian schools in England and some Methodist schools but historically the Dual System was founded on Church of England and Roman Catholic provision. Broadly, the Dual System allows for the church governance of schools, admissions policies that allocate school places on the basis of faith, and the teaching of religious education (RE) in line with denominational tradition. Broadly, state-funded church schools are obliged to follow a nationally prescribed subject curriculum and they are subject to statutory frameworks of assessment and inspection.

The Forster Act of 1870 introduced the principle of universal state-funded education for children aged between five and twelve in England and Wales. Prior to 1870 the Church of England's National Society, founded in 1811, had been at the forefront of the drive to utilize education as a means to alleviate poverty and address the perceived moral degradation associated with the rapid expansion of the industrial urban poor. The government had already provided money to the National Society to build schools and in practical terms the provision of mass education would have been impossible without utilizing existing church charitable provision. Chadwick[5] argues, however, that the Dual System was more than a practical arrangement;

1. Office for National Statistics, "2011 Census, Population and Household."
2. Green and Cooling, *Mapping the Field.*
3. Church of England, "Academies."
4. Catholic Education Service, "Academies."
5. Chadwick, "Conflict and Consensus," 43–57.

she writes that a commitment on behalf of the Church of England to the education of the nation paved the way for a unique partnership between the state and the established church. From its inception this partnership has not been without its tensions; in the nineteenth century tensions were predominantly sectarian. Protestant non-conformist denominations protested vehemently against the use of their rates (local taxes) to fund Church of England schools. A special clause had to be written into the legislation that guaranteed the rights of parents to withdraw their children from RE and ensure that in secular state elementary schools no catechism and no denominational religious instruction would take place. The clause was named the Cowper-Temple Clause after its architect, William Cowper-Temple, a Liberal Party member of Parliament (MP). This illustrates that some fundamental differences about the nature and mission of church schools underpin different denominational models. Chadwick points out that whilst the National Society has always maintained the dual mission of educating the whole nation and educating children in the doctrines of the Church of England, the "Roman Catholics primarily created schools to protect their interests as a minority discriminated against in society."[6]

A major reform of public welfare services took place in the UK at the end of the Second World War. The 1944 Education Act, also referred to as the Butler Act after R. A. Butler, the Conservative Party MP who introduced it, further cemented the Dual System. It raised the school leaving age to fifteen and mandated that every school begin the day with a non-denominational act of worship. Church schools were affirmed alongside secular state schools as integral to provision but offered a choice of status either to be "Voluntary Aided" (VA) or "Controlled" (VC). In VA schools the governing body employs the staff, the school sets its own admission arrangements, and buildings and land are owned by a charitable foundation. All Roman Catholic schools that remained state-funded became VA because the Roman Catholic Church wished to keep control of its schools and continue denominational religious instruction. In VC schools, local education authorities (LEAs) remain in control of staffing and admissions; denominational religious instruction was guaranteed if parents specifically requested it, otherwise RE is taught according to a locally agreed syllabus. Whilst these designations remain, today the picture has become even more complex and the original partnership of the 1944 Act has been eroded with the creation of new designations of schools such as academies, trust and foundation schools many of which are privately run but funded by the state. These complexities are a direct result of policies that privatized public

6. Ibid., 44.

services and introduced school choice. An overview of these policies will be presented in the following section and the contemporary implications for church schools will be explored in the final section of this chapter.

An Overview of School Choice

In the UK the right of parents to choose the school that their children attend is a relatively recent policy development when set against a 150-year history of universal free education. Prior to major reforms set in motion by the Conservative government under Prime Minister Margaret Thatcher in the 1980s, the UK had a comprehensive system of education. In 1988 a major education reform act marked a significant shift in the direction of education policy. The twin themes of the 1988 Reform Act, as it is known, were privatization and centralization. At first glance these might appear contradictory, but the aim was to centralize the curriculum with the introduction of a National Curriculum yet privatize the delivery of services. This was done by introducing the local management of schools and parental choice; hence the creation of a market in educational provision. Bypassing LEAs and teaching unions to make new providers directly accountable to central government fitted with Conservative party belief in small government and faith in choice and competition. In 1988 these reforms were hugely controversial but they have rapidly become the dominant way of thinking about education. Under successive Labour Party and Coalition (Conservative Party and Liberal Democrat Party) governments, these structures have been extended and the principle of private sponsorship for schools is now well embedded in the system. As of the beginning of May 2013 there were 2,924 academies open in England[7]. Academies are independent schools that receive per capita funding from the state. The academies program has been one of the central planks in the reform of educational provision. An extensive review of these policies is beyond the scope of this chapter but an excellent summary can be found in Sally Tomlinson's book *Education in a Post-Welfare Society*. In the second part of this section we will turn our attention to some of the key critiques of school choice as they relate to church school education.

To some extent church schools have been able to take refuge in the creation of the internal market in education and the expansion of the education policy discourse of "choice and diversity."[8] For example, Ruth Deakin[9] builds her defense of faith-based education firmly on the rights of parents

7. Department for Education, "Open Academies."

8. Department for Education, *Choice and Diversity.*

9. Deakin, *New Christian Schools.*

to choose an education for their children in accordance with their religious beliefs, and argues that diversity of provision best represents ethnic, racial, and religious diversity. This argument is commonly evoked by those already involved in the provision of education for minority religious or ethnic groups. The argument that to deny, for example, a Muslim parent the right to a state-supported religious education for their child when Church of England and Catholic parents enjoy such provision is considered by some a pragmatic rather than an ideological argument, but it is one that is nevertheless difficult to counter. However, emphasizing the rights of parents only evokes part of the argument presented by writers such as Hargreaves[10] who also believe that diversity and competition raise standards in schooling.

The assumption that school choice improves the quality of educational provision is hugely contested within the educational community in the UK. Adnett and Davies,[11] Gorard,[12] and West[13] have concluded that the privatization of services and competition between schools actually leads to a decline in academic standards in some schools. Reay and Ball[14] have further argued that middle-class parents are better positioned to exercise choice and that as a result structural class inequalities are perpetuated by school choice policies. Two significant charges are levied against church schools in particular. The first is that they perpetuate structural inequalities in the system by actively selecting their pupils; the second is that they actively foster segregation along sectarian lines. The final section of this chapter considers the implications of school choice and these charges in particular for the contemporary Dual System.

Contemporary Themes

The Church of England is now the largest provider of academy schools; it runs 256 academies and the Roman Catholic Church runs 148.[15] Under the academies program new non-denominational Christian providers such as Oasis Community Learning (OCL), United Learning Trust (ULT), the Grace Foundation, and the Emmanuel Schools Foundation (ESF) have also taken on responsibility for state provision and between them run a total of

10. Hargreaves, "Diversity and Choice."

11. Adnett and Davies, "Competition Between or Within Schools?"

12. Gorard et al., "Does School Choice Lead to 'Spirals of Decline'?"

13. West, "School Choice, Equity and Social Justice."

14. Reay and Ball, "'Making Their Minds Up.'"

15. Figures correct at January 2013. Sources: Church of England and the Catholic Education Service.

51 academies.[16] This raises three critical questions in relation to the Dual System and school choice: First, how do church schools answer the charges of perpetuating structural inequality and sectarian division? Second, what is distinctive about church school provision in the marketplace? And third, what might be the disadvantages of a close partnership with the government? A comprehensive examination of all of these questions is not possible within this chapter, but comments in relation to each will be offered using the lens of recent research carried out in the UK. A full review of the research evidence can be found in Green and Cooling.[17]

In 2001 serious disturbances along racial lines occurred in some northern towns and cities in England. Key reports produced in the wake of the riots argued that division along race, ethnic, class, and religious lines can be perpetuated by separate educational provision and conversely that tolerance can be promoted by mixed schooling.[18] As a consequence of the 2001 riots the government required the Office for Standards in Education (Ofsted) to inspect all schools on their contribution to community cohesion. Morris et al.[19] analyzed the published data from Ofsted inspections. The analysis showed the Catholic sector to be more effective in contributing to social cohesion than other state-funded schools. Other work by Morris and Godfrey[20] found that secondary-school pupils in state-funded Catholic secondary schools were performing, on average, better than those attending non-Catholic schools even when adjustments were made for factors known to affect levels of achievement, such as prior attainment or socioeconomic status (SES). This is significant because the charge commonly levied at church schools is that they select pupils with a social class, cultural, and economic advantage, but Morris[21] found that pupils who were more socially disadvantaged, on average, did better in Catholic secondary schools. Similar work carried out by Arthur and Godfrey[22] in Church of England secondary schools does much to empirically support the claim that pupils have higher achievement and demonstrate more progress than pupils in secular state schools. They acknowledge, however, that some of the statistical difference could be accounted for by prior attainment and might relate to the SES of pupils. What this illustrates is that the picture is complex and that church

16. Figures correct at May 2013. Sources: OCL, ULT, Grace Academies, and ESF.
17. Green and Cooling, *Mapping the Field.*
18. Ousley, *Community Pride Not Prejudice.*
19. Morris et al., "Promoting Community Cohesion."
20. Morris and Godfrey, *Statistical Survey of Attainment in Catholic Schools.*
21. Morris, "Academic Standards in Catholic Education."
22. Arthur and Godfrey, *Statistical Survey of the Attainment and Achievement.*

schools do need to be able to demonstrate how they are contributing to social cohesion in the national context. This leads us to our second question: What is distinctive about church school provision in the marketplace?

Church schools position themselves in the UK educational marketplace as offering a distinctive ethos and values. Green and Cooling write that "the perception remains that Christian ethos schools achieve higher educational standards and produce pupils with a reassuring sense of values and civic responsibility."[23] Two major reviews of its educational provision by the Church of England in 2010 and 2013 have taken as their central theme the "distinctive" contribution that their provision offers via ethos, religious education, and collective worship.[24] The picture provided by the research evidence, however, is less clear about the nature of the distinctive provision and whether it is well understood by school leaders. Jelf's[25] research into the Christian distinctiveness of Church of England primary schools found that the schools had not attempted to critique the dominant educational discourse within which they operated. She argued that Christian character was thus compromised "by an unwitting compliance with values and principles that may compromise those they seek to promote."[26] Research based on interviews with church school principals suggests that school leaders lack theological literacy, are unclear about the nature of a distinctively Christian ethos, and in some cases are uncomfortable with explicitly linking school values to Christianity.[27] In her research carried out in the new Christian-sponsored academies, Green[28] found little evidence that a distinctive Christian ethos and values impacted the subject curriculum; she also concluded that it had little impact on student culture. This suggests that institutional structures and practices may mitigate against the intended theological aims of Christian educational providers. Green argues that "this is significant because Christian schools justify their mission in these terms and successive government policies have been committed to their expansion."[29] This leads us to consider our third question: What might be the disadvantages of a close partnership with government?

The expansion of church school provision in the current policy context of school choice may have made the sector more dependent on government

23. Green and Cooling, *Mapping the Field*, 14.

24. Dearing, *Way Ahead*; Chadwick et al., *Church School of the Future Review*.

25. Jelfs, "Is It the Dance of Life Miss?"

26. Ibid., 2.

27. Street, "Impact of The Way Ahead."

28. Green, "Research in the new Christian Academies."

29. Ibid, 395.

through the partnership model. Chadwick points out that "in the process of gaining more independence, church schools have inadvertently made themselves more vulnerable to a future government whose policies might be less sympathetic to Christian education."[30] This model of partnership also makes church schools subject to the same measures of accountability and modes of discourse associated with choice and competition. To what extent are they able to critique the view of personhood and aims of education that lie behind such measures? Cooling has argued that "education is always based on a vision of what it means to flourish as a human being."[31] He contests the utilitarian conception of education as a means to pass on knowledge and skills and argues that church schools have a vital role in supporting "people in the process of making their own wholesome interpretations of human knowledge and of applying those in their lives."[32] In the present policy climate in the UK this would require church schools to subvert dominant discourses that emphasize productivity, performance and individual choice.

In conclusion, this chapter has briefly sketched out the history of the Dual System and the evolution of school choice policies in the UK, with particular reference to the situation in England. The partnership of church and state remains a significant part of current educational provision, but the distinctive nature of church school provision faces both challenges and opportunities in the present policy climate and requires much critical reflection.

Reflection Questions

1. Do children belong to their parents, the state, themselves, or to God? What implications does your answer to this question have for the UK model of partnership between government and church in education?
2. Is it legitimate to admit students to a school on the basis of their faith, or the faith of their family?
3. Are choice and competition in education compatible with the values of the gospel?

30. Chadwick, "Conflict and Consensus," 57.
31. Cooling, *Doing God in Education*, 40.
32. Ibid., 39–40.

Recommended Reading

Cooling, Trevor. *Doing God in Education*. London: Theos, 2010.

Green, Elizabeth, and Trevor Cooling. *Mapping the Field: A Review of the Current Research Evidence on the Impact of Schools with a Christian Ethos*. London: Theos, 2009.

Tomlinson, Sally. *Education in a Post-Welfare Society*. 2nd ed. Maidenhead: Open University Press, 2005.

Bibliography

Adnett, N., and P. Davies. "Competition Between or Within Schools? Re-Assessing School Choice." *Education Economics* 13 (2005) 109–21.

Arthur, J., and R. Godfrey. *A Statistical Survey of the Attainment and Achievement of Pupils in Church of England Schools*. Canterbury: National Institute for Christian Education Research, 2005.

Catholic Education Service. "Academies." Online: http://www.catholiceducation.org.uk/academies.

Chadwick, P. "Conflict and Consensus in the Dual System." In *Anglican Church School Education: Moving Beyond the First Two Hundred Years*, edited by Howard J. Worsley, 43–57. London: Bloomsbury, 2012.

Chadwick, P, et al. *The Church School of the Future Review*. London: Church of England, Archbishops' Council Education Division, 2012.

Church of England. "Academies." Online: http://www.churchofengland.org/education/national-society/academies-(1).aspx.

Cooling, Trevor. *Doing God in Education*. London: Theos, 2010.

Deakin, Ruth. *The New Christian Schools: The Case for Public Funding*. Bristol: Regius, 1989.

Dearing, R. *The Way Ahead: Church of England Schools in the New Millennium*. London: Church House Publishing, 2001.

Department for Education. *Choice and Diversity*. London: HMSO, 1992.

———. "Open Academies and Academy Projects in Development." Online: http://www.education.gov.uk/schools/leadership/typesofschools/academies/b00208569/open-academies.

Gorard, Stephen, et al. "Does School Choice Lead to 'Spirals of Decline'?" *Journal of Education Policy* 17 (2002) 367–84.

Green, Elizabeth, and Trevor Cooling. Mapping the Field: A Review of the Current Research Evidence on the Impact of Schools with a Christian Ethos. London: Theos, 2009.

Hargreaves, D. "Diversity and Choice in School Education: A Modified Libertarian Approach." *Oxford Review of Education* 22 (1994) 131–41.

Jelfs, H. "Is It the Dance of Life Miss?: An Exploration of Educational Paradigm and Pedagogical Practice in Church of England Schools." PhD diss., University of Bristol, 2008.

Morris, A. "Academic Standards in Catholic Education in England: Indications of Causality." *London Review of Education* 3 (2005) 81–99.

Morris, A., et al. "Promoting Community Cohesion in England." *School Leadership and Management* 31 (2011) 281–96.

Morris, A., and R. Godfrey. *A Statistical Survey of Attainment in Catholic Schools in England with Particular Reference to Secondary Schools Operating Under the Trust Deed of the ARCHdiocese of Birmingham.* Canterbury: National Institute for Christian Education Research, 2006.

Office for National Statistics. "2011 Census, Population and Household Estimates for England and Wales." Online: http://www.ons.gov.uk/ons/rel/census/2011-census/population-and-household-estimates-for-england-and-wales/index.html.

Ouseley, H. *Community Pride Not Prejudice: Making Diversity Work in Bradford.* Bradford Vision, 2001. Online: http://www.bradford2020.com/pride/report.pdf.

Reay, D., and S. Ball. "'Making Their Minds Up': Family Dynamics of School Choice." *British Educational Research Journal* 24 (1998) 431–48.

Street, R. W. "The Impact of The Way Ahead on Headteachers of Anglican Voluntary-Aided Secondary Schools." *Journal of Beliefs and Values* 28 (2007) 137–50.

Tomlinson, Sally. *Education in a Post-Welfare Society.* 2nd ed. Maidenhead: Open University Press, 2005.

West, A. "School Choice, Equity and Social Justice: The Case for More Control." *British Educational Research Journal* 54 (2006) 15–33.

14

The Global Electric Republic

Teaching the Timeless in the Digital Age

GRANT N. HAVERS

WHEN WE ASK "TIMELESS questions," we are posing questions that are of importance to all human beings in every historical period. "What is justice?" "What is the good life?" "What do we know about God?" All of these are questions that have preoccupied human beings from classical antiquity all the way down to the modern age. In order to ask these questions in a serious way, one must step outside of one's own historical context in order to recognize that the meaning of justice or the good life may transcend one's own parochial perspective. It is not obvious, for example, that the twenty-first century possesses an understanding of justice that is superior to other historical periods. Although the historical context in which we live may consist of fleeting and changeable moments and events of finite importance, it is important to consider at least the possibility that the true meaning of justice or the good life transcends the assumptions and ideas of a particular historical period. This last fact is particularly important for Christians to understand, since we have been taught to believe that the truth of the Bible is the truth revealed for *all* ages, not simply a collection of teachings that was only meant for the Jews and Gentiles who lived in the Biblical Era.

One serious challenge that arises in our own twenty-first century is this: How does a scholar-teacher teach awareness of the timeless in an age of constant change? Why is it even necessary to do this? Is the timeless timely (that is, relevant) anymore? The mass media of the electric age make these questions both difficult and yet necessary to answer. They are difficult to answer because these media transmit information so instantaneously that they create the understandable impression of constant transformation. Yet these questions are also necessary to answer because it is important, as Christians, to understand how the timeless—the eternal—transcends this recurrent pattern of flux. God, after all, is the ultimate unchanging reality that stands above all change in the universe.

There are exactly two ways of understanding and teaching the timeless in the digital age. The first method is to understand ideas of the timeless as merely effects, or epiphenomena, of mass media. The Canadian Catholic media theorist Marshall McLuhan (1911–1980) popularized this method of study in the 1950s and 1960s. McLuhan constantly emphasized that all ideas, including ideas of the eternal, are reflections of a particular media age. In short, we can only have timely notions of what is timeless. His famous aphorism, "the medium is the message," essentially summarizes his overall theory of media: the message (content) of our ideas is the direct result of the medium in question; the medium creates the message, not the other way around. For the sake of simplicity, I shall call this approach the *historicist* method, since McLuhan's focus is on the manner in which a medium in a given historical period shapes and even causes particular ideas to come into being.

The second method is to understand the timeless as a reality that is distinct from what is merely timely or changeable. The German-Jewish philosopher Leo Strauss (1899–1973) was one of the most famous defenders of this method. Strauss taught that the most intelligent minds of the philosophical tradition have understood the need to distinguish what is timeless from the timely. If human beings know nothing but their own period of history—the timely—then their knowledge will be limited to a rather narrow horizon. Worst of all, the very notion of what is good for all human beings throughout history would no longer be well understood. Strauss believed that certain questions, such as "What is the good?" or "What is justice?," are important to all human beings, regardless of when or where they lived. There is a universal human nature that is eternally open to these questions. Strauss, in other words, was a critic of historicism who presented a philosophical reading of Plato, one that is devoted to the search for the eternal amidst constant flux. I shall call this approach the *philosophical* method of understanding the timeless or eternal.

Both McLuhan and Strauss have a deep interest in the ancient Greek thinker Plato (427–347 BC), who was the foremost philosopher of the distinction between the timeless and the timely (or the eternal and the changeable). Plato, whose philosophy has had a strong influence on many Christian thinkers throughout history, insisted that an infinite reality existed above and beyond the merely finite. It is useful to compare and contrast McLuhan and Strauss, since they were both interested in the vast differences between antiquity and modernity as well as examining what moderns could learn from the ancients.[1] McLuhan's and Strauss's approaches to Plato plainly reveal just how different historicism and philosophy truly are from each other. Whereas McLuhan understands Plato's philosophy as a historic product of his age, Strauss portrays this great Greek philosopher as a figure who sought to transcend the biases and conventions of his age altogether.

McLuhan's Historicist Method

Historicists of all types generally believe that no idea can claim to be valid beyond its specific historical context.[2] McLuhan's theory of media is historicist in this sense because it emphasizes the utter power of the media to create the ideas that human beings hold throughout history. When McLuhan famously quipped that "the medium is the message," he meant that the media "work us over completely . . . they leave no part of us untouched, unaffected, unaltered."[3] In order to support his premise that the media decisively cause our ideas of reality, McLuhan advanced a stage theory that divided up history according to the prominence of certain types of media.[4] There are four stages in all:

1. See McLuhan, "Ancient Quarrel in Modern America"; Strauss, "On Classical Political Philosophy."

2. This is Leo Strauss's definition of "historicism," to which I adhere throughout this essay. See Strauss, "Political Philosophy and History," 63.

3. McLuhan and Fiore, *Medium Is the Massage*, 26. For a critical discussion of McLuhan's historicist method, see Fekete, "McLuhanacy."

4. See McLuhan, *Gutenberg Galaxy*.

1. the oral age (6000–3500 BC)
2. the writing age (3500 BC–AD 1455)
3. the print age (AD 1455–1844)
4. the electric age (1844–present)

In each period, a particular medium tended to hold sway over the institutions and even ideas of the time. For example, in the oral age the speaking and singing of words dominated all communication. In the writing age, pictographs, followed by the alphabet, became the dominant media. At the start of the print age, Johannes Gutenberg's invention of the printing press in 1455 made mass literacy possible, since human beings could read books in their own languages for the first time in history. Finally, the electric age, which commenced with Samuel Morse's invention of the telegraph in 1844, ushered in the age of instantaneous communication in which we now live.

One important implication to draw from McLuhan's method here is that there is no such thing as an eternal or unchanging concept of reality, unless of course a particular historic period happens to believe in one. Still, saying that it is eternal does not make it eternal. Although he considered himself a believing Christian, McLuhan doubted that there is such a thing as a permanent "nature" that transcends or resists change. In fact, the new mass media were "nature," since they exerted more authority over human nature than nature itself.[5] Moreover, the very idea of a permanent "nature" is a fiction, according to McLuhan, that was invented by Greek philosophers such as Plato in order to impose order onto a chaotic cosmos. McLuhan chided Plato for ignoring the real order of the universe, one that is imposed by "man-made technologies."[6]

Does the philosophy of Plato, then, according to McLuhan, have anything to teach moderns who are used to understanding all ideas as subject to historical change? McLuhan's answer is that Plato helps moderns understand historic changes in his age that perhaps parallel the upheavals of our own time, since we are all subject to the twists and turns of technological change. Plato not only lived in the transitional period between the oral age and the writing age. According to McLuhan, Plato even helped to advance the displacement of oral speech by writing.[7] Although Plato, in his dialogue

5. McLuhan, *Essential McLuhan*, 272.

6. Ibid., 360–61.

7. Ibid., 120–21. McLuhan's understanding of Plato was heavily influenced by the classical scholarship of Eric Havelock, particularly his study *Preface to Plato*. Leo Strauss, by contrast, was opposed to Havelock's scholarship, which he considered "historicist." See Strauss, *Liberalism*, 29–30.

The Phaedrus, has Socrates (his famous teacher and the main speaker in most of his dialogues) warn about the negative impact of writing on memory (275a–e), his attack on the power of the poets of his time arguably contributed to the rise of writing. Poetry, which in ancient Greece was sung out loud, was gradually displaced by writing as the new dominant medium of communication.[8] Ultimately, Plato's dream of an ideal republic governed by philosophers, as he famously described in *The Republic*, required the rule of philosopher-guardians over the poets, whom Plato threatened with exile if they did not agree to the rule of philosophers (*Republic* 607c). Of course, all of these assumptions presupposed a rather small regime in which philosophers knew the citizens that they governed.

If McLuhan is right, then Plato's philosophy is most intelligible to a particular period in history, and one that is long past. McLuhan also insists that only moderns living in his age can understand great ancient thinkers like Plato. As he once famously put it, reality can be understood only after the fact, as in a rearview mirror. In fact, McLuhan makes a key historicist assumption when he suggests that he understands Plato better than Plato understood himself, since this ancient Greek was unaware of the massive technological shifts from speech to writing that were affecting his philosophy. Only in the electric age of media can human beings (that is, moderns) fully comprehend the hidden and biased effects of technological change.[9]

Is Plato, then, relevant anymore to the electric age, which is more concerned with the instant flow of communication than with the deep thinking that is required in philosophical speech and writing? In his classic *Understanding Media: The Extensions of Man* (1964), McLuhan provided an ambivalent answer to this question. On the one hand, he portrayed Plato as an adherent of "old-fashioned tribal ideas of political structure." By "tribal," McLuhan meant the idea of a closely knit political regime in which citizens knew each other. Since this idea once fitted the small city-states of ancient Greece, McLuhan was inclined to believe that Plato's philosophy has no relevance to the age of mass populations, which the print age and electric ages had ushered into being. On the other hand, he left open the possibility that "radio, because of its ease of decentralized intimate relations with both private and small communities, could easily implement the Platonic political dream on a world scale."[10] In short, electric mass media may make an "electric" Platonic republic into a reality that even Plato did not anticipate.

8. See Postman, *Amusing Ourselves to Death*, 12–13.

9. Targeting Plato's unsuccessful attempt to impose a "natural" order on change and chaos, McLuhan writes: "The world of men's artifacts was considered neutral until the electric age" (*Essential McLuhan*, 361).

10. McLuhan, *Understanding Media*, 307.

Two lessons can be drawn from McLuhan's understanding of Plato. First, Plato's philosophy corresponds most closely with the age of writing, in which a relatively small number of people could read and write (and, in the case of the philosopher-guardians, govern). Second, Plato's philosophy could only become relevant again if a medium like the radio recreated small regimes that parallel his philosophical republic. In short, the truth of Plato's philosophy is far less important than the historic periods that either gave birth to it or revive its influence. One way or the other, technological change alone determines the relevance and importance of his thought. This conclusion is a typically historicist one.

Strauss's Philosophical Method

According to Leo Strauss, philosophy is concerned with understanding what is true for all human beings, not what is simply true for a particular historic period. While he was not opposed to the study of history, he strenuously argued that the historical period in which one lived does not have final or even correct answers to all questions, especially the timeless questions of the ages. It was not obvious to Strauss that the modern age in particular provided an adequate answer to questions about the meaning of justice or the good life, since moderns tended to understand the good as identical to the maximization of self-interest. The difference between the premoderns and moderns amounted to a vast difference over what constitutes *nature*. From a premodern perspective, nature is an eternal necessity, created by God, which dictates what the purpose (*telos*) of human life is as well as standards of virtue that all human beings must follow in order to live a good life. "All natural beings have a natural end, a natural destiny, which determines what kind of operation is good for them."[11] Since nature is eternal, these standards do not change over time even if human beings violate or ignore them. The highest level of knowledge, according to the premoderns, must be knowledge of what is invisible and even immeasurable by the standards of physical science. Justice and the virtuous life are concepts that are infinite and transcendent, not to be understood through the finite means of physical science. By contrast, nature, from a modern perspective, is simply the physical stuff of the universe that teaches nothing about how human beings ought to live their lives. Nature, including human nature, is finite, measurable, raw material that can be understood as well as controlled through the

11. Strauss, *Natural Right and History*, 7.

means of modern science and technology.[12] These two profoundly divergent approaches to nature lead to two equally distinct views of the meaning of both knowledge and the good life.

Whereas classical and medieval authors had taught that the good is identical to the pursuit of virtue or the cultivation of one's character, moderns were content to teach that the good is equivalent to one's fulfillment of the human desire for material goods. Human nature, like animal nature, is preoccupied with mere survival, not virtue. Our modern "right" to life replaces the premodern focus on our "duty" to uphold virtue.[13] Strauss drew another contrast between the premodern (including ancient and medieval) and modern ways of thinking. Whereas the premoderns had taught that knowledge of the most important things (e.g., justice, virtue) never truly changes from one historical period to another, the moderns believed that knowledge "progressed" from a state of backwardness in antiquity all the way to a state of advancement and sophistication in the modern age. The moderns believed this because they identified knowledge with the scientific method that helps us understand the physical facts of the universe, whereas the premoderns identified the highest level of knowledge with the practice of virtues that are right and good for all human beings. From a modern perspective, real knowledge (science) must study what is measurable, which is the material universe. Since the premoderns were technologically and scientifically backward, according to modern philosophers, they taught nothing of importance to human beings in the modern age. According to Strauss, then, it is not surprising that the modern identification of knowledge with science leads to historicism, or the belief that knowledge is relative according to the time in which one lives. According to historicism, then, "Every doctrine, however seemingly final, will be superseded sooner or later by another doctrine."[14]

The problem for moderns, according to Strauss, is that their overreliance on modern science and technology as the foundation for all knowledge leads to considerable uncertainty over what the good life is. Can science alone teach us the moral standards by which we are to live? Since the moderns believed that nature has nothing to teach human beings about virtue, they concluded that questions about living the good life are best left to the personal choices of human beings. Although scientific and technical knowledge was far more preoccupied with understanding and controlling nature, moderns nevertheless were confident that, as humanity progressed

12. Ibid., 1–34.

13. Strauss, "Progress or Return?," 271.

14. Strauss, *Natural Right and History*, 21. See also Strauss, "Progress or Return?," 261–63.

in a scientific manner, it would also progress in a moral vein as well. As a witness to the horrors of world war and genocide in the twentieth century, Strauss was far from confident that the mere advancement of scientific and technological knowledge led to improvements in human character as well. For this reason, Strauss chastised the moderns for facilitating the "emancipation of technology, of the arts, from moral and human control," a project that has contributed to the "dehumanization of man" in our age.[15]

Given his doubts about the modern mind, Strauss turned to the philosophy of Plato for an alternative way of understanding the highest goals of human life. Unlike McLuhan, who takes the modern view that Plato's philosophy is a mere reflection of the ancient period in which Plato actually lived, Strauss contends that his modern contemporaries need to rediscover the timeless importance of Plato's teachings. In other words, it is wrong for moderns to dismiss Plato as a thinker that wrote his numerous dialogues only for his contemporaries. Plato's condemnation of murder, theft, and adultery in his work *The Laws* constitutes a moral teaching that, like the Ten Commandments, applies to all human beings, not just the ancient Greeks.[16]

Strauss is interested in Plato for another reason. In *The Republic*, his most important philosophical work, Plato famously tells a story about the two worlds in which human beings exist. This section is known as the "Cave Allegory," a narrative in which Plato compares most of human life to living in a cave. This story illustrates the differences between human beings as to their understanding of realities that are both permanent and changeable (*Republic* 514a–517b). According to Plato, most human beings live inside a cave, which is barely lit by a small fire. The people inside the cave are mainly focused on the shadows on its walls, which are cast by the dim light of the fire. These shadows are images, or merely changeable imitations of the objects that exist inside the cave. Outside the cave, however, there is a realm of pure light that represents the unchanging truth. Only a fortunate few, mainly philosophers, get the chance to leave the cave and look into this blinding light, in which they can access the highest principles (or what Plato calls the "Forms") of justice and virtue. The rest of humankind are forever trapped inside the changeable realm of the cave, in which they are ignorant of this outside reality.

What does this have to do with the modern mind? Strauss believed that modernity was "a second, much deeper cave," which moderns have constructed for themselves.[17] This cave focused simply on what is change-

15. Strauss, *What Is Political Philosophy?*, 37.

16. Strauss, "Progress or Return?," 274.

17. Strauss, *Early Writings*, 215.

able, the material facts of the universe: these are the modern "shadows" that bewitch the modern mind. As a result, moderns are oblivious to what is truly "timeless," the light of virtue and justice that exists outside of the cave. (McLuhan may have had a point when he compared Plato's cave to the audience's experience of the movies today: "The dreaming eye of the movie god casting his images on the dark screen corresponds to that image of human life offered to us by Plato in the *Republic*."[18])

Although Strauss never wrote on the media revolution in the modern age, he clearly believed that the modern dependence on science and technology as the only pathway to knowledge had led to a new and deeper kind of cave. While he never wrote on McLuhan, it is likely that Strauss would have interpreted McLuhan's historicist method as yet another attempt by moderns to create a cave.[19] To teach, as McLuhan does, that there is no truth or knowledge beyond the changeable patterns of media that determine a particular historical period is to restrict human knowledge to whatever is relevant in a given time frame. Any notion of the good or virtuous life, then, is subject to whatever a particular period understands as good or virtuous. In short, the cave that is constructed by mass media today encourages moral relativism.

Conclusion

McLuhan may well fault Strauss for paying insufficient attention to the massive technological upheavals that shaped and inspired both the age of Plato and his philosophy. Critics of Strauss often contend that he is unjustifiably disinterested in the historical context in which philosophers lived and thought.[20] The challenge that Strauss presents to McLuhan is whether historicism alone can help moderns navigate through the upheavals of the modern age. If McLuhan is right that all ideas are completely subject to technological change, then it must follow that his own ideas are the mere effects of the electric age of media. As Strauss once put it, "Historicism is not a cab which one stops at his convenience. Historicism must be applied to itself."[21] Yet if McLuhan's ideas are only correct insofar as they mirror the

18. McLuhan, "Catholic Humanism and Modern Letters," 165.

19. Strauss's student Allan Bloom astutely notes that the modern mind, as shaped by the Enlightenment, would promise the liberation of all human beings from the "cave," presumably through the power of modern science. See Bloom, "Interpretive Essay," in his translation of Plato's *Republic*, 403.

20. Gottfried, *Leo Strauss and the Conservative Movement in America*; McIntyre, "'What's Gone and What's Past Help.'"

21. Strauss, "Political Philosophy and History," 72–73.

transitory assumptions of the electric age, then they themselves are stuck within the assumptions of that age. If historicism is true, then it is also only temporarily true and thus incapable of demonstrating whether it is true at the moment or true for all time. This is a problem for McLuhan's thought, since he tried to understand the past stages of history from a perspective that is shaped only by his own finite period of history. Therefore, McLuhan and other historicists need to address the question that is posed by Leo Strauss: If all ideas are true only insofar as they reflect our period of history, then how do we know for certain that our age has the truth?

Reflection Questions

1. What are the main differences between the philosophical and historicist methods of reading and interpreting a philosophical text?
2. If the historicist method were applied to the Bible, which conclusions would modern readers have to make about the relevance of Scripture in our time?
3. What does Plato's story of the cave teach about human existence and, in particular, the power of images over humanity?
4. From a premodern perspective, what are the problems with an educational program that is modeled solely on science and technology?

Recommended Reading

Havers, Grant. "Leo Strauss, Willmoore Kendall, and the Meaning of Conservatism." *Humanitas* 18/1–2 (2005) 5–25.

———. "The Right-Wing Postmodernism of Marshall McLuhan." *Media, Culture, & Society* 25/4 (2003) 511–25.

McLuhan, Marshall. *Essential McLuhan*. Edited by Eric McLuhan and Frank Zingrone. Toronto: House of Anansi, 1995.

———. *The Gutenberg Galaxy: The Making of Typographic Man*. Toronto: University of Toronto Press, 1962.

———. *Understanding Media: The Extensions of Man*. With a new introduction by Lewis H. Lapham. Cambridge, MA: MIT Press, 1994.

Plato. *The Laws of Plato*. Translated with notes and essay by Thomas L. Pangle. Chicago: University of Chicago Press, 1980.

———. *Phaedrus*. In *The Collected Dialogues of Plato, Including the Letters*, edited by Edith Hamilton and Huntington Cairns, 475–525. Princeton, NJ: Princeton University Press, 1980.

———. *The Republic of Plato*. Translated with notes and essay by Allan Bloom. New York: Basic Books, 1968.

Strauss, Leo. "Plato." In *An Introduction to Political Philosophy: Ten Essays by Leo Strauss*, edited by Hilail Gildin, 167–245. Detroit: Wayne State University Press, 1989.

———. "Political Philosophy and History." In *What Is Political Philosophy? and Other Studies*. Chicago: University of Chicago Press, 1989.

Bibliography

Fekete, John. "McLuhanacy: Counterrevolution in Cultural Theory." *Telos* 15 (1973) 75–123.

Gottfried, Paul E. *Leo Strauss and the Conservative Movement in America: A Critical Appraisal*. Cambridge: Cambridge University Press, 2012.

Havelock, Eric. *Preface to Plato*. New York: Grosset and Dunlap, 1963.

McIntyre, Kenneth B. "'What's Gone and What's Past Help . . .': Oakeshott and Strauss on Historical Explanation." *Journal of the Philosophy of History* 4/1 (2010) 65–101.

McLuhan, Marshall. "An Ancient Quarrel in Modern America." In *The Interior Landscape: The Literary Criticism of Marshall McLuhan*, edited by Eugene McNamara. Toronto: McGraw-Hill.

———. "Catholic Humanism and Modern Letters." In *The Medium and the Light: Reflections on Religion and Media*, edited by Jacek Szklarek, 153–74. Eugene, OR: Wipf & Stock, 2010.

———. *Essential McLuhan*. Edited by Eric McLuhan and Frank Zingrone. Toronto: House of Anansi, 1995.

———. *The Gutenberg Galaxy: The Making of Typographic Man*. Toronto: University of Toronto Press, 1962.

———. *Understanding Media: The Extensions of Man*. With a new introduction by Lewis H. Lapham. Cambridge, MA: MIT Press, 1994.

McLuhan, Marshall, and Quentin Fiore. *The Medium Is the Massage*. New York: Bantam, 1967.

Plato. *The Laws of Plato*. Translated with notes and essay by Thomas L. Pangle. Chicago: University of Chicago Press, 1980.

———. *Phaedrus*. In *The Collected Dialogues of Plato, Including the Letters*, edited by Edith Hamilton and Huntington Cairns, 475–525. Princeton, NJ: Princeton University Press, 1980.

———. *The Republic of Plato*. Translated with notes and essay by Allan Bloom. New York: Basic Books, 1968.

Postman, Neil. *Amusing Ourselves to Death: Public Discourse in the Age of Show Business*. New York: Penguin, 1985.

Strauss, Leo. "On Classical Political Philosophy." In *What Is Political Philosophy? and Other Studies*. Chicago: University of Chicago Press, 1989.

———. *The Early Writings (1921–1932)*. Translated and edited by Michael Zank. Albany: State University of New York Press, 2002.

———. *Liberalism: Ancient and Modern*. Chicago: University of Chicago Press, 1995.

———. *Natural Right and History*. Chicago: University of Chicago Press, 1953.

———. "Progress or Return? The Contemporary Crisis in Western Civilization." In *An Introduction to Political Philosophy: Ten Essays by Leo Strauss*, edited by Hilail Gildin. Detroit: Wayne State University Press, 1989.

15

Religion, Secularity, and Education

On Not Taking Things for Granted

DOUG BLOMBERG

HAVING BEEN A RESIDENT of three countries—Australia (my birthplace), the United States, and Canada—I am often surprised that societies with so much in common also differ in significant respects. On my first trip to the States in the mid-1970s, I was amazed to learn there was widespread opposition to laws mandating the wearing of seatbelts, because this was considered an infringement of personal liberty. Nowadays, however, buckling up seems second nature to the Americans I know and most whom I have observed. It might be that, in a generation or so, even universal public healthcare will be taken for granted, as it long has been in other developed countries.

What Is "Secular"?

Of course, history is littered with assumptions later forsaken. One such was the long-held conviction in Europe that belief in God is intrinsic to what it means to be human. Charles Taylor defines our "secular age" as an era in which this conviction has been overturned.[1] But people's lives nonetheless remain grounded in and directed by fundamental commitments, and we still have not resolved the issues surrounding the proper relations between the state and various believing communities within its borders. Thus, Taylor argues in a recent paper that we need to radically redefine our notion of *secularism*, so we are clear that "in fact it has to do with the (correct) response of the democratic state to diversity."[2] State neutrality towards religion is not satisfied by constructing a "wall of separation" between government institutions and churches. Rather, regimes deserve to be deemed "secularist" only when they are "conceived not primarily as bulwarks against religions but as good faith attempts to . . . shape their institutional arrangements . . . to maximize the basic goals of liberty and equality between basic beliefs."[3]

In common parlance, the secular realm is that which is not "religious." Christians have to live in both realms, but with a neutral or often negative attitude towards the former, considered a lower mode of existence than that which is accessed through religious practices. Thus, John Peck and Charles Strohmer suggest "life's highway" comprises many lanes, but that most Christians consider the imperatives of the gospel to apply only to a couple of these.[4]

To the north of Toronto is a multilane highway reputed to be the busiest corridor in North America. If you imagine yourself driving on Highway 401, it would be as if the speed limit were to apply in just one lane eastbound and one lane westbound. Outside these lanes you could travel at whatever speed took your fancy. The two lanes in which God's laws of love for life are thought to apply are the "moral" and "spiritual"; the rest are "secular." God reveals his guidance for two lanes, but elsewhere we move in the realm of common sense, natural reason, and personal freedom. Our primary responsibility in these areas is to witness to Christ, and as long as we have a fish emblem on the back of the car—or even better, a bumper sticker that invites, "Honk if you love Jesus"—we are doing our Christian duty. (The number of times I have seen drivers of these "Christmobiles" speeding and swerving dangerously from lane to lane suggests the "two lanes" view of life is discouragingly prevalent.)

1. Taylor, *Secular Age*.
2. Taylor, "Why We Need a Radical Redefinition of Secularism," 36.
3. Ibid., 56.
4. Peck and Strohmer, *Uncommon Sense*.

"Give Back to Caesar What Is Caesar's"

If we may paraphrase theologian and statesman Abraham Kuyper in the context of this metaphor, he would say, "There is not one lane on the highway of life that is not God's." In other words, there is no law by which life should be ordered than that revealed in God's integral revelation in Christ, Scripture, and creation. Even the speed limits posted are an expression of this order, because governments derive their authority from God and are accountable to him for how they use it. If a Christian were asked, "What are the limits to God's authority?" we would rightly expect the answer to be, "None!" Nevertheless, it is customary in many circles to interpret Jesus' response to the question as to whether or not we should pay taxes as pointing to just such limitations, with authority divided between a realm that belongs to God and a realm that belongs to Caesar (Matt 22:15–22).

Could this really be what Jesus meant when he asked whose image and inscription were on the coin? Yet the assumption of two realms is so pervasive that we readily ignore an answer that stares us in the face. We even remember Martin Luther for his conviction that "it is not impossible for a prince to be a Christian, although it is a rare thing and beset with many difficulties."[5] He was in part reacting to the then prevalent assumption that the realm of nature and reason was a substructure functioning as a gateway to the supernatural realm of faith and grace. This seemed to Luther a denial of the radical effects of the fall, which he believed made it impossible for humans to please God by any natural means.

Rendering unto Caesar what is his is not an acknowledgement of an authority parallel to God, but of a limited and delegated authority under God. Thus, Luther, Dietrich Bonhoeffer, or Martin Luther King Jr. could claim that disobedience to authority illegitimately exercised is at the same time obedience to God. A Quaker or a Mennonite who withholds the portion of her taxes that would be used to fund military expenditures is not merely exercising a personal right of conscience but is doing what she is convicted the Word of God demands—rendering her life to God.

Confessing God's comprehensive sovereignty implies that nowhere have we been left in the dark. God's light shines everywhere, if only we have eyes to see. It illuminates every facet of our lives. This means we should live every dimension of life in response to God, which is what renowned Calvin College philosophy professor H. Evan Runner had in mind whenever he would thunder, "Human life in its entirety is religion!" He wished to make it clear that "religious" is not just an adjective applied to some aspects of life

5. Luther, "Temporal Authority," in *Martin Luther's Basic Theological Writings*, 450.

or to some people but not to others. No, life *equals* religion: all of life is to be in service of the triune God. In this fallen world, however, it is too often in service of a substitute god; but it is a spiritually directed life, a life of religion, just the same. Elijah challenged the people of Israel to make up their minds which of two gods they would serve, for only one can be followed (1 Kgs 18:21). Jesus made it clear we cannot serve two gods, but will end up hating one of them (Matt 6:24). There are no neutral areas in respect to the service the "whole self" offers to God or to an idol (Rom 12:1–2).

Serving God wholeheartedly comes neither automatically nor readily to us. It is a transformation that occurs by the ongoing renewal of our hearts and minds as we submit ourselves to the Spirit who works in us. The temptation to wander off after other gods remains with us life-long, until Christ's kingdom comes in its fullness. In the between times, we must exercise the continuous discipline required of those who would bear the name (and cross) of "disciple."

The comprehensive character of God's rule resounds in the repetition of "all things" in the hymn to Christ that Paul includes in his letter to the Colossians (1:15–20). It is a sovereignty that goes back to the very foundation of the world, when God called into being all things by the power of his Word, which has continued to sustain them. The Word who is Christ has come to restore all things to what they were meant to be, by reconciling them to God and to one another.[6] Reconciliation is God's embrace of the world. It is an embrace that—like those of lovers, of parents and children, of loyal friends—leaves no space between. Nothing is excluded from an embrace that would gather up the beloved in nurturing arms. There can be no secrets, no part of life withheld in this face-to-face commitment of one to the other.

Education and Schooling

One of the most significant institutional developments over the past century and more has been the rise of systems of schooling under the control of and funded by the state. At its extreme, this has led to what might be described—in the precise sense usually reserved for religious institutions—as the "establishment" of schools. Not only is schooling legally compulsory for many years of children's lives, state schools are accorded a privileged position, with the expense of attending alternative schools beyond the means of most. Even though many parents would elect not to send their children

6. See Pss 33:6–9, 147:17–19, 148:8, John 1:1–3, 1 Cor 8:6, Eph 1:9–10, 3:8–10, Heb 1:3, 2 Pet 3:5–7.

to government schools, because they embody a conception of life they reject, they are effectively often compelled to do so. Such schools are not truly "public"—open to all—if they represent only one sector a society's array of fundamental convictions.

American educationalist Svi Shapiro is a staunch supporter of public schooling, but it was not until the decision loomed concerning where to send his daughter to high school that he recognized the full force of the potential clash between his generalized "moral, ideological, and political considerations" and the particularities of his daughter's life.[7] Convinced that being Jewish is not a Shabbat-only concern, he wished his "daughter's heart and soul to be shaped and nurtured by a Yiddishkeyt that would ensure her allegiance to a Jewish identity."[8]

Schooling is indeed a powerful shaper of identity. An important justification for "free, compulsory and secular" or "common" schooling, in British colonies and the United States respectively, was the potential that such schools had to nurture children from diverse cultural, ethnic, and religious backgrounds to participate harmoniously in public life. But there are numerous issues to be addressed in negotiating between the right of parents to choose the kind of education their children receive and the state's expectations for its citizens.

Shapiro understands schooling to be not just a utilitarian concern, but induction into a way of life. Schooling construed as primarily utilitarian, designed to "produce" graduates who have the skills necessary to be economically productive and responsible citizens, is itself such an induction. But it is a way of life that, taking material prosperity and democratic decision making as its goals, runs counter to ways of life that regard non-material goods and transcendent values as having priority. Schooling that focuses on the transmission of knowledge and skills while purportedly eschewing the formation of character is formation unto a particular view of what it means to be a mature person. And achieving maturity is not the result of lifting oneself up by the bootstraps, as if there were a pre-existent, self-sufficient individuality; it is a cultural (necessarily religious) heritage for which an individual is invited to take responsibility, albeit critically.

7. Shapiro, "Parent's Dilemma," 231.

8. Ibid., 232.

Structural Pluralism in Schooling

If religion or spirituality is a life orientation that comes to expression in all domains, legislated impartiality of governments towards religious institutions is quite a different matter from spiritual neutrality in the public domain, as Taylor explains. The latter needs to be seen within the context of institutional differentiation, in which structural pluralism could provide a framework within which cultural and confessional pluralism flourishes. In other words, we require faith-based public schooling if we are justly to accommodate all citizens and their children in religiously plural societies. The devolution and distribution of authority—as advocated in the Catholic concept of subsidiarity or the Reformed notion of sphere sovereignty—is essential to the increasingly diverse societies that many have become or are becoming.

There are numerous jurisdictions in which schools supported by different faith and/or ethnic communities receive substantial if not full public financial support. In the province of Ontario, there are only two such communities (for historical reasons, naturally). This hardly represents the cultural mosaic Canada purports to honor, though neither is it an American melting pot. One could discuss in terms of natural justice the inequity of funding Catholic and secular systems and not Jewish, Islamic, Waldorf, or Hindu schools, for example. There is a straightforward way to disestablish Ontario's two school systems. This is by not merely regulating and authorizing but financially empowering all schools. Michael Merry argues that schools (and his particular focus is on what are currently the most controversial of these in Western countries, Muslim schools) accredited by government agencies as viable educational providers ought to be afforded funding that enables them to provide resources on a par with those available to government schools.[9] It is an argument articulating what has been long accepted elsewhere, but not one readily heard by those who regard certain statements of principle (such as the U.S. First Amendment) as inviolable. But principles are never simply instantiated in practice; their expressions are always historically forged, in a struggle between competing interests and interpretations. A reconceived secularism is one such principle, requiring institutional embodiment.

9. Merry, *Culture, Identity*.

God and Schools

Schools too are cultural products, given shape in particular and almost invariably contested situations. As noted, the universal public and usually secular schooling systems of which the West is so proud are concerned with the practical things of this life, like reading, calculating, preparing for a job, and being a citizen, with the bonus of acquiring some of the refinements of civilization if time and talent allow. Are schools not a matter for Caesar?

It is tempting to decide that schools are "of this world," merely a pragmatic response to needs that have arisen in the industrial and post-industrial eras, like trade unions and transnational corporations, and of little significance for the life to come. Yet sentiments such as these take us out on the divided highway again, where we are guilty of limiting God's authority to a couple of lanes. We drive a wedge between "natural" or "creational" institutions, such as marriage and family on the one hand, and "cultural" institutions on the other. Though we may not confess it in our churches, in our practice we become deists. It's as if we believe that God finished the work of creation and then left the world to develop howsoever it would, forgetting that it was the task of filling the earth with "culture"—agriculture and political culture, family life and works of music and art, for example—for which God created humankind. The story of the fall is in part the story of how our first parents thought they could carry out their mandate without recourse to God in deciding what was good and what was evil. But we do not build culture *ex nihilo*, we only shape what God has put into our hands as potentialities; everything lives and moves and has its being only because it is sustained by him. And we *should* not build culture in ways disobedient to God's desire for justice, mercy, and humble service of his purposes. This includes, most emphatically, the culture of schools.

We also limit God's authority by restricting it to the hearts of individuals rather than acknowledging that it holds for communities, organizations, and institutions. Indeed, the story of God's dealing with humankind is one of calling out communities to be his people for the blessing of others, from Abraham through Jacob and David and the people of Israel to Jesus and the new Israel, the Body of Christ. The individualistic spirit of our age often blinds us to this communal dimension to Christ's work of redemption, but it certainly was not ignored by Christians of earlier eras. Leaders such as John Calvin, John Wesley, William Wilberforce, Lord Shaftesbury, Leo XIII, Tommy Douglas, and Martin Luther King Jr. recognized the reformation of social structures is as imperative as "saving souls."

Education is an induction into a way of life. It is the passing on of what has been found meaningful, and ultimately, of convictions about the source of this meaning. No culture, nor the knowledge it embodies, is agnostic with respect to these questions of meaning. Knowledge develops within a matrix of assumptions about the character and origin of order and meaning, the nature of humanness, the purpose, task, and way to flourishing of human life. It is not a passive recording of an objective world, but an active shaping and interpreting in accord with presuppositions about what it all means.

Not a Controlled Experiment, But . . .

Too often we have taken for granted a particular understanding of secularity. As Taylor says, it is an understanding we need to rethink radically. What most intrigues me about national differences with respect to systems of schooling is how Australia and the United States, with virtually identical constitutional provisions concerning religion, have yielded such different outcomes. Section 116 of the Australian Constitution is a "fairly blatant piece of transcription" of the First Amendment to the US Constitution.[10] Yet the High Court of Australia's interpretation of the establishment clause has been much narrower—and that of free expression seemingly much broader—than the US Supreme Court's. With respect to schools, the High Court for some decades now has upheld Australian government funding of non-government, predominantly religiously oriented schools, in which approximately 34 percent of children are enrolled. In the United States, however, private schools are by definition those that receive no such (direct) funding and their population comprises about only 11 percent of those of school age. This is an amazing disparity, especially when one recalls that the comparison is between a notoriously secular Australia and an overtly religious United States of America. It proffers evidence to sustain the hope that the principle of secularism can find historical embodiment in ways that "maximize the basic goals of liberty and equality between basic beliefs."[11]

We have placed our faith in education in the modern West (and elsewhere). We have not, however, sufficiently recognized that education is always in service of a faith, of religion conceived as basic beliefs or fundamental convictions. Shapiro realized the full force of this in the face of his daughter; it is imperative that all parents—Christian and otherwise—come to the same realization.

10. Pannam, "Travelling Section 116," 41.

11. Taylor, "Why We Need," 56.

Reflection Questions

1. What does it mean to be "religious" or "spiritual"?
2. Is schooling necessarily an induction into a way of life?
3. Taylor argues that "separation of church and state" is insufficient "to maximize the basic goals of liberty and equality between basic beliefs." What kinds of "institutional arrangements" are most likely to secure these goals?
4. Christians have acted politically to challenge many legalized social practices, such as slavery, underage labor, abortion, and preferential funding for government schools. Do you think such action is justified biblically (in general terms) with respect to school funding (in particular)?

Recommended Reading

Clouser, Roy A. *The Myth of Religious Neutrality: An Essay on the Hidden Role of Religious Beliefs in Theories*. 2nd ed. Notre Dame, IN: University of Notre Dame, 2005.

McCarthy, Rockne, Donald Oppewal, Walfred Peterson, and Gordon Spykman. *Society, State, and Schools: A Case for Structural and Confessional Pluralism*. Grand Rapids: Eerdmans, 1981.

Wolters, Albert M. *Creation Regained: Biblical Basics for a Reformational Worldview*. 2nd ed. Grand Rapids: Eerdmans, 2005.

Wolterstorff, Nicholas. *Educating for Life: Reflections on Christian Teaching and Learning*, edited by Gloria Goris Stronks and Clarence Joldersma. Grand Rapids: Baker Academic, 2002.

Bibliography

Luther, Martin. *Martin Luther's Basic Theological Writings*. Edited by Timothy F. Hull and William R. Russell. 3rd ed. Minneapolis: Fortress, 2012.

Merry, Michael S. *Culture, Identity, and Islamic Schooling: A Philosophical Approach*. New York: Palgrave Macmillan, 2007.

Pannam, Clifford L. "Travelling Section 116 with a U.S. Road Map." *Melbourne University Law Review* 4/1 (1963) 41–90.

Peck, John, and Charles Strohmer. *Uncommon Sense: God's Wisdom for Our Complex and Changing World*. Sevierville, TN: Wise Press, 2000.

Shapiro, H. Svi. "A Parent's Dilemma: Public vs. Jewish Education." In *Critical Social Issues in American Education: Transformation in a Postmodern World*, edited by H. Svi Shapiro and David E. Purpel, 231–40. Mahwah, NJ: Erlbaum Associates, 1998.

Taylor, Charles. *A Secular Age*. Cambridge: Harvard University, 2007.

———. “Why We Need a Radical Redefinition of Secularism.” In *The Power of Religion in the Public Sphere*, edited by E. Mendieta and J. VanAntwerpen. New York: Columbia University, 2011.

16

Walking Humbly, Listening Compassionately and Living Justly

A Way Forward in Our Relations with Aboriginal Peoples in Canada

David Long *and* William Van Arragon

Introduction

In his novel *Illusions: Adventures of a Reluctant Messiah*, Richard Bach writes that "we teach best what we most need to learn."[1] Although the two of us agree that we learn something in every university course that we teach, two courses in particular have brought the truth of Richard Bach's observation to life in our teaching. One is a senior sociology course that engages a broad set of issues involving Aboriginal people in Canada, while the other is an interdisciplinary course that examines historical and contemporary issues related to the work of this country's Indian Residential School Truth and Reconciliation Commission (TRC). That we have each learned a great deal teaching these two courses is in part due to their

1. Bach, *Illusions*, 48.

subject matter, which is fascinating and wonderfully complex. We have also found that gaining new understanding of issues involving Aboriginal people in Canada can be a challenging and at times deeply unsettling experience for us and our students. For one thing, it confronts us with some of the pain, suffering, and brokenness experienced by generations of Aboriginal individuals, families, and communities in this country. It is also somewhat disconcerting to learn of the central role played by Western European Christians in the colonization of Canada, since it provides the rather sobering reminder that much of the way we currently view "Aboriginal issues in Canada," and therefore the way we think and act in relation to Aboriginal people in this country, were passed down to us from our colonizing ancestors. As we discuss throughout this chapter, our paraphrased invitation to students from the Old Testament prophet Micah to "walk humbly, listen compassionately, and live justly" helps to not only guide our teaching and learning in relation to a wide variety of complex socio-historical issues; it more importantly enables all of us to see a way forward in our relationships with our Aboriginal sisters and brothers in our everyday lives.

The Freedom in Walking Humbly

A first step towards reconciliation and moving positively forward in all our relations is to acknowledge our human limitations, including our brokenness and lack of understanding. Indeed, we are of the mind that embracing our limitations liberates teachers and students from the bonds of self-centered learning. Admitting that our self-centeredness and our brokenness go hand in hand also helps us to acknowledge our complicity in what is wrong in the world and to embrace the hope of accepting our responsibility to do what we can to make things right.

We have certainly learned a great deal through our reading of historical and contemporary issues involving Aboriginal people in Canada. However, we recognize that we gain much deeper understanding of some of the profound similarities and differences between our own religious, familial, educational, economic, and cultural experiences and those of our Aboriginal sisters and brothers when we engage in humble, respectful dialogue with them. Engaging in respectful dialogue also benefits us in a number of other, significant ways. For one, it helps us to see that we share this world with many "others." This helps us to understand how those we are in dialogue with often view us, which can of course remind us in rather startling and sometimes unsettling ways that we too are different and "other." Most importantly, engaging in mutually respectful dialogue transforms our learning from a formal, largely impersonal educational activity that focuses on hearing information and stories *about* Aboriginal people to the much more challenging, personal experience of learning to walk *with* Aboriginal people. Along with engaging us with Aboriginal people's experiences and perspectives on life and history in deeply personal ways, learning to walk *with* one another helps us all to better understand ourselves and our common humanity. The clear benefit of doing so is that we see a more hopeful way forward on our journey of reconciliation.

Walking humbly on our journey of reconciliation also requires that Canadians unlearn much of what is commonly taken for granted as the history of our country. It was, in part, the task of the Royal Commission on Aboriginal Peoples (RCAP) to help Canadians both unlearn and relearn their country's history. The RCAP was a massive four-year undertaking during the mid-1990s that involved hundreds of public meetings in which commissioners heard thousands of accounts and stories from Aboriginal and non-Aboriginal people throughout Canada. More recent efforts to help cultivate a new understanding of our shared past and a way forward in our current relations are evident in the work of the TRC. Much like their RCAP predecessors, those involved in the TRC understand that Aboriginal stories must become an integral part of Canada's story if their work is to bring healing and hope.

In both of our courses, students learn to understand that language matters deeply because it shapes what and how we know; stories matter greatly because they reflect as well as form the worlds in which we live. We thus highlight that walking humbly along the path of reconciliation requires that we learn to use new language and to tell new stories. One scholar, Paulette Regan, has suggested that stories involving relations between Aboriginal peoples and the rest of Canada should "unsettle the settler within." As a non-Aboriginal participant in a number of reconciliation activities between church and Aboriginal groups, Regan "learned that reconciliation is not a goal but a place of encounter where all participants face our shared history honestly without minimizing the very real damage that has been done, even as we learn new decolonizing ways of working together that shift power and perceptions."[2] One of the most significant stories we need to unlearn, which we describe at greater length below, is the "myth of the savage." This myth needs to be unlearned not only because it reinforced the policies and practices that led to the creation of Indian residential schools in Canada, but

2. Regan, *Apology Feast*, 42.

also because it continues to inform the way many non-Aboriginal people in Canada think and speak about as well as act towards Aboriginal people in this country.

So how do we learn to walk in humility and acknowledge our lack of understanding in ways that will give us hope? Consider how those of us who are non-Aboriginal are apt to hear as well as cast the story of relations between Aboriginal and non-Aboriginal peoples in terms of conquered and conqueror, or victim and villain, and how our use of these categories leads many of us to ignore or discount the experiences, perspectives and stories of Aboriginal people altogether. This observation was brought home during a visit by the TRC class to Blue Quills First Nations College, a vibrant institution in St. Paul, Alberta, that once was an Indian residential school. The hospitality we received was warm and wonderful; we smudged and talked, some of us participated in a sweat and others engaged in rudimentary lessons in Cree. And we heard heart-breaking stories from survivors—former students who had lived at Blue Quills under its colonial, residential school regime. At the end of the day, however, the Elder talked with us and gestured to the campus. "Don't think of us as stuck in the past," he told us. "We're not there anymore. We've moved on." The "lesson" we experienced from the Elder was that if we continue to think of our collective history as a story of victims and villains, then we ourselves become part of a narrative that is essentially fixed, static and hopeless. In contrast, if we are to share new stories that give us hope, they must be stories—however difficult they might be to speak and hear—in which all people are treated with respect, dignity, and compassion.

The Challenge of Listening Compassionately

It is unfortunately the case that the majority of students in our courses are familiar with a less than hopeful story of relations between Aboriginal people and the rest of Canada. We often begin each course by asking students what comes to mind when they hear the terms "Aboriginal" or "native." Students invariably respond by sharing what they have heard in the news, read in their high school textbooks, or in a few cases what they have experienced. Given these sources of information, it is hardly surprising that students often paint a picture of poor, lazy, uneducated, violent, and broken people that appear to have little sense of hope and direction in their lives. Many students are therefore quite surprised to hear that this view of Aboriginal people has been shaped by a number of "colonial filters" passed down for over four centuries by our European ancestors. One such filter is the myth of the savage, while another that informs most historical, sociological, and legal understandings is the practice of narrowly defining "truth telling" through rational, objective, and neutral analysis and critique. Our view is that if reconciliation through compassionate listening is to redress our conflicted history, then our practices of truth telling and "critical dialogue" must include stories that embrace the oral histories, cultural and religious traditions, and legal concepts that are foundational to Indigenous peoples.[3]

As our students become open to honoring Aboriginal peoples' ways of being, knowing, and storytelling, they gradually learn to see that their own filters often act as blinders. Unlearning the myth of the savage then becomes possible as students come to understand that the societies of many First Peoples[4] of North America were well organized, culturally distinct, and economically viable prior to European contact.[5] Students also read and hear that most First Peoples shared the Indigenous view that humans inhabit a materially, socially, and spiritually integrated world ecosystem in which, ideally, we exist in equal and respectful relationship to every living and non-living being and entity in creation.[6] We contrast this worldview with that of sixteenth-century Western Europeans, whose perspective on the relationship between humans and nature was drawn largely from the Judeo-Christian teaching that humans were charged by God to have dominion over the earth and every living thing. Although there are obvious differences between the two worldviews, students are often quite surprised to learn that the French and the British developed the "myth of the savage" out of their worldview in part to legitimize the colonial expansion of their Christian empires. They see that the myth was based on a variety of measures that quantified a people's humanness and level of civilization, and therefore come to understand why, given these measures of "civilization," French as well as British explorers, missionaries, and government representatives commonly referred to the "Indians" as relatively innocent children of nature at best or savages at worst.[7] They are also confronted by the rather uncomfortable fact that defining the First Peoples of this land in this way justified any and all attempts by the French and the British to Christianize/

3. Regan, "Apology Feast," 43, 52.

4. The term "First People" is commonly used when speaking about the First Nations and the Inuit, and sometimes includes the Métis.

5. Dickason and McNab, *Canada's First Nations*, 4.

6. Bopp et al., *Sacred Tree*, 7.

7. Dickason, *Myth of the Savage*, 8.

civilize *l'Homme sauvage*, and that their hope in doing so was to eventually eradicate "the Indian problem" altogether. [8]

Being confronted by their own colonial preconceptions also unsettles students in a number of more positive and hopeful ways. For one, it enables them to see that the narrative of Canada does not have to be fixed and hopeless, but that it can and ought to be fully shared, active and hopeful. Many students also come to understand that they have never listened with compassionate hearts and minds to our whole history, and that this has prevented us all from being able to collectively grieve that which is lamentable and celebrate that which is noble and good in our shared past. As students learn to listen respectfully and compassionately to the stories, both past and present, of Aboriginal people in Canada, they also learn that the future of our journey together depends on how we choose to act in relation to one another now.

The Hope in Living Justly

Our hope is that our students will learn to know that it is a privilege to be invited into the life and story of another. As an Elder shared during one of the sociological issues classes, however, it is disrespectful and hurtful to expect a people to share their stories of pain and suffering over and over again and then fail to act. Simply listening to the story of another, however compassionate and sorrowful one might think they are being, traps the listener in a world in which they remain both isolated as well as insulated from the experience of the one who has told their story. In contrast, learning to listen compassionately with a heart that is committed to living justly frees us as individuals from the hopeless trap of living for ourselves. The desire to live justly not only opens our eyes to the common ties of our humanity that bind us, it also helps us begin to understand what justice and reconciliation look and feel like in very concrete, practical terms.

We also seek in our courses to challenge and invite students to humbly embrace the risks and uncertainty that flow from a commitment to live justly. For example, students learn to see how the compensation payments made to almost 80,000 residential school survivors as part of the 2006 settlement agreement with the government of Canada are contributing in some ways to the healing of individuals, families, and communities. They also learn to understand why it is so important for churches, communities, and the Canadian government to offer formal apologies for the pain and

8. LaRocque, "Conversations with Olive Dickason," 81.

suffering their actions and those of their ancestors have caused for generations of Aboriginal people. However, we also seek to challenge students to reflect on why the offering of formal apologies and monetary payments are not sufficient to bring about justice and reconciliation. Particularly when they are in the presence of someone who is telling their story, students begin to see why formal apologies offered by the churches and the Canadian government, powerful and eloquent as they may be, are woefully inadequate if they are not offered in the context of ongoing, mutually respectful relationships. "The burden of this experience has been on your shoulders for far too long," Prime Minister Stephen Harper told former students of Indian Residential Schools in the government's 2008 apology. He continued, "The burden is properly ours as a Government, and as a country. . . . You have been working on recovering from this experience for a long time and in a very real sense, we are now joining you on this journey."[9] Prime Minister Harper's apology certainly appeared to express sorrow as well as convey the government's commitment to join this country's Aboriginal people on a journey of healing and reconciliation. Unfortunately, subsequent actions by the Harper government indicate that his apology was less than sincere and that his government's commitment to move positively forward in their relations with this country's Aboriginal people was short lived.

Examining the lives of this and many other similar "apologies and promises" enables us to impress upon our students that living justly in relation to Aboriginal people is not simply a matter of humbly and compassionately listening to their stories, offering an apology for our complicity in their ongoing suffering, and agreeing out of our position of power and privilege to take on their burdens. Rather, our students learn to understand that living justly and creating hope requires that we commit ourselves to *living fully within and then beyond our apologies* in ongoing relationship.

We therefore find Paulette Regan's insights on "living the apology" to be instructive for students, teachers, and Christians generally. She sees reconciliation not as a one-time experience or transaction, but as *critical pedagogical practice* that is a continuing and fully respectful, learning encounter. She describes an apology feast in Hazleton, British Columbia, in which representatives of the United Church of Canada and the Canadian government met with Gitxsan survivors of Indian residential schools in a reconciliation potlatch. An irony here was that the traditional potlatch ceremony was abolished by the Canadian government in 1885 in an attempt to "civilize" Indian peoples. In a further inversion, the Gitxsan elders asked the Canadian representatives to act as hosts of the potlatch, thus moving

9. Harper, "Statement of Apology."

the apology from Western to Gitxsan legal protocols. While this potlatch was only a beginning, Regan describes how the encounter was an experiential, pedagogical tool that required Canadian participants to relinquish their power, thereby enabling everyone to engage in deep dialogue about historical injustice on indigenous terms. "If reconciliation is to be more than a soothing balm for white guilt," Regan argues, then "Canadians must offer more than token 'gifts.'" Regan suggests that Indigenous legal and oral traditions "should be central to reconciliation processes because they are uniquely well suited to the deeply transformative work of authentic reconciliation between peoples."[10] The experiences and lessons of the reconciliation feast described above illustrate well the kinds of learning we hope occur in our classes as well as the everyday lives of our students.

On the occasions in which we discuss these issues in our classes, well-meaning, thoughtful students sometimes ask, "When can we stop saying 'sorry'?" Some students ask the question out of irritation, out of a sense of impatience that the apologetic gestures made so far have not been accepted as sufficient. Others ask it more out of a sense of resignation and weariness since they feel that the task is so immense and the problems so intractable that it seems hopeless to even try to embark on the journey. Their recognition of the difficulty of the work is not unwarranted, of course. In a presentation to one of our classes, the chair of the TRC, Justice Murray Sinclair, told us that Aboriginal peoples were under the regime of residential schools for seven generations, and that it will take seven generations to undo the damage and to heal.

Given this formidable challenge, we think it important to frame the call to reconciliation in the language of hope. Approaching reconciliation not as a distant goal but a place of immediate, hopeful encounter[11] invites students and teachers to privilege ongoing relations and face-to-face communication in much the same way that Aboriginal people have long passed on traditional knowledge and teachings. It also places truth telling and reconciliation in the context of loving relationships, and indeed many of our students attest to how they have been blessed by the smudge, the sweat, the pipe ceremony, listening to the stories of their Aboriginal sisters and brothers, and learning from the wisdom of the Elders. The way forward in all our relations embraces the risks and relinquishes power by seeing the process of reconciliation as gift and as grace. There is a gospel here, good and hopeful news for those who are open to walking humbly, listening compassionately, and living justly—hand in hand with all our neighbors.

10. Regan, "Apology Feast," 49.

11. Ibid., 42.

Reflection Questions

1. Reflect for a moment on the words and images that come to mind when you hear the terms *Aboriginal*, *native*, and *Indian*, and also where in your life you think those words and images came from. In what ways might those words and images affect the way you think about and relate to Aboriginal people in your everyday life?
2. Many New Testament stories describe the Pharisees ignoring certain individuals or groups of people, and sometimes that they even treated them with disdain, because they were "other" than Jewish or they were simply judged to not be religiously pure (i.e., the Samaritan, the woman caught in adultery, the Roman soldier). How are the attitudes and actions of many Canadians towards Aboriginal people similar to those of the Pharisees?
3. Many of Jesus' own people, including some that were very close to him, were critical of the way he related to certain "types" of people. In what ways does Micah's invitation provide insight into the way Jesus related to these "others"?
4. Read and reflect on some of the recent public apologies to Aboriginal peoples (from Prime Minister Stephen Harper on behalf of the Government of Canada, for example, or from the United Church of Canada). How do these statements lay out a way forward to reconciliation? What commitments were made? What challenges do you see in living out these apologies?

Recommended Reading

Brant Castellano, Marlene, et al., editors. *From Truth to Reconciliation: Transforming the Legacy of Residential Schools.* Ottawa: Aboriginal Healing Foundation, 2008.

Canada. *Final Report of the Royal Commission on Aboriginal Peoples.* Ottawa: Queens Printer Press, 1996.

Long, David, and Olive Dickason, editors. *Visions of the Heart: Aboriginal Issues in Canada.* 3rd ed. Toronto: Oxford University Press, 2010.

Regan, Paulette. *Unsettling the Settler Within: Indian Residential Schools, Truth Telling, and Reconciliation in Canada.* Vancouver: University of British Columbia Press, 2010.

Bibliography

Aboriginal Affairs and Northern Development Canada. *Report of the Royal Commission on Aboriginal Peoples*. Ottawa: Queens Printer Press, 1996.

Bach, Richard. *Illusions: The Adventures of a Reluctant Messiah*. New York: Delacorte, 1977.

Bopp, Judie, et al. *The Sacred Tree: Reflections on Native American Spirituality*. Lethbridge: Four Worlds International Institute, 1984.

Dickason, Olive Patricia. *The Myth of the Savage: And the Beginnings of French Colonialism in the Americas*. Toronto: Oxford University Press, 1984.

Dickason, Olive Patricia, and David McNab. *Canada's First Nations: A History of Founding Peoples from Earliest Time*. 4th ed. Toronto: Oxford University Press, 2009.

Harper, Stephen. "Statement of Apology—to Former Students of Indian Residential Schools." June 11, 2008. Online: http://www.aadnc-aandc.gc.ca/eng/1100100015644/1100100015649.

LaRocque, Emma. "Conversations with Olive Dickason—A Tribute to a National Treasure." *Native Studies Review* 21/2 (2012) 81–84.

Regan, Paulette. "An Apology Feast in Hazelton: Indian Residential Schools, Reconciliation, and Making Space for Indigenous Legal Traditions." In *Indigenous Legal Traditions*, by the Law Commission of Canada, 40–76. Vancouver: UBC Press, 2007.

———. *Unsettling the Settler Within: Indian Residential Schools, Truth Telling, and Reconciliation in Canada* Vancouver: UBC Press, 2010.

17

Educating for Public Life

Angus Brook

> For, inasmuch as every family is a part of a state, and these relationships are the parts of a family, and the excellence of the part must have regard to the excellence of the whole... children must be trained by education with an eye to the constitution, if the excellences of either of them are supposed to make any difference in the excellences of the state. And they must make a difference: for the children grow up to be citizens . . .[1]

Introduction

This essay will address the topic of educating for public life. As with any short text, it must approach the topic from a limited point of view and with a limited objective in mind. The claim that education is intrinsically tied to public life is associated with the earliest accounts of education in ancient Greece and is taken up by both the sophists and the philosophers in different ways. This early account of education has been one of the most dominant forces in the history of educational theory: its influence can be traced from ancient Greece to the development of the liberal arts in Rome, which in turn was taken up in medieval education,

1. Aristotle, *Politics*, 1260^{b}9–1260^{b}20.

was dominant at the time of the first universities in Europe, and is the theoretical underpinning of the idea of liberal education in the development of Northern American colleges. This, then, will be the limit of this essay: an examination of the ancient, medieval, and some of the contemporary arguments regarding liberal education—an education for public life. I will be taking up and offering a brief account of the liberal education tradition as an educating for public life through an examination of the philosophical arguments offered by some of the greatest liberal educational theorists in Western history.

Arguments about Educating for Public Life

Plato: Education as a Freeing Up for Public Life

The idea of educating for public life was a common and often celebrated feature of ancient Greek civilization founded upon their ideal of a free citizen with the leisure to study.[2] There were, however, at least two distinct approaches to educating for public life in ancient Greece; the rhetorical model of the sophists and the philosophical model of those like Socrates and Plato.

The sophists, or those who called themselves "wise," travelled extensively around the Mediterranean offering public lectures much like the inspirational speakers in our contemporary world, but in their travels were generally employed and housed by wealthy families to train their children in the art of rhetoric, the art of convincing others of their position in public democratic debate or in the context of legal disputes.[3] This mode of approaching education for public life was primarily oriented towards the self-interest of the powerful, of winning court cases and convincing others to agree with one's interests in democratic debate.[4] Educating for public life, within the sophistical tradition, signified an education in the basic arts such as grammar, law, and rhetoric with an orientation towards self-interested engagement in public life.

Amongst those who reacted against the self-interested model of educating for public life, Plato provided an alternative account of education. In Plato's case, the account of education for public life was reoriented towards a notion of freeing up a human being, through the investigation of reality and

2. See Kimball, *Orators and Philosophers*, for an excellent overview of this view of education.

3. Dillon and Gergel, *Greek Sophists*, x–xiii.

4. This is clearly articulated in Thrasymachus' arguments in Plato's *Republic*.

a pursuit of virtue, for an appropriately reasoned commitment to public life. Plato's philosophical account of education, provided in the *Republic*, proved to be the foundation for a model of educating for public life within a love of truth, a commitment to a good human life (a life of virtue), and a notion of contribution to the common good.

In the *Republic* Plato provides the infamous allegory of the cave in which he describes the process of becoming wise, which is also about becoming truly human, and also at the same time about the nature of education.[5] The allegory, to put it in modern terms, works in a similar way to going to a movie theatre. When we enter a movie theatre, we are engrossed in the images on the screen in front of us and therein we suspend our judgments about what we see and take those images to be true even if what we see, such as the contents of a science fiction movie, are patently fictional. We know that the movie is fictional and yet, in our engrossment in what we experience on the screen, we can't help but treat the movie as if it were true.

Plato's allegory parallels our experience of a movie theatre except he thinks that our physical or sensuous experiences in general—not just in a movie theatre—lead us to suspend our judgment about the apparent reality of our experiences.[6] This engrossment in the content of our physical experiences often leads us to treat difference and change as the basic characteristic of reality and therein conclude that the issues that concern us in public life, like piety, justice, friendships, and so on, are merely matters of custom. In more modern terminology we might say that Plato claimed that where we base our conception of reality on our physical and sensuous experience alone we arrive at the view that our values and beliefs are relative to culture or are merely subjective.

Plato thinks that the position that promotes the rule of custom—or ethical and cultural relativism—is a dangerous position to hold if one is to be truly committed to public life because your education will only be oriented towards your own self-interest and will tend to simply reproduce the rule of the powerful. Someone educated by the sophists will not be concerned with the common good or the needs of all individuals in the community.

Plato's allegory of the cave can be read, as such, as an explicit rejection of the possibility that a subjective or even culturally relative education will properly educate for public life. Rather, according to Plato, the first stage of *paideia*—of education for public life—is to detach oneself from the appearances of things and to realize that custom or culture is an insufficient explanation of our need for education and, moreover, our commitment to

5. Plato, *Republic*, 514a–519d.

6. Ibid., 514b.

public life. The first stage of education for public life, in the allegory of the cave, is thus to turn one's back on appearances and to seek the common ground or unifying concepts that underlie our need for education.[7]

The second stage of education entails the movement from physical appearances and experience to an understanding of concepts, in particular concepts that enable us to understand the reality we all share and the moral values and goals that all humans hold in common. Education, in this sense, is all about a search for the common ground, the unifying principles that underlie our different experiences of the world.[8] For Plato, then, education entails a twofold commitment towards common or universal concepts: (i) concepts that enable us to know the truth about the reality in which we live, and (ii) concepts that enable us to live well.

The third stage of education indicated in the allegory of the cave is transformative; that is, when we learn about reality and about a good human life the truth we find transforms our sense of self and therein our approach to life.[9] In learning about these common or universal concepts we begin to know ourselves beyond changing appearances and this frees us from our slavery to appearances and change; we are freed from the appearance of custom or cultural relativism. This freedom is not empty of content, for we are freed from appearances for the sake of the truth, goodness, beauty, etc.

The fourth and final stage of education according to Plato's allegory of the cave then flows from freedom to a commitment to the attainment of good in others. A person who has been freed from their engrossment with physical appearances will be able to commit fully and appropriately to a public life, for they have come to know themselves, the reality in which they live, and the goods that are common to all humans. In other words, we might say that education for public life according to Plato entails being freed from a particular view, whether it be individual or cultural, in order to gain an appropriately universal reasoned and moral view of human nature upon which one can fully and freely commit oneself to the common good.

Aristotle: Education and the Public Pursuit of Happiness

Aristotle's approach to educating for public life is inherently tied up with his view of the nature of human persons. Human persons, he argued, are born with certain potentialities or capacities to achieve purposes and goals. It is the task of a human life to make these purposes and goals actual. The means

7. Ibid., 518d.
8. Ibid., 519a–d.
9. Ibid., 518c.

by which we attain the goals and purposes that are intrinsic to our nature is what we call education. What, then, are the goals of human nature?

The first and essential goal of human nature is reason. Humans are reasoning animals according to Aristotle; that is, we are animals who are defined as different to other animals because of our capacity for reason. In the *Nicomachean Ethics*, Aristotle distinguishes what it is in reason that defines the basic goals of human life: "animals lead for the most part a life of nature. . . . Man has reason . . . and for this reason nature, habit, reason must be in harmony with one another . . . (and this) . . . is the work of education . . ."[10] There are, as such, three intrinsic goals of education: (i) to educate our natural inclinations, (ii) the education of good habits (virtues), and (iii) the education of reason itself (wisdom and prudence). The final goal of education—the harmony of these three goals—is to become happy or to flourish as a human being (*eudemonia*).

Rather than provide an extended interpretation and argument about what Aristotle will say about education, it is worthwhile focusing on why Aristotle will claim that all education is fundamentally an education for public life. Below you will find a "standard form" argument that will provide you with a synopsis of Aristotle's argument about educating for public life:

P_1. All humans by nature desire the good (happiness).

P_2. Happiness requires the formation (education) of good moral and intellectual habits.

P_3. Humans are by nature social (we are dependent upon other humans for our happiness).

P_4. Human happiness will only be found through our relations with others (public life).

Therefore, education must be an education for public life in which students are provided with formation in the necessary moral and intellectual habits that will enable them to flourish as individuals and to commit to the flourishing (or happiness) of other humans.

It is important to note here that where Aristotle and Plato talk about the common good they are not referring to anything in addition to the individuals who form the society. Humans require each other; we depend upon each other for the pursuit of a good life (a flourishing or happy life). For this reason, the common good refers to this interdependency in the pursuit

10. Aristotle, *Nicomachean Ethics*, 1332b[<superscript b]4–10.

of happiness, and further, the need for society to be structured in such a way that it enables flourishing for all of its citizens. To take part in public life, for Aristotle and Plato, is as such to commit to a mutually supportive pursuit of a good life in community with others. To be educated for public life, therefore, is to be educated for the common good.

The quote provided at the beginning of this short essay, from Aristotle's *Politics*, aptly sums up Aristotle's view of educating for public life. The quote, it seems to me, suggests that human happiness (in the sense of a fully flourishing human life) is not merely dependent upon our social life, but is actually achieved within a deep and rich commitment to others in our contribution to the public life of the particular community in which we are citizens. Education, as such, is not merely a moral and intellectual formation within a society for public life but is also more specifically an education for public life within the particular constitution to which we belong as a citizen.

St. Thomas: A Universal Christian Vision of Education for Public Life

The approaches to educating for public life discussed thus far were both philosophical and non-Christian. However, both Plato (via St. Augustine) and Aristotle (via the Islamic philosophers) were of fundamental importance to the development of the universal Christian vision of education for public life developed by St. Thomas Aquinas.

St. Thomas Aquinas is infamous for his synthetic approach to thinking and arguing; his ability to bring together all of the great philosophical and theological arguments in history, whether they came from a pagan, Jewish, Muslim, or Christian background. Of all the philosophers prior to St. Thomas, it will be Aristotle, Plato, and St. Augustine that have the most influence on his approach to education.

From Aristotle, Thomas will take the view that education is primarily the formation of potentialities for ends (or purposes),[11] that humans are sociable by nature, and that the final and unifying end of education is happiness.[12] From Plato, Thomas will take the view that education for moral virtues entails the formation of the cardinal virtues of temperance, courage, justice, and prudence.[13] From Augustine, Thomas will also take the notion of a necessary relation between happiness, God, and the theological

11. Thomas Aquinas, *Disputed Questions on Truth*, vol. 2, q. 11: "The Teacher."

12. Thomas Aquinas, *Summa Theologiae*, Ia, q. 117; IaIIae, q. 1.

13. MacIntyre, *God, Philosophy, Universities*, 87.

virtues.[14] These will all serve as important points in Thomas' development of an implicit notion of educating for public life.

All human actions according to Thomas aim at happiness. However, to become truly happy humans first need to have our potentiality for happiness developed and formed through education. Education, as such, is the means by which humans learn (or are taught) the necessary conditions for happiness. Human happiness is achieved in two interrelated ways: the first, imperfect happiness, is found in human nature itself; the second, perfect happiness, is found in attaining an object of eternal or transcendental happiness (an object of religious faith).[15]

Imperfect happiness requires, in the same vein as Aristotle's *Nicomachean Ethics* and *Politics*, the formation of moral and intellectual habits necessary for human fulfilment in community. In this respect, educating for public life intrinsically contains three key interrelated phases: (i) the formation of individual moral and intellectual habits, (ii) the formation of habits necessary for human social life, e.g., friendship, family, moral virtues, etc., and (iii) the formation of habits necessary for public life.[16]

Thomas then divides these necessary habits into two types: those of practical reason , which are oriented towards the good, and those of theoretical reason, which are oriented towards the truth.[17] The practical dimension of educating for public life revolves primarily around the formation of the cardinal virtues. Prudence (or practical wisdom) is the foundation of our human reasoned commitment to the public good through action. Courage and temperance, in their own fashion, enable humans to act well in relation to other humans (and themselves) in ruling and measuring human appetites and desires. Finally, justice enables the commitment to other humans through action and social relations; to give to others their due.[18] The cardinal virtues are the basis for a proper commitment to the common good and to human happiness—but these virtues must be learned. Educating for public life, in the first instance, is a matter of acquiring through teaching (and learning) the cardinal virtues.

Human happiness also depends upon the formation of our capacity for intellectual habits, those habits or virtues that orient us towards the truth. The final end of truth, and a necessary condition of happiness, is the point at which the intellect arrives at God (or something like God), which serves

14. Ibid.,87.

15. Thomas Aquinas, *Summa Theologiae*, IaIIae, q. 1.

16. Thomas Aquinas, *Commentary on Aristotle's Nicomachean Ethics*, 3.

17. Ibid.

18. Thomas Aquinas, *Summa Theologiae*, IIaIIae, q. 58, art. 1.

as an ultimate explanation of the universe and human life and therein becomes the ultimate object of human happiness.[19] It is important to note here that this ultimate end of the intellect is not a purely solitary activity, for humans are by nature social animals. It follows from this that any discussion of ultimate happiness cannot be completely detached from public life. This is why, for example, Thomas argues that the virtue of religion (or proper religion) is a communal and relational virtue that falls under the cardinal virtue of justice; it is done in public with other humans for the sake of a right relationship with God.[20]

It is at this point that reason and faith emerge as the pivotal co-conditions of human happiness and thus educating for public life. In the *Summa Contra Gentiles* Thomas argues that both faith and reason are necessary for our search for the ultimate truths about ourselves, a moral life, and the universe, truths upon which all of our happiness rests.[21] Reason is a necessary condition for our pursuit of the truth as humans. Faith, in turn, is a necessary condition for our access to truths that surpass our capacity to attain via reason. These truths of faith, while they surpass our capacity to attain via reason, and that we hold by assent and trust, are nonetheless absolutely essential for human happiness.

The final dimension of education, in this sense, involves the mutual interdependency of the cardinal and theological virtues. The theological virtue of faith, according to Thomas, supplements and fulfills the virtue of reason (or wisdom). On the other hand, the theological virtue of charity underpins all moral virtues, in particular the cardinal virtues.[22] Human happiness, both imperfect and perfect, are thus intertwined. Our imperfect happiness, as humans, is a necessary condition of and points towards perfect happiness. At the same time, however, the hope for perfect happiness, via the theological virtues, serves as an educational foundation for our pursuit of human happiness, e.g., faith, hope, and charity serve as instructional guides in the pursuit of human happiness.

For Thomas, as it was for Aristotle, education is at its very basis an educating for public life. For this reason, Thomas' account of education is firmly oriented towards teaching and learning the moral and intellectual habits necessary for a public life of commitment to the common good. For Thomas, unlike Aristotle, educating for public life also transcends human nature without contradicting it. Education, in short, is universalized; it

19. Thomas Aquinas, *Commentary on Aristotle's Nicomachean Ethics*, 56–57.

20. Thomas Aquinas, *Summa Theologiae*, IIaIIae, q. 81.

21. Thomas Aquinas, *Summa Contra Gentiles*, bk. 1, chs. 3–8.

22. McCabe, *On Aquinas*, 92.

recognises the universal desire for happiness in all humans and recognizes the universal importance of religion as an intrinsic aspect of the pursuit of happiness in the public life of a society. Educating for public life, for Thomas, is the pursuit of truth, goodness, and beauty that unifies and orders human communities towards the universe and the universal.

Key Issues in Educating for Public Life in the Contemporary World

It appears difficult to reconcile the ancient and medieval accounts of educating for public life with our contemporary Western democratic societies, given our emphasis on individuality, rights, and freedom. Nonetheless, it is quite clear with some critical reflection and analysis that to be an active and engaged citizen in contemporary democratic societies does require certain moral and intellectual habits. In this section of the essay I will briefly point out two themes of contemporary theory about educating for public life.

A democratic society requires certain moral and intellectual habits to function well. John Dewey, for example, claimed that a democracy relies on the formation of normative habits of cooperation, industry, and dependability,[23] and elsewhere suggests that education is at its heart about the formation of intellectual habits, such as critical thinking, reflection, and sustained inquiry. John Dewey claims that these habits are all necessary conditions of full participation in democratic life.[24] Likewise, Martha Nussbaum claims that education for public life in a democratic society requires such intellectual habits as critical thinking and reflection, of a capacity to argue and analyze, and to understand the basic principles of democratic government.[25] Martha Nussbaum also argues that citizens in democratic society must be educated for public life with particular moral habits or dispositions in mind, habits such as the capacity to value the equality of human life and a disposition to care for other humans.[26] In short, even with its emphasis on individuality, rights, and freedom, a democratic society nonetheless requires of its citizens that they be educated for public life through the formation of certain intellectual and moral habits.

23. Boisvert, *John Dewey*, 67; see also John Dewey, *Democracy and Education*, ch. 7.

24. Dewey, *How We Think*, 13.

25. Nussbaum, *Not for Profit*, 26.

26. Ibid.

A second key feature of our contemporary world is the rapid changes brought about by new technologies and the corresponding capacity to exchange and store information. This has led some to ask what qualities we need to promote in educating for public life in a "super-complex" society.[27] There is a danger, in a world saturated with information communications technologies, that the citizens of society may become lost in the sheer amount of data available to them and may even become unable to tell the difference between information and meaning, fact and explanation. For this reason, it has become increasingly apparent that educating for public life, in particular for work life, requires a formation of intellectual habits oriented towards a mastery of information.[28]

Conclusion

This short essay has attempted to provide a brief introduction to the classical arguments about educating for public life. In the process, I have tried to draw out some of the key elements of educating for public life, which include: (i) a need to be freed from subjectivism and relativism which prevents our commitment to public life; (ii) a need to learn key moral and intellectual habits which enable a full commitment to the common good via public life; and (iii) a need to recognize that the human pursuit of happiness, pursued through for formation of intellectual, moral, and religious habits, is the basis of educating for public life.

Reflection Questions

Plato's theory of educating for public life hinges on the argument that we need to be freed from our individual and cultural opinions about reality and the good life, which prevent us from appropriately and freely committing to the common good. This suggests some further questions for reflection:

1. Is education primarily about freeing us from our individual or cultural perspectives?
2. Do we need to be freed from our individual and cultural perspectives to be properly committed to public life?
3. Is public life about pursuing the common good or is public life about the self-interested relations between individuals?

27. Barnett, "Learning for an Unknown Future."
28. Star and Hammer, "Teaching Generic Skills," 240.

Aristotle's account of education suggests that we are educated for public life only insofar as we are educated in the necessary moral and intellectual virtues required for a commitment to the common good as it is expressed in our particular community's constitution. This claim suggests that we need to ask some further questions:

1. Do we need to be educated in moral and intellectual virtues in order to take part in public life?
2. Does education need to be specifically tailored to the constitution of our community or nation?

Questions about Thomas Aquinas' account of education for public life:

1. Is religious faith just as important as moral and intellectual habits in public life?
2. Should religious education be included as an essential feature of educating for public life?

Recommended Reading

Coulter, David L., Gary D. Fenstermacher, and John R.Wiens. *Why Do We Educate?: Renewing the Conversation*. Hoboken, NJ: Wiley-Blackwell, 2009. See particularly chapter 4.

Dewey, John. *Democracy and Education*. New York: Floating Press, 2009.

Kimball, Bruce A. *Orators and Philosophers: A History of the Idea of Liberal Education*. New York: Teachers College Press, 1986.

MacIntyre, Alisdair. *God, Philosophy, Universities: A Selective History of the Catholic Philosophical Tradition*. Lanham, MD: Rowman & Littlefield, 2009.

Newman, John Henry. *The Idea of a University*. New Haven, CT: Yale University Press, 1996.

Nussbaum, Martha. *Cultivating Humanity: A Classical Defense of Reform in Liberal Education*. Cambridge, MA: Harvard University Press, 2003.

———. *Not for Profit: Why Democracy Needs the Humanities*. Princeton, NJ: Princeton University Press, 2010.

Bibliography

Aristotle. *Nicomachean Ethics* and *Politics*. In *The Complete Works of Aristotle: The Revised Oxford Translation*, edited by Jonathan Barnes. Princeton, NJ: Princeton University Press, 1995.

Barnett, Ronald. "Learning for an Unknown Future." *Higher Education Research & Development* 23/3 (2004) 247–60.

Boisvert, Raymond. *John Dewey: Rethinking Our Time*. New York: State University of New York Press, 1997.

Dewey, John. *Democracy and Education*. New York: Floating Press, 2009.

———. *How We Think*. London: D.C. Heath, 1909.

Dillon, John, and Tania Gergel. *The Greek Sophists*. London: Penguin, 2003.

Kimball, Bruce A. *Orators and Philosophers: A History of the Idea of Liberal Education*. New York: Teachers College Press, 1986.

MacIntyre, Alisdair. *God, Philosophy, Universities: A Selective History of the Catholic Philosophical Tradition*. Lanham, MD: Rowman & Littlefield, 2009.

McCabe, Herbert. *On Aquinas*. London: Continuum, 2008.

Nussbaum, Martha. *Not for Profit: Why Democracy Needs the Humanities*. Princeton, NJ: Princeton University Press, 2010.

Plato. *Republic*. Translated by G. M. A. Grube. In *Complete Works*, edited by John M. Cooper. Indianapolis: Hackett, 1997.

Star, Cassandra, and Sara Hammer. "Teaching Generic Skills: Eroding the Higher Purpose of Universities, or an Opportunity for Renewal?" *Oxford Review of Education* 34/2 (2008) 237–51.

Thomas Aquinas. *Commentary on Aristotle's Nicomachean Ethics*. Translated by C. I. Litzinger. Notre Dame, IN: Dumb Ox Books, 1993.

———. *Disputed Questions on Truth*. Translated by James V. McGlynn. Chicago: Regnery, 1953.

———. *Summa Contra Gentiles*. Translated by Anton C. Pegis. Notre Dame, IN: University of Notre Dame Press, 2009.

———. *Summa Theologiae*. Notre Dame, IN: Ave Maria Press, 1948.

18

The School as Community

Learning for Service in an Era of Educational Narcissism

STEPHEN FYSON

The Context

SCHOOL STUDENTS ARE PERSONS who, like all of us, desire purpose and hope in life. This search for purpose and hope is carried into the classroom. However, much of what happens in Western-style classrooms today works against learning for such heart level meaning. This is because current Western secular thinking and teaching practice is often based on rationalism, individualism, and self-advancement (often expressed as being "financially secure").[1]

Rationalism in this context is that form of science that is sometimes called "naturalism." It is science that assumes the only reality is the physical one, i.e., there is nothing in existence other than physical elements in combination forming various forms and structures of being. Therefore, we live

1. The focus of this paper is to review the impact of these things pastorally in terms of classroom practice rather than a theoretical exploration. See the bibliography for philosophical readings.

in a closed-box universe where there is no guidance from a greater Mind of any kind and we are a result of *unguided* evolutionary processes.

A consequence of this thinking is that in the Western-style classrooms around the world, anything to do with deep purpose, meaning and calling in life is increasingly seen as an "add-on" activity, rather than being integrated into the core business of the content and processes of teaching and learning. In many places, the attempt to do anything beyond relativistic process-based ethics courses is quickly diminishing (like in my home state of New South Wales, Australia).[2]

Without conceptualizing life in more profound terms, teachers are left with pragmatism ("do what works for you") in discussions about morality in the classroom. Of course, such pragmatism helps to promote the student being encouraged that they are the center of their decision-making universe, and individualism becomes more prevalent.

Individualism at its source is an outworking of the temptation to make ourselves the center of the moral universe as described in Genesis 3:6–7. It is the lie so close to the truth that it is an incredibly appealing lie. We are respected enough by the Creator to be allowed to decide for ourselves how we shall live. The consequences of these decisions are therefore appropriately ours (although as faithful sons and daughters of Adam and Eve, we like to try to "pass the buck'"—see Genesis 3).

The implications for the classroom are again profound. It seems that teachers can promote hope based on a historically revealed and personal faith (we do not have time to compare other faith propositions in this essay), or else give up on any systematic promotion of anything but individually focused reasons for advancement. My observations over thirty years is that it is the second belief system that has become increasingly prevalent in school curriculum at large, and even faith-based schools are struggling to counter it in the conceptualization of their subjects and topics of study.[3]

Self-advancement is caught by our students in Western-style classrooms when students learn, however subtly or explicitly, that they are simply physical matter making their way through an unguided universe,[4] and their decisions are therefore the acceptable center of the moral universe.

2. For example, trying to define the good becomes difficult, if not impossible; see Hare, *Why Bother Being Good*.

3. Brian Hill outlined the failure of schools to come to grips with the importance of teachers not drawing on the deeper issues of life (beyond the individual) in "Talking Point at Last."

4. I do not have time to explore the lack of coherent internal frame of reference in assuming that individuals can make autonomous decisions in a totally closed and unguided universe. See for example O'Hear, *Beyond Evolution*; and Plantinga, *Where the Conflict Really Lies*.

I am not in any way suggesting that we should not be interested in the progress of individuals in their learning. I am stating that the biblically assumed *purpose* within the teaching and learning process is love of God and brother and sister.[5] It is the process of becoming more mature in this love that we are called to celebrate.

Kenneth Sirotnik summarized the tension well when he noted the tendency to focus on technologically based teaching and learning such that:

> We are apt to reject the importance of community in favor of ourselves and the importance of ethical foundations in favor of radical individualism. This will be a series of serious mistakes . . .[6]

I suggest that one of the most important aspects of community—using whatever gifts we have to serve others[7]—needs to be rediscovered in our schools. To aid in this process, common practices that promote individualized self-advancement (which is called "educational narcissism"') are described. Suggestions about how to invite students into learning for service are then presented. Note the assumption in this essay is that this endeavor is just as necessary for teachers working in Christian schools or other schools.

A Summary of Educational Narcissism in the Classroom

The first thing to note is that educational narcissism cannot be described by simply reviewing whether the students are being compliant or whether they are achieving well in the tests that are being given. Students can stay compliant and successful in tests, particularly in a well-managed school, but hide their non-engagement. One researcher described the subtle form of how these experiences were manifested for emerging adolescents:

> Although most students are not openly rebellious or misbehaving, they clearly identify ways in which schooling is alienating and unrewarding . . . [they] are working in structures that thwart.[8]

5. Ps 119; Matt 22:37–39.

6. Goodlad, Soder, and Sirotnik, *Moral Dimensions of Teaching*, 321. Also see Twenge and Campbell, *Narcissism Epidemic*, "Introduction."

7. 1 Pet 4:10–11.

8. Hatton, "Middle School Students' Perceptions of school organization." *Unicorn*, 21, 17–26."

A Checklist of "Ifs" to Test for Educational Narcissism

Taking the lead from Henri J Nouwen,[9] I suggest the following if we wish to test whether teaching is promoting educational narcissism in a classroom:

- *If* the teaching is equated with the transfer of information (of cognitive only knowledge and skills) . . .
- *If* the result of teaching is me, the student, getting ahead of those who do not have as much information as me . . .
- *If* I as the student never have to consider, or more strongly, be confronted by the implications of what I might do with the information that I have—particularly by my peers or parents . . .
- *If* it is assumed that the process of information "sharing" is on a one-way path—that I only need to discover the agenda of what the expert knows in all things . . .
- *If* learning is seen as being apart from the rest of life that involves meaningful relationships with people . . .
- *If* learning means that I can hate my teacher if I choose, and ignore the needs of my fellow students or anyone else in my life world . . .
- *If*, in the quest to *not* become meaningfully involved with others, particularly my teacher (yuk!), I assume that I do not have to review any insights that might cause me pain in any way . . .

Then sadly we have a teaching and learning environment that promotes educational narcissism. That is, for many of our young people at school, the teaching is about information transfer according to a rigid agenda that is shallowly presented in an environment of competition that is targeted solely on self-advancement. Such self-aggrandizement is the opposite of the purpose of teaching as a Christian, which has as its goal "service of God and His creatures, so that His justice and *shalom* might be at least pastorally restored."[10]

Moreover, in the context of educational narcissism, *the students do not have to think deeply about what they believe and why they believe it.* To do so would bring into question the focus and purpose of the teaching and learning relationship. This would take the instructional relationship into the realm of teaching, which the overly fragmented and shallow world of Western secular education is not equipped to do.

9. Nouwen, *Creative Ministry*, ch. 1.

10. Blomberg, "Knowing and Learning," 84.

The problem that we have been describing can be summarized well by this quote from Hargreaves and Ryan:

> The quest for self-fulfillment has, in many respects, been subsumed in a sea of individualism and isolation. . . . They experience this alone in the culture of individualism or within the refuge of a student counterculture. What they experience little of is care, concern or community.[11]

We will now explore what might help in the classroom.

Elements to Promote Service Learning

I suggest that two questions about learning—*what is it that I am actually trying to learn?* and *why am I learning it?*—are critical if we want to achieve meaningfulness in learning as a starting point for preventing educational narcissism. Moreland and Beckwith noted in the early centuries of Christianity, focusing on the truth and wisdom in Jesus was the basis of learning wisdom, and suggested that:

> Our schools need to recapture and propagate this broader understanding of following Christ if they are to be thoroughly Christian in their approach to education.[12]

What is being suggested here is the lack of deep learning when schools become too focused on cognitive only knowledge and skills, overspecialization, and competitive self-advancement. Others have explored the deeper philosophical and sociological considerations of this lack of focus on wisdom within our classrooms.[13] Below is a more pastoral description of a teacher who can be holistic in their conceptualization of teaching and learning and holistic in conceptualizing the content and contexts in which this occurs.[14]

For some schools, attempts at introducing such holism come in the form of extra-curricular activities and programs. With teachers who care for the deeper things of life, these activities can have a profound impact on the life orientation learning for many students. However, the thesis in this

11. Hargreaves and Ryan, *Schooling for Change*, 32

12. Moreland and Beckwith, Series Preface in *Psychology in the Spirit*, 15.

13. See for example Blomberg, *Wisdom and Curriculum.*

14. The need for students to be involved in more than information and skill acquisition was well first described in recent times in Wolterstoroff, *Educating for Responsible Action.*

essay is that such elements can be integrated into the overall social regularities of school life. Some of these key features will now be described more fully.

The Holism of Heart, Heads, and Hands

One way of describing educational holism is that there is a focus on soft hearts (a humble spirit), strong minds (deep thinking), and serving hands (making a difference in the world, from within the classroom and outside of it).[15]

A. The Relational Holism of a Soft Heart

One way of expressing deep and meaningful learning is that it is "heart learning." Basically this is a learning environment where the teacher models an appropriate humility in the process of teaching that is evidenced in providing a certainty about how to demonstrate respect and safety.

A soft-hearted teacher is concerned about the life orientation of their students whilst setting boundaries for safety for everyone in the classroom. The students are not a means to an end, for example, "showing that I am a good teacher," "demonstrating that my techniques work," or "getting the school a good reputation." All of these may be good outcomes. However, if they become the primary driving force for the teacher, the deep life of the student will be buried in the pursuit of these other targets. Thus the hearts of the students will not be heard or responded to.

Being a soft-hearted teacher creates vulnerability, for to share things of the heart is to place one's own life at the hands of potentially fickle, immature, and sometimes just mean-spirited youth, which is why many experienced teachers simply tell inexperienced ones, "Don't do it."

What I learned (after more soul searching) is that being soft-hearted is not simply about me being willing to tell personal stories from my life to students (although rightly timed, this can be a very powerful connector with their hearts). Being soft-hearted means the willingness to be in touch with the students' hearts first of all, so that I increasingly know what engages them because it meets some needs of their hearts. To be a soft-hearted teacher is to be committed to listening to what is important to the hearts of their students. To be soft-hearted is the equivalent to being discerning.

15. The relational challenges of what is about to be described pastorally can be explored in depth theologically, e.g., Grenz, *Created for Community*, or philosophically, e.g., Wolterstorff, *Justice in Love*.

Jesus repeatedly demonstrated this by telling parables in teaching moments, rather than responding to questions and issues by simply quoting from the Torah.

B. The Relational Holism of Strong Thinking

The phrase "deep thinking" that is used in this essay is sometimes called the "intellectual quality" that a teacher brings to the teaching and learning process (for example in the "NSW Quality Teaching Framework"). It can incorporate descriptors such as deep knowledge, deep understanding, and more substantial conceptualizing of language and problem solving.

In this context however, it also refers to the ability to bring such things to the heart of the students. This intentional heart teaching is in order to *invite a love and awe of learning*, whilst guiding them through *the prescribed content* of any compulsory curriculum. It is during this process that *knowledge can start to become wisdom*—what the Bible refers to as the wellspring of life. It enables the student to start understanding how they are meant to live *with reference to the Creator's intent*, given the complexities of the necessary everyday compromises of life.

Such wisdom enables students to start to see the *relationship between the deepest general principles of Truth and the particularities of the content at hand*. It helps them move from being disconnected with life and relationships to being engaged with people. It starts with stilling one's own heart as a teacher so that the hearts of the students can be known. It then progresses to bringing knowledge to bear to this heart to heart relationship.

What are the signs of teaching that is focused on developing strong minds? I would suggest the following:

- The philosophy of the classroom revolves around "looking not only to your own interests, but also to the interests of others," "doing unto others as you would have them do unto you," and "use whatever gifts you have to serve others."[16]
- The teaching methods create an invitation to individually learn consistently, well and deeply in order to contribute to humanity and to care for its environment.

The classroom content is linked to the deep principles above.

What can then drive home the heart to heart connection for deep learning beyond these core classroom practitioner elements? It is creating an environment that invites students to discover a context greater than the

16. These principles of life are described in various parts of the Bible, e.g., Phil 2:4; Matt 7:12; and 1 Pet 4:10, respectively.

textbooks and workbooks, which takes us to considering the nature of service within learning.

C. The Relational Holism of Serving Hands

Over time, if we listen in discerning ways (have a soft heart in our teaching) and teach deeply and enquiringly into the Truth, then this invites students to develop a discernment to choose well with reference to submitting to the Truth while learning to meet the needs of people (their needs and the needs of others).[17] Such is the basis of constructive compromise in life. It is built upon a willingness to serve others rather than to feed one's own willfulness and sense of entitlement. This commitment to service is what the Bible calls *doing good*, which is a repeated phrase in the New Testament.[18]

This seems to be the hardest of the three engagement dynamics to implement into schools. The structure and relational norms of the self-focused classroom seem, for most teachers, to be the defining restricting boundary that inhibits them being able to encourage students' engagement with life more fully. I suspect that is why holistic engagement attempts are mostly structured as extra-curricular activities outside of the classroom—the creative and performing arts and sport programs in particular. These settings do allow for more naturally flexible interpersonal relationships. However, to give up on incorporating the "serving hands" into the classroom would be to give up on the greatest time opportunity in our young people's lives to bring to fulfillment the purpose of soft hearts and strong minds.

Within a learning for service environment, teachers have a constant orientation for making a real difference in other people's lives by offering them their gifts of learning in grace. This is the spirit of 1 Peter 4:10–11, with which we started this essay. This verse reminds us that it is God's grace (*charis*) that allows us to develop our gifts (*charismata*). It is the recognition that our differences provide the opportunity to serve each other.[19]

Whenever an individual succeeds in learning, the class can be thankful that they have more opportunity to help others. The class practices this serving tradition within the classroom, and goes outside of the classroom to make a difference serving others. The vision is simple. The outcome is profound. Anyone who wishes to grow this in their class must expect other people to question and challenge them. May God's grace sustain them in the journey of learning for service to Him and others.

17. Eph 5:21.
18. See, for example, Paul's letter to Titus.
19. Broughton Knox, *Everlasting God*, 129–46.

Our Concluding Choice

Seymour Sarason from Yale University was one of the first in the field of contemporary psychology to start interest in the field of what is helpful in engaging students. Some of his conclusions were that:

> I believe that subject matter is essential . . . [but] belief that such mastery is critical for adaptation over one's lifetime drove me to the conclusion that far from facilitating mastery over subject matter, the classroom extinguishes interest. . . . What so many scientists fail to understand is that at its root education is a moral enterprise and that by glossing over that fact we sustain fruitless controversy and continued failure.[20]

And so we are left with a choice: do we want to see schools as information and skill factories, or as one of the critical mediating structures of our society? This search for understanding, within a world that is both transcendent and rational, is not a new concern. Howie recorded the following as one of Augustine of Hippo's contributions to education:

> . . . he declared that wisdom . . . is the ultimate goal of education. Wisdom is a higher value than science, the former being "the intellectual understanding of eternal [transcendent] things," and the latter the "rational understanding of temporal things." Therefore, as educators we must maintain a sense of proportion.[21]

Which wisdom will we follow? Or will we simply not try to change, and let reductionist information transfer rule the day?

Response Questions

1. Can you think of and describe examples of rationalism, individualism, and self-advancement that were present in your educational experiences?
2. How do you think this had an impact on your approach to learning?
3. Reflect on and describe teachers who were able to encourage you to think about *why* you were studying something.

20. Sarason, *Schooling in America*, 142–65.
21. Howie, *St. Augustine on Education*, 27.

4. Can you think of any examples in your learning experiences when you were encouraged you to serve others with what you have learned? Were there aspects that engaged your heart, head, or hands in this experience?
5. What do you think would be hardest aspects of orienting your classroom or school to learning for service?

Recommended Reading

Hare, John. *Why Bother Being Good: The Place of God in the Moral Life*. Downers Grove IL: InterVarsity, 2002.

Twenge, Jean M., and W. Keith Campbell. *The Narcissism Epidemic: Living in the Age of Entitlement*. New York: Free Press, 2009.

Stark, Rodney. *The Victory of Reason: How Christianity led to Freedom, Capitalism, and Western Success*. New York: Random House, 2005.

Plantinga, Alvin. *Where the Conflict Really Lies: Science, Religion, and Naturalism*. New York: Oxford University Press, 2011.

Zacharias, Ravi. *The Real Face of Atheism*. Grand Rapids: Baker, 2004.

Bibliography

Avenall, Ken. "Deep Learning, Rich Understandings." *The Australian Education Leader* 32 (2010) 27.

Bateman, Helen Vrailas. "Sense of Community in the School: Listening to Students' Voices." In *Psychological Sense of Community: Research, Applications, and Implications*, edited by A. T. Fisher, C. I. Sonn, and B. J. Bishop. New York: Plenum, 2002.

Blomberg, Doug. "Knowing and Learning in Biblical Learning." In *Reclaiming the Future*, edited by Ian Lambert and Suzanne Mitchell. Sydney: CSAS, 1996.

———. *Wisdom and Curriculum: Christian Schooling after Postmodernity*. Sioux Center, IA: Dordt College Press, 2007.

Broughton Knox, D. *The Everlasting God*. Homebush West: Lancer Books, 1988.

Crawford, M., and G. Rossiter. *Reasons for Living: Education and Young People's Search for Meaning, Identity and Spirituality: A Handbook*. Sydney: ACER Press, 2006.

Downey, Patrick. *Desperately Wicked: Philosophy, Christianity, and the Human Heart*. Downers Grove, IL: InterVarsity, 2009.

Eckersley, Richard. *Never Better—or Getting Worse?: The Health and Wellbeing of Young Australians*. Online: http://www.australia21.org.au/pdf/Youth%20Health%20Text%2008.pdf.

Etzioni, Amitai. *The Spirit of Community: The Reinvention of American Society*. Sydney: Simon & Schuster, 1993.

Flew, Antony, and Roy Abraham Varghese. *There Is a God: How the World's Most Notorious Atheist Changed His Mind*. New York: HarperCollins, 2007.

Frankl, Victor. *Man's Search for Meaning*. New York: Pocket Books, 1959 [1984].

Fullan, M. *The NEW Meaning of Educational Change*. 4th ed. New York: Teachers College Press, 2007.

Goodlad, John I., Roger Soder, and Kenneth A. Sirotnik. *The Moral Dimensions of Teaching*. San Francisco: Jossey-Bass, 1990.

Grenz, Stanley J. *Created for Community: Connecting Christian Belief with Christian Living*. Grand Rapids: Baker, 2000.

Hare, John. *Why Bother Being Good: The Place of God in the Moral Life*. Downers Grove, IL: InterVarsity, 2002.

Hargreaves, Andy. *The Fourth Way of Educational Reform*. ACEL Monograph Series 45. Penrith, NSW: Australian Council for Educational Leaders, 2009.

Hargreaves, Andy, Lorna M. Earl, and James Ryan. *Schooling for Change: Reinventing Education for Early Adolescents*. London: Falmer, 1996.

Hatton, E. "Middle School Students' Perceptions of School Organization." *Unicorn* 21 (1995) 17–26.

Hill, B. A. "Talking Point at Last: Values Education in Schools." *Journal of Christian Education* 48/3 (2005).

———. "Whose House Do You Live In?: A Brief for Religious Education In Schools." *Journal of Christian Education* 48/2 (2005).

Hinck, S. S., and M. E. Brandell. "Service Learning: Facilitating Academic Learning and Character Development." *National Association of Secondary School Principals Bulletin* 83 (1999) 16–25.

Hirsch, E. D. *The Schools We Need And Why We Don't Have Them*. New York: Anchor, 1999.

Hollis, Shirley A. "Capturing the Experience: Transforming Community Service into Service Learning." *Teaching Sociologically* 30/2 (2002) 200–213.

Howie, George. *St. Augustine on Education*. Chicago: Regnery, 1969.

Machuga, Ric. *In Defense of the Soul: What It Means to Be Human*. Grand Rapids: Brazos, 2002.

Moreland, John P., and F. J. Beckwith. Series Preface. In *Psychology in the Spirit: Contours of a Transformational Psychology*. Downers Grove, IL: InterVarsity, 2010.

Nouwen, Henri J. *Creative Ministry*. New York: Image, 1973.

O'Hear, Anthony. *Beyond Evolution: Human Nature and the Limits of Evolutionary Explanation*. Oxford: Clarendon, Oxford University Press, 2002.

Peck, M. Scott. *People of the Lie*. London: Arrow, 1990.

Pianta, R. C. "Applying the Concept of *Resilience* in Schools: Cautions from a Developmental Systems Perspective." *School Psychology Review* 27 (1998) 407–28.

Platinga, Alvin. *Where the Conflict Really Lies: Science, Religion, and Naturalism*. New York: Oxford University Press, 2011.

Rappaport, J. "Community Narratives: Tales of Terror and Joy." *American Journal of Community Psychology* 28 (2000).

Rhodes, J. E., P. M. Carnic, M. Milburn, and S. R. Lowe. "Improving Middle School Climate through Teacher-Centered Change." *Journal of Community Psychology* 37/6 (2010) 711–24.

Sarason, Seymour Bernard. *Schooling in America: Scapegoat and Salvation*. New York: Free Press, 1983.

———. *The Predictable Failure of Educational Reform* San Francisco: Jossey-Bass, 1990.

Scherer, M. "Do Students Care About Learning?: A Conversation with Mihaly Csikszenmihalyi." *Educational Leadership*, September 2002, 12–17.

Sergiovanni, Thomas J. *Building Community in Schools.* San Francisco: Jossey-Bass, 1994.
Stark, Rodney. *The Victory of Reason: How Christianity Led to Freedom, Capitalism, and Western Success.* New York: Random House, 2005.
Twenge, Jean M., and W. Keith Campbell. *The Narcissism Epidemic: Living in the Age of Entitlement.* New York: Free Press, 2009.
Weintstein, Rhona S. *Reaching Higher: The Power of Expectations in Schooling.* Cambridge, MA: Harvard University Press, 2002.
Wilhoit, James. *Christian Education and the Search for Meaning.* Grand Rapids: Baker, 1986.
Wolterstorff, Nicholas. *Educating for Responsible Action.* Grand Rapids: CSI, Eerdmans, 1980.
———. *Justice in Love.* Grand Rapids: Eerdmans, 2011.
Zacharias, Ravi. Grand Rapids:
———. *The Real Face of Atheism.* Grand Rapids: Baker, 2004.

Index